CAN YOUR TEN- TO FOURTEEN-YEAR-OLD MAKE YOU A HAPPIER, LESS STRESSED, AND MORE EFFECTIVE PARENT? YOU BET! FIND OUT ABOUT—

•Junk food . . . your kid loves it, but is it causing hidden problems with big consequences? *See pages 189–90, 210, 299.*

•Your child's body type: round and plump or bony and angular . . . does it predict behavior, temperament, and more? *See pages 208–9.*

•Bifocals for thirteen-year-olds? Find out when vision problems are behind headaches and poor athletic performance. *See pages 117–18.*

•A vitamin to stop nervous tics and twitches for kids under tension? It's true! *See page 117.*

•Long hair, peculiar behavior, strange clothes . . . is it drugs, or just part of the normal search for self? *See pages 220, 286–89.*

•The simple powerful sentence that can really get your kids to start talking to you . . . about worries, sex, or feelings. *See page 87.*

. . . and more!

YOUR TEN- TO FOURTEEN-YEAR-OLD

"I think [these books] are delightful and likely to capture the imagination of young parents enough to get them through these years. . . . I think the books will be both a pleasure and support for many parents."—T. Berry Brazelton, M.D., author of *Toddlers and Parents* and *Infants and Mothers*

"These are cheerful, optimistic books. . . . I agree with just about everything they say."—Lendon Smith, M.D., author of *Feed Your Kids Right*

Books from the Gesell Institute of Human Development

YOUR ONE-YEAR-OLD
Ames, Ilg, and Haber
YOUR TWO-YEAR-OLD
Ames and Ilg
YOUR THREE-YEAR-OLD
Ames and Ilg
YOUR FOUR-YEAR-OLD
Ames and Ilg
YOUR FIVE-YEAR-OLD
Ames and Ilg
YOUR SIX-YEAR-OLD
Ames and Ilg
YOUR SEVEN-YEAR-OLD
Ames and Haber
YOUR EIGHT-YEAR-OLD
Ames and Haber
YOUR NINE-YEAR-OLD
Ames and Haber
YOUR TEN- TO FOURTEEN-YEAR-OLD
Ames, Ilg, and Baker

YOUR
TEN- TO
FOURTEEN-YEAR-
OLD

by
Louise Bates Ames, Ph.D.
Frances L. Ilg, M.D.
Sidney M. Baker, M.D.
Gesell Institute of Human Development

A Dell Trade Paperback

A Dell Trade Paperback

Published by
Dell Publishing
a division of
Bantam Doubleday Dell Publishing Group, Inc.
1540 Broadway
New York, New York 10036

Portions of this book appeared in a different form in *Youth: The Years from Ten to Sixteen*, by Louise Bates Ames, Ph.D., Frances L. Ilg, M.D., Sidney M. Baker, M.D., and Arnold Gesell, M.D. (Harper & Row, 1956).

Excerpts from THE GOOD HIGH SCHOOL by Sara Lawrence Lightfoot. Reprinted by permission of *Daedalus*, Journal of the American Academy of Arts and Sciences, Cambridge, MA.

Excerpts from TIMES THREE by Phyllis McGinley
Copyright © 1952 by Phyllis McGinley. Renewed © 1980 by Julie Elizabeth Hayden and Phyllis Hayden Blake.
Originally published in *The New Yorker*.
Reprinted by permission of Viking Penguin Inc.

ISBN: 0-440-50678-6

Reprinted by arrangement with Delacorte Press

Printed in the United States of America

Published simultaneously in Canada

April 1989

20 19 18 17
BVG

Sincere thanks are due to the following colleagues and educators for invaluable help in gathering data on our most recent group of subjects.

Hollis Block/Lustig
Pamela Barry
Richard Dolven
Deborah Falcigno
Bette Hamlin
Dennis A. Hinricks
Richard Myers
Nancy Richard
Carole Sabin
Albert J. Wojtcuk

CONTENTS

PART THREE
Maturity Trends and Selected Growth Gradients

PART FOUR
After Fourteen

APPENDIXES

PREFACE

The chief purpose of this book, as of many Gesell publications, is to describe the characteristic changes in human behavior which take place from year to year, in this instance in the years from ten to fourteen.

Since our original study of adolescence was published in 1956, we have obtained additional information from interviews with more than one thousand of today's young people and with some of their parents. These interviews have provided a basis for comparison of teenage behavior in the early fifties with that of young people in the late seventies and early eighties.

It is our definite impression that, fundamentally, human behavior has not changed in the past few decades! Pregnancy in most women still lasts for nine months. The age of sexual maturing is not notably different from what it was twenty or thirty years ago. Preschool behavior changes, as we have observed them in depth, have been strikingly similar during these years.

Teenage behavior seems, in many ways, to be much the same as we found it to be in the early 1950's. The major tasks of adolescence remain (a) getting free of one's parents, (b) establishing a feeling about one's own personality, (c) becoming interested in and gradually relating to the opposite sex.

However, strong and consistent as basic growth changes may be, it is generally acknowledged that human behavior results from an interaction between organism and environment. The same individual may behave quite differently in one environment from the way he behaves in another. And it must be admitted that the world of the teenager in the 1980's is in many ways quite different from what it was in the early fifties.

As Dr. Ralph Rutenber puts it:

This is part of the mythology of the Sixties and Seventies—that young people today are a different breed from their predecessors. Actually they are no different from their predecessors. *But they operate in a different world*—a world in which their elders are not certain of their own beliefs. *They* would be more sure of *their* values if *we* were more sure of ours.[1]

There are probably many areas in which the changing values of the adult world do not substantially alter the behavior of teenage boys and girls from what it was earlier. Perhaps our changing values have influenced them most in such sensitive areas as sex, drinking, and the use of drugs. Attitudes toward marriage and parenthood do not seem to have changed substantially in teenagers, in spite of Women's Liberation and the efforts of feminists. Girls increasingly plan to invade the formerly mostly-male bastions of law and medicine, but marriage and motherhood remain a major goal of the majority.

One of our New Haven mothers, a writer herself, gave this helpful comment:

Your earlier book *Youth: The Years from Ten to Sixteen* is an impressive and enduring work. Where it has not endured is in those passages discussing areas most affected by cultural change. I find it hard to assess how deep this change cuts into the lives of young people.

Perhaps something like this might be true: Adolescents are subjected to somewhat different messages concerning sex, marriage, roles of men and women; and some of them, probably a minority, act on these messages in a way that would not have been possible twenty years ago. Or would have come at a later age. Many, probably most, do not, but I think they have to contend in their heads with these messages.

Another way of putting it might be this: There are new ways of testing the margins of acceptability and the edge of daring and personal limits. From the point of view of anyone my age or older, these new possibilities involve risks, or at least are strong stuff.

My thirteen-year-old, for instance, is in the category of those who contend without so far experimenting, other than occasional rudeness. She fits your developmental portrait very closely. Nevertheless she is having to make sense of, and locate herself in relation to, messages which I think would have been nonexistent in this city in the fifties. Some of her classmates use dope; some of them cut classes; many are pretty rude and ragged. I doubt that any of them have had intercourse, but on the basis of what I know of the children of friends, this is probably only a year or so off for a few, rather than, say, three or four years off, as it might have been for comparable kids in the fifties.

And there is much talk about homosexuality, much referring to classmates as "that faggot." I think that the volume of talk reflects the anxiety the subject arouses, and that the accusation is a way of keeping oneself safe.

I'm sure adolescents have always bucked authority and that the way they do it today differs from twenty years ago in degree and not in kind, but degree can become significant. At times adults are battered badly enough so that only the very stalwart can stand up to the bucking they get—the nonnegotiable-demand phenomenon.

Be that as it may, though some of our subjects (or their friends) admitted using drugs and/or being sexually active, none to our knowledge went beyond mild juvenile delinquency to actual criminality. Child abuse was not admitted by any of our parents, nor did parents admit they were physically abused by any of our subjects. In our observations of school behavior, neither teachers nor fellow students were physically harmed by subjects.

In view of the marked unrest in the world today, in homes as well as in the schools and on the streets, some readers may find our subjects and their families to be conservative indeed. One of our chief purposes in writing this book was to describe the intricacy, complexity, and difficulty of growing up even when family and home background are stable and secure.

Needless to say, in homes stressed by poverty, unemployment, divorce, by the presence of only a single parent, by crime and unrest in the household or neighborhood, by extreme adolescent rebellion, what we have found to be more or less normal or ordinary parent-child tensions will be exaggerated.

Readers whose teenage boys and girls are deeply in trouble—heavily involved with drugs or drinking or sex, physically violent, runaways, lawbreakers—may find our descriptions of teenage behavior inappropriately bland. There are probably two main reasons for this seeming blandness. One is that although in writing this book we added a current group of more than a thousand boys and girls, our original subjects lived in a time when society was more protective and more supportive than it is today. The second is that, for the most part, they came from rather stable families.

We believe that the age changes described in this book do hold true for the majority of today's young people, even though when things go dreadfully wrong, the knowledge that a child is behaving like a typical twelve-, thirteen-, or fourteen-year-old may not be of much consolation to a parent.

For those whose teenagers are disruptively out-of-bounds, we recommend three extremely helpful publications. The first and strongest of these is entitled *Toughlove: An Effective Program for Parents of Unruly Teenagers by the Founders of the National Toughlove Movement,*[2] by Phyllis and David York and Ted Wachtel.

This Toughlove movement in some ways resembles Alcoholics Anonymous except that here it is the parents of people in trouble who band together in support groups. These groups recognize that unacceptable behavior is for the most part not the parents' fault, but is encouraged by today's culture. The authors suggest ways in which parents can change this destructive cultural pattern by making their children responsible for their own negative actions and the consequences of these actions. At the heart of the Toughlove program is a method by which parents in a community form their own support system and learn how to precipitate crises for their teenagers which will lead to positive changes.

A second book which can be helpful to parents of teenagers who are in slightly less serious trouble is *How to Deal with Your Acting-Up Teenager*, by Robert and Jean Bayard.[3] These authors suggest that instead of trying to push misbehaving teenagers into shape, parents should ask themselves, "What can we do in this situation that would contribute to our child's being more responsible and able to make his own decisions?"

They advise making a list of all the things your teenager does that bother you. Go over this list and pull out for a separate list all the things he does which do not affect *your* future life. Then drop the responsibility for the items that are in your child's pile and that do not totally influence you. Given the responsibility for these items, he may eventually, it is hoped, make the right decisions.

A third, equally realistic book is called *How to Survive with Your Teenager*, by Joel Wells.[4] Among the topics covered are suicide, runaways, drugs and drinking, and trouble with the law.

We maintain that the changes in behavior with age which we will describe in this book hold true regardless of home situation. It is our hope that an understanding of these biologically-based changes will help readers to achieve good parent-child relationships regardless of family background or situation.

Even the healthiest and most stable adolescent does need to achieve separation and autonomy from his parents. When parents are informed enough to permit "normal" teenage rebellion, many of the more destructive kinds of rebellion may be prevented or forestalled. It is the purpose of this book to provide this kind of information.

PART ONE
Our Research on Teenagers

chapter one
ORIENTATION

The basic theme of this book is growth—the growth of body, mind, and personality. The book itself is a product of growth which traces its origins to previous studies. For more than sixty years the authors have been making systematic observations of normal child development. During that time we have been observing the procession of behavior patterns which begin to unfold even before birth and which assume such varied forms throughout infancy, childhood, and adolescence.

This present volume carries our studies of age changes in behavior into the preadolescent and adolescent years. We have been particularly interested to determine the influence of age on the organization of behavior under the conditions of contemporary American culture.

In spite of the gradualness of the child's behavior growth, we found that each year of maturity brings characteristic traits and trends in these older years, just as is the case in the first ten years of life. Ten marks a turn in the spiral course of development, with the behavioral beginnings of adolescence appearing at about eleven. The adolescent cycle continues through the teens well into the twenties, but the same kinds of age changes that appeared earlier are still evident: ages of relative equilibrium alternate with ages of disequilibrium; expansive ages alternate with times of inwardization.

How do the mechanisms, patterns, and laws of growth manifest themselves in the transitional years from ten to fourteen? Answers to this question became the goal of this investigation.

SETTINGS AND SUBJECTS

A fortunate combination of circumstances enabled us to maintain research contact with a large number of the same children whose development we had already followed up to age ten. These children, along with siblings and peers, constituted our original core group of 115 subjects, seen repeatedly throughout adolescence. To these were added fifty children seen at one age only. All told, there were 545 contacts with these children over a span of ten years.

With few exceptions, the families lived in New Haven, Connecticut and its suburbs. Some who moved away returned periodically for the half-day visits required by our investigation. All had demonstrated a genuine interest in the methods and aims of our research. A supplementary group of more than one thousand subjects was added in the years 1977-1978. These young people each responded to a questionnaire which covered aspects of social and sexual behavior (See Appendix A). These subjects came from communities which ranged geographically from the East Coast to the West Coast of the United States.

Intellectually, our original group of subjects was well above average, as tested on the Wechsler-Bellevue Intelligence Scale. The average IQ for the ten-, eleven-, and fourteen-year-olds was 117; for the twelve-, thirteen-, fifteen-, and sixteen-year-olds, the average IQ was 118. The socioeconomic status of the original families was generally favorable. The method itself—requiring contacts over a span of years—tended to select families of stable position in the community. The majority of the parents were in professional, semiprofessional, managerial, and skilled occupations. The children were representative of a high average to superior level of school population in a relatively prosperous community. The socioeconomic status of our 1977-1978 subjects ranged from upper class to welfare.

We were, of course, dealing with presumably normal children, and we shared the parents' avid interest in the child's behavior in terms of individuality and growth characteristics. Each visit in our original study included a detailed behavior and personality examination, an interview with the parents, and a personal interview with the child. (See Appendix A for details.) The parents were eager to observe the developmental examination (which they did through a one-way screen) and were enthusiastic and helpful in the parent conference which followed. The interview with the child was conducted in privacy between an interviewer and the boy or girl. The entire visit required, on each occasion, a full half day.

Readers will undoubtedly be aware that throughout this book we speak, for the most part, as if every boy or girl had a mother and father living in the household. And for our original group of subjects, those whom we studied in the most detail and whom we knew best, this was the case. Our second (more recent) group of subjects were known to us only through their responses to our questionnaire. We did not meet their parents or know, in most instances, whether these children lived in an intact two-parent home, a stepfamily, or a single-parent home.

Thus we do not in this book give special information about the particular problems which exist in stepfamilies or in single-parent families. Such information, however, is available in several of the books included in our reference list. Our interest here was in the young people themselves and in the way things changed with them from age to age—not in the particular kind of family they grew up in.

THE INTERVIEWS

The personal interview with our subjects and the interview with their parents were an organic part of the investigation program. These interviews were carried on independently of each other. Leading questions were kept at a minimum. The procedure was informal and favored free and easy conversation. There was no rigid standardization, but the questions embraced the eight basic developmental areas considered in the present volume, under the following headings: (1) Total action system, (2) Self-care and routines, (3) Emotions, (4) The growing self, (5) Interpersonal relationships, (6) Activities and interests, (7) School life, (8) Ethical sense.

Subject interview:

The subject was at once reassured that the questions were not tests and that we were not looking for right or wrong answers. We were simply interested to know how he thought and felt. He need not answer if he so chose, and he could add anything he wished to talk about. The questions were formulated briefly and directly. For example, when emotions were under discussion the subject was asked, "What do you do when you get angry?" "Do you ever cry and, if so, what about?" "How about competition?" and so forth. Intellectual areas were explored with similar directness. The child gave us his ideas about time, space, war, ethics. As he grew older, phases of the interview might reverse direction, and he would ask for the opinion of the examiner. In general, the children appeared to find the interview an interesting experience, and seemed gratified that their ideas were important enough to be recorded.

We have sometimes been asked if this very awareness of our interest did not distort the response of our adolescents. Were they really telling us the truth? We believe that our subjects responded to our interview with the truth as they experienced it; each responded in accord with his inner picture of self as a person.

Parent Interview:

This interview was an important part of each yearly visit. It was a two-way arrangement which invited eager questions and comments. Parent and interviewer had reciprocal reasons for defining the individuality and progress of the child whose behavior had just been witnessed in the standardized setting of the developmental examination.

The parents were encouraged to report their own observations, lively anecdotes, problems or concerns, and any noteworthy happenings of the year just past. We found that the conference, which was quite informal, could admit the humorous as well as the serious aspects of domestic problems.

ANALYSIS OF DATA

From this account of the ground plan of our adolescent study, it is evident that we spread a wide net to gather our data. The records on our original subjects were voluminous. For the children whose development we had followed since their earliest years, the documentary file for a single individual assumed the proportions of a biography. For the thousand or so boys and girls who responded to our questionnaire in the late 1970's, only the questionnaire was available for analysis.

Our task was to analyze and interpret this formidable mass of data and to reduce it to a meaningful pattern. Our method involved the determination of a series of growth gradients and maturity profiles.

SCOPE AND PLAN OF THE BOOK

We have formulated the findings of our study from three converging angles of approach as follows:

1. *Maturity Profiles* Portrayals of the maturity characteristics of seven yearly age norms from ten through fourteen years.

2. *Maturity Traits* Behavior patterns and symptoms in eight major areas for each age zone: (1) Total Action System, (2) Routines and Self-Care, (3) Emotions, (4) The Growing Self, (5) Interpersonal Relationships, (6) Activities and interests, (7) School Life, (8) Ethical Sense.

3. *Maturity Trends* The sequences and gradients of growth for the sector of years from ten through fourteen.

The governing concept is that of growth—growth as a patterning process. Even a young adolescent becomes somewhat more understandable when he is considered from the standpoint of growth—of immaturity and of relative maturity.

But growth is subtle and often elusive. It takes time. We can scarcely perceive it without the perspective which comes with the passage of time.

Part Three of the present volume provides another approach from which the trends of maturity can be examined in greater detail. A separate chapter is devoted to each of the eight major areas of behavior development. Instead of focusing on a single age zone, we look at the sequences of growth in longitudinal perspective and tabulate the growth gradients for some forty distinguishable fields of behavior. A growth gradient is the series of stages or degrees of maturity by which a child progresses toward a higher level of functioning.

Note: The maturity profiles, the maturity traits, and the maturity trends described here are not to be regarded as rigid age norms or as models. They simply indicate the kinds of behavior—desirable or otherwise—which tend to occur at certain stages and ages under contemporary cultural conditions. Every child has an individual pattern of growth unique to him or her. The profiles, traits, and trends are designed to suggest the various maturity levels at which young people may function. The "ages" denote approximate zones rather than precise moments in time.

chapter two

DEVELOPMENT:
A KEY CONCEPT

It has long been our belief that behavior, like physical growth, develops in a patterned, predictable way. In fact it appears that behavior is, to a large extent, a function of structure. We behave as we do primarily because of the way our bodies are built. True, the individual body continues, in spite of changes with age, to have many stable characteristics, evident at all ages. But the chronological age of the growing person to a very large extent determines the ways in which he may be expected to behave.

This appears to be a primary rule of development. However, for those who wish to anticipate the ways in which growing human behavior is likely to change, a second rule must be kept in mind: Behavior as it matures does not necessarily improve and does not always continue in the same direction.

Rather, it appears that ages of equilibrium tend to alternate, as the individual grows older, with ages of disequilibrium. Ages when behavior forces are expansive and directed outward seem to alternate with those in which these same forces are inwardized. This alternation of direction, this shift in course, has been noted in children of younger ages than those being considered here, but it clearly continues into the age period of ten to fourteen.

In very brief summary, we give here a preview of what we shall tell you about the succeeding ages during this eventful time in life. We have found Ten to be an age of equilibrium, of good adjustment, of comfortable functioning not only within the individual but also between the child and those around him.

Eleven is quite the opposite. It is a time of breaking up, of discord and discomfort. Gone is the bland complaisance of the typical ten-year-old. Eleven is a time of loosening up, of snapping old bonds, of trial and error as the young child tests the limits of what authority will and will not permit.

The typical twelve-year-old tends to be smoother in his relationships, more positive in mood, more enthusiastic about life. Whereas Eleven seemed to live with a perpetual chip on his shoulder, Twelve can be remarkably tolerant, even when the adult errs or falls short of perfection. And Twelve shows an outgoing enthusiasm for new adventure.

Thirteen, in contrast, is likely to be extremely inwardized, withdrawn. He not only spends much time alone, away from other people, but also appears to be painfully self-conscious, thoughtful, and moody. Thirteen's unwillingness to cooperate expresses itself not so much in reacting against the adult, as at Eleven, as in simply withdrawing from any and every unnecessary contact.

Perhaps predictably, the next age change is once again in the direction of expansion. Fourteen tends to be all over the place, not only physically but in enthusiasms. Fourteen loves the new and different—new activity, new friends, and any new adventure. Energy seems boundless. Parents, it's true, can bring a frown, but for almost anybody and anything else there is a ready welcome.

The notion that behavior in the teens actually does change from year to year in these very striking ways may be hard for some to accept. It was even a little difficult for us to accept the evidence of our eyes and ears that this actually should be the case. It seemed almost too pat.

Acceptance of what we seemed to be seeing was made easier by the fact that we had, after all, seen it before. The yearly alternations of outwardized and inwardized behavior change had been observed by us twice before—in the years from five to ten and, before that, in earliest childhood. (Infancy too reveals this kind of change, but it seems to us less clear.)

This intriguing repetition of a highly patterned sequence of behavior change thus appears to occur three times between the ages of two and sixteen, as shown below in Table 1:

Our description may make behavior appear to be rather more stereotyped and predictable than it actually is. What we have described is a sequence of developmental stages which we believe most growing human beings share. But as will be elaborated on in the following chapter, not every growing boy or girl follows this common path with accuracy or precision. We have described behavior changes in terms of calendar years. However, not every ten-

---

Table 1

Cyclic Changes in Behavior Pattern

	Equilibrium, Good Adjustment	Breaking Up	Equilibrium, Expansion	Inwardization	Vigorous Expansion	Inward	Equilibrium
Age in Years	2	2½	3	3½	4	4½	5
	5	5½–6	6½	7	8	9	10
	10	11	12	13	14	15	16

---

year-old behaves for an entire year in the ways we describe as characteristic of Ten. Nor does he change from the inwardness and complexity of Nine to the calm equilibrium of Ten right on his tenth birthday.

In fact, the child may never quite hit the pinnacle of smooth existence which we describe as normally characteristic of Ten. Some children by nature seem always to live on the "disequilibrium" side of existence. In others, good equilibrium never breaks up excessively. Timing is as individual as the quality of behavior. Some boys and girls seem to speed through early life, always a little ahead in their behavior. Others, equally normal, are always a bit on the immature side, being always a bit "young" for their age.

Perhaps more often than not, however, growing boys and girls follow more or less along the path we have described. It is our hope that knowing what, in general, one may expect at any given age may be of use to parent and teacher alike in living and dealing with that elusive and fascinating creature, the teenager.

To fully understand any boy or girl, one needs to know about at least three things—the child's basic individuality, what to expect of anyone of his particular age level, and what kind of environment he finds himself in. These three factors interact at all times. For full understanding, we need to know about all three.

The present volume briefly mentions individual differences, but emphasizes age changes in behavior as they characteristically occur in our American culture. We do not discuss the way in which children from other cultures behave. But it is our hope that an understanding of the kind of behavior which one can, in general, expect from the child of different ages will help you to do a better job in living with your own boy or girl.

chapter three
INDIVIDUALITY

Every human being is an individual. The tendency of our physical body to be different from that of every other person creates a basis for a kind of loneliness that is experienced deeply as the adolescent discovers that he is a unique person. The tendency of the sequences and rhythms of the events of our lives to be similar to those of every other human provides a reassuring counterbalance to the isolation of our individuality. Growing boys and girls show their individuality in the way they progress from stage to stage of maturity. Thus not everyone will go through the stages we describe in this book in exactly the way pictured here. Some will be ahead of the more or less typical pattern which we describe; some behind it. Some will emphasize the stages of withdrawal; others the outgoing stages. Some swing wildly from one extreme to another; others proceed along on a more or less even keel.

Even within a family you will see differences. Dr. T. Berry Brazelton of Harvard has made the extremely insightful observation that in addition to the differences which exist among individuals, differences also exist among mother-child couples.[5] The same mother may find that she gets along very easily with one of her children, but has much trouble with another. This parent-child relation is one of the many factors which influences the way any given child will behave as he or she goes through the often difficult teen years.

In fact, this very parent-child area is one in which tremendous individual differences can be observed. Some young people remain calm and friendly, an integral and even affectionate and respectful member of the family group well past sixteen. Others in the very early teens take a big step in that process of separation which makes life so difficult in many families.

We cannot predict for sure. We can merely outline a more or less typical series of stages which perhaps the majority of children go through as they move through those fateful years from ten to sixteen. We present a basic map or ground plan, but we cannot guarantee precisely what life during these years will be like for you or your particular girl or boy.

Variations of individuality will be discussed briefly under the following headings: (1) Sex differences, (2) Physique and temperament, (3) Intelligence, (4) Style of growth, (5) Adjustment to society, (6) Individuality of the decade.

Sex differences:

The most far-reaching constitutional factor which divides the whole of humanity into two groups is that of sex. True, many of the behaviors commonly associated with being male or female are at least to some extent a product of culture—of customs and expectations and also of subtle pressures from parents, age-mates, and society at large.

But the earliness and persistence of many sex differences indicate that many of the traits do have a constitutional basis and that the encouragements and prohibitions of the culture do not so much cause as reinforce them. The manner of expression of such traits is patterned by society; but their sources lie deep in the organism.

Girls, for example, generally mature earlier than boys in total physical development and behavior. In a revision of our 1940 preschool behavior norms, we were able to make fifty-nine objective comparisons of the two sexes. Boys were ahead in seven instances, girls in fifty; the two sexes were equal in two.

Comparisons which we described in our earlier book *Youth*, in our experience, still hold good today. Thus we found that girls in general are more interested in the person, in social relationships; boys are more interested in objective reality, in mechanics, science and engineering, and sports. Girls tend to prefer indoor activities and recreations; boys prefer those outdoors. This difference is plainly exhibited in magazine reading, the tendency of boys to elect sports and science, and girls' preference for fashion and romance. Girls begin dating at an earlier age. In our group, girls proved to be earlier and more articulate than boys in making ethical distinctions between right and wrong. They seem more adept at sizing up and responding to the implications of life and conduct.

Sex differences can easily be overstated; the lines of demarcation are not sharp. Every individual has a combination of so-called masculinity *and* femininity traits—in body chemistry as well as in behavior. There are many such composite traits, and they vary enormously from individual to individual. On the whole, boys and girls meet most stages of development in a highly comparable manner. But girls in general are slightly precocious when compared with boys, especially in physical growth and social development, as well as in many other areas. A tempering of the gradients of this book, then, toward the expectation of slight acceleration in girls and slight retardation in boys will help to make the age assignments more appropriate.

Physique and Temperament:

W. H. Sheldon approaches the problem of adult individual differences and deviations from the standpoint of varieties of physique and temperament.[6] According to him, there are three major body types: the roundish endomorph (soft body, short neck, small hands and feet), the squarish mesomorph (firm body with rugged muscles), and the spindly ectomorph (slender and delicate in construction). Pure types are rare. Individual differences in physique are usually manifested in mixtures of the basic body types. Similarly, there are three temperamental types. Temperament denotes the distinctive mental character of a person. The temperamental traits combine in widely variegated degrees in different individuals. The extreme endomorph tends to have a good digestive tract. He is good-natured, relaxed, sociable, communicative. The pronounced mesomorph is active, energetic, assertive, noisy, and aggressive. The fragile ectomorph is restrained, inhibited, tense: he may prefer solitude to noise and company. He is sensitive and is likely to have allergies.

Though all individuals present complex mixtures of components, the "typical" endomorph, mesomorph, and ectomorph tend to express the ground plan of growth in characteristic ways which are now being investigated at childhood and youth levels. In the area of emotions, for example, the endomorph tends to show his feelings easily at any age. Other people are too important for him to withdraw very far, even in the most "withdrawing" phases of growth. The mesomorph, even at an age generally described as less competitive, is noncompetitive only in a comparative sense—compared, that is, with *himself* at other ages. The ectomorph is quicker to withdraw when troubled, takes more pains to hide his feelings. He may show alertness and fast reaction, but in many areas he tends to show immaturities. He seems to need more time to grow than do others. Our observations indicate that the gradients of growth take on added meaning when interpreted in the light of constitutional individuality.

Intelligence:

Variations in human intelligence have always been an area of particular interest to psychologists, educators, and parents. Though some groups oppose so-called intelligence testing, there is no question that intellectual ability is important in determining the life success of any girl or boy.

Perhaps more research effort has been expended on this aspect of individuality than on all others combined. Such study continues today—now focused not only on general intelligence but also on more specific aspects of intelligence such as verbal, numerical, and spatial abilities, form perception, and a number of other such factors.

Indeed, intellectual growth itself has sometimes been considered to be *the* course of development, with "mental age" its main measure. But a normal ten-year-old with a mental age of fourteen does not necessarily act like a fourteen-year-old. He tends to act more like a bright ten-year-old. Within the normal range, intelligence is not so much related to the *speed* of the course of development as to its *fullness*. The superior child tends to portray the developmental characteristics of any given age with a special vividness.

Style and growth:

Every individual has a distinctive style of growth which is revealed when the progressive course of development is viewed in perspective. Some individuals, for example, develop in a smooth, gradual, step-by-step fashion; others seem to move in spurts, hardly changing for long periods of time, then acquiring new behaviors in a sudden flood. Again, some individuals show wide swings of behavior as they proceed from stage to stage of maturity, highlighting the extremes of each phase, while others, by contrast, show only a slight gravitation toward the prototypes of behavior along their overall course. Growth patterns such as these are often characteristic of the individual from earliest infancy throughout life.

Another dimension appears when the growth course is viewed over a longer timespan. A majority of individuals appear consistent in overall rate of development, showing a more or less constant degree of earliness or lateness in reaching critical points in the growth cycle. Others show variations in this respect. One pattern is that of rapid early development which does not later fulfill its apparent promise. It may seem as if the individual failed to clear a crucial hurdle in the early stages of development, and, though his growth proceeded in many ways, he remains handicapped by a lack in some particular aspect of organization. Another variation is exemplified in the immature individual. Slowness of development is sometimes a feature of generalized retardation, in which the individual never reaches an adult level of functioning. But sometimes it is a more benign immaturity, in which later stages of growth are either accelerated or prolonged, allowing the eventual achievement of average or even superior status. The "superior-immature" individual, the child of above-average intelligence who shows a total functioning more characteristic of a younger developmental level, presents special problems and a special challenge to the educational system.

Adjustment to Society:

One further dimension in which any growing child will function is the extent to which he is able to adapt to the customary demands of society. The behavior of girls and boys described in this book may seem exceedingly bland to some anxious parents. And it is true that our basic, original group of research subjects were, indeed, an unusually stable group of young people from extremely stable homes. Also, they were studied some years ago. And our supplementary group of more than one thousand interview subjects were all volunteers. One may hazard the guess that the more unstable or, especially, the more antisocial did not volunteer.

At any rate, regardless of the stability of our own research subjects, it is obvious that young people—like adults—range in social stability from the extremely well-adjusted to the highly antisocial; in personality adjustment, from "normal" to psychotic and from outgoing to withdrawn, depressed, or even suicidal. They range from those who exhibit normal, everyday rebellion to those who cannot, and often do not want to be, contained within the home.

Individuality of the decade:

Though this book deals primarily with the individual child as his or her behavior changes from year to year, it is obvious that, at least to some extent, any human being of any age does react to cultural forces. Today's teenager quite clearly lives in a somewhat different world from that of the boys and girls originally studied by us.

In *The Good High School,* Sara Lawrence Lightfoot describes recent cultural changes at the high school level as follows:

> After a conservative period in the sixties, when "athletics were important, student council was big . . . and a great emphasis was put on prom queens and cheerleading," students abruptly lost interest in the traditional high school activities. They moved into what many teachers refer to as "the hippie period," when they rebelled against conservative attitudes reflected in the curriculum and structure of the school. Football and cheerleading were no longer activities of status, it was hard to get students to run for student council, and student garb changed from neat to purposefully sloppy. Some teachers remember this period as a time when students were "threatening and menacing," when discipline seemed to break down. "You didn't dare tell kids to pick up the orange peel they just dropped on the floor . . . you feared repercussions." During the tumultuous seventies, the students turned away from math and science and demanded more nontraditional courses. "There was an awful lot of pressure to do away with sex-bias courses . . . Girls enrolled themselves in auto mechanics and boys in child development." A few daring boys chose to take home economics—long the exclusive preserve of "feminine" girls.
>
> Now in the seventies the pendulum has swung back and once again students are making the more conservative choices. For the first time in several years a large group of girls showed up for cheerleading tryouts and the competition was stiff. Seniors brag about the great success of Homecoming Day this year. They worked hard on elaborate floats, costumes and activities. . . .The new glimmer of school spirit is accompanied by a great preoccupation with grades, class standing, and "courses that count." Almost no boys appear in child development and interior design courses anymore, and girls are content to avoid learning the "masculine" skills of industrial arts and auto mechanics. There is a noticeable return to conservative attitudes and traditional roles.[7]

All of these factors and many, many more must be considered in any effort to truly understand any growing boy or girl. Understanding the common or typical age changes which occur is only a small beginning of any effort to understand your own individual teenager. But it is at least a beginning. The picture we give represents a ground plan which most young people have in common. Age changes are the things which perhaps the majority of young people *do* have in common. Individuality is the uniqueness with which each growing organism interprets for itself the common ways of growing.

Keep this in mind as you read: Every person, young or old, is primarily an individual.

PART TWO
Maturity Profiles and Traits

chapter four
THE TEN-YEAR-OLD

MATURITY PROFILE

There's nobody nicer than a ten-year-old. If now and then your own Ten's behavior is less than ideal, keep in mind that growing up isn't easy, nor is family living. But Ten withstands both very well because the child of this age loves his family. In fact, he loves life and shares it enthusiastically with those near and dear.

The outstanding thing about the typical ten-year-old is a certain goodness, a smoothness, a friendliness, an acceptance of things as they are. He loves and admires his parents; enjoys friends; even accepts self as a comfortable person to be with. For this year, at least, things for most boys and girls have reached a wonderfully enjoyable state of equilibrium.

Most delightful from a parent's point of view is Ten's admiration for, even adoration of, his mother and father. Father's word is definitely law, though mother is the person most often quoted—perhaps because she is usually the one who gives the most directions. "Mommy says it's okay for me to go downtown alone," Ten will tell you. Or, "Mommy says I'm not ready" (for this or that). And when mommy says "No," Ten will tell you this without resentment. That's just the way things are.

Actually, most ten-year-olds love their whole family. "Best family in the world." And Ten loves family activities and outings. "Every Sunday *our whole family* goes for a ride." However, in spite of this, relations with siblings are not always smooth. With his typically balanced approach, Ten will tell you of sibs, "Sometimes I get on with them and sometimes I don't."

Grandparents, as earlier, are still admired and enjoyed. Ten, with stars in his eyes, likes to show grandma something that he has constructed, or perhaps share something that he has purchased with her. Ten also enjoys the company of grandpa. This enthusiasm for sharing things that are important to him (that neat exhibit at the Science Fair) is one of Ten's most lovable traits.

Outgoing as he is in many ways, Ten does much of his playing in his own neighborhood; in fact seems to feel most at home close to home. Boy or girl shows, as yet, no desire to escape the family sphere of influence.

As to friends, boys in typical ten-year-old fashion tend to get on harmoniously with friends of the same sex. Girls, however, are not as smooth in their friendships. Relationships among girlfriends tend to be complex and intense—with much getting mad, not speaking, making up.

The majority of both sexes are now a million miles from dating. Girls may say, "Oh, we don't like boys. They can be really mean." (Pull hair, chase, push, act rough, throw food at parties.) The slightly more mature girl may comment, "We aren't interested in boys *yet!*" A typical boy will tell you, "I don't like girls. Period. They're tattletales." However, in a neighborhood group, girls may be accepted in a sandlot baseball game, especially if an extra player is needed.

Most Tens are rather good eaters. If they dislike food they may tell you so dramatically (pretending to vomit.) But in general they are not picky about their eating. Bedtime and bath both may still be resisted. There is, as yet, no appreciation of the need to be rested or clean.

Though Tens, especially girls, may have special likes and dislikes when it comes to what to put on, their care of clothes and of room is now at a dismal low. Ten admits that "My room is a mess. If it was neat I couldn't find anything." And like Eleven, Ten may even express a preference not to make his bed. "I don't like to sleep in a made bed."

Ten doesn't as a rule resist parental directives as will be the case at eleven, but like a younger child Ten still needs considerable supervision to get through daily routines.

Most Tens like school, are reasonably satisfied with their teacher, and are easy to teach. Most respect their teacher and may consider her word the law.

At school as at home, boy or girl may still need a considerable amount of supervision to be sure that everything gets done. Tens are most comfortable if the teacher follows a rather set schedule of activities so that they will know what is coming next.

Outside of school, ten-year-olds usually find plenty to keep them busy, since interests and enthusiasms are many. Play is paramount in their lives, and they enjoy doing almost anything. Outdoors, both boys and girls are very active. Ten moves around a good deal, often just for the sheer joy of movement rather than to conform to any special rules of a game. The sheer pleasure of exercising one's body is enough.

Indoors, collections may hold first place in Ten's heart, but he enjoys almost anything that comes up: table games, making gadgets or models, sewing, cooking, drawing, reading, and, of course, television: "I have all the programs memorized so that I know just where each program is. I can just turn on the set and go zip—and find my program."

Though Tens are basically well-adjusted and happy, and will tell you "I don't like to be cross," when provoked girl or boy can be very cross indeed. Response to anger, when it comes, is violent and immediate and rather surprising: "I beat them up," "Hit and kick and bite," "Kick the place around." Even if they merely leave the room when angry, as they will when older, they first stamp their feet or explode verbally. Some even plot revenge, though it is seldom carried out.

Your typical ten-year-old, as dear and satisfactory as he is in most respects, is not at his best as a humorist. In fact, in terms of humor, one may fairly say that the child of this age has all four feet on the ground. Ten's idea of a big joke may be to say that there is lots of mail in the mailbox when actually there is none. And Ten is not good at taking jokes on himself; in fact, he is a bit afraid that somebody may make fun of him.

This is, nevertheless, a rather happy age. Ten will tell you, "Most of the time I'm real happy." Nor do Tens worry much, as they will later, about self or personality. They take themselves much for granted, just as they tend to take the rest of the world. Asked to respond to any specific question about preferences or likes or usual way of doing things, Ten tends to shrug his shoulders and say, with his typical sense of balance, "Sometimes yes, sometimes no."

Ethically, as one would expect, Ten is a very nice person. A boy of this age will admit that he cannot always tell right from wrong, so he usually goes by what his mother tells him. Or by what he learns in Sunday school, or possibly by what his conscience tells him. "Conscience usually tells me if it's wrong, and then I wait till Mommy bawls me out to see if it is."

Fairness is very important to Ten. He tries to be fair to others, and is very insistent that they be fair to him. He feels that cheating is "awful."

The typical ten-year-old is at heart a very positive person—friendly, secure, outgoing, accepting, trusting of others, and, for the most part and within reason, trustworthy. Boy or girl still needs a good deal of supervision and direction, and is usually ready and willing to accept both. Some parents quite naturally wish, as their children grow older and are less friendly and comfortable, that their son or daughter could go back to earlier, easier ways.

MATURITY TRAITS

1. Total Action System

The taut-string quality of the nine-year-old is at ten giving way to looser, softer structure. This is expressed in Ten's general demeanor as well as in changes in bodily structure. He meets situations head-on with sincerity and without embarrassment.

There is a certain poise in Ten as he works at a table or sits in a chair. Head movements are marked as the child shifts from side to side either because of shift of gaze or possibly shift of thought.

Ten prefers to be active, and the outdoors is his greatest love. Tens love most to play outdoor gross-motor games and ride bicycles, but they are not overly active. There is a congeniality that speaks of smoothness in whatever they do.

Health General health is veering toward the "good now" or "better than before." Many of the somatic complaints so common at nine (stomachaches, sick headaches, dizziness, leg pains) are now lessening or disappearing. Even though some of these symptoms may persist, the urge to go out to play overpowers the demands of the symptoms.

Even at ten, just over fifty percent of boys and girls admit that at least "some of the kids" they know smoke at least an occasional cigarette. However, only about one third of each sex say that any of their friends drink alcoholic beverages. Twelve percent of each sex claim to have classmates who use drugs.

Tensional Outlets There may be an increase of fingers-to-mouth activity, including fingernail biting or playing with hair, but on the whole tensional outlets are less evident at ten than they were at nine. The drawing in of lips so common at nine is now less evident and will soon give way to a greater tendency to extend or pout the lips. If thumb-sucking still persists, a real effort may be made by the child to resolve this habit. Increased fidgeting, hopping on one foot, never being still, does not usually occur until mid-ten and is then more common in girls than in boys.

Vision The visual behavior of the ten-year-old tells us much about other inner functioning. Ten accepts a visual examination by a vision specialist for as long as an hour or more without fatigue. Tens are complacent visually and rarely report visual symptoms (such as blurring, doubling, eye-watering), even though tests show that the majority of ten-year-olds depart In some way from theoretical "ideal" vision. But it is always necessary to differentiate what is real trouble from what is a passing (often necessary) phase of development.

Tens are best in their fixation mechanism. They can locate. Their eyes rove around a room or landscape, picking up this or that visually. But general behavior often suggests that they do not wish to penetrate deeply or define sharply. And certainly their focusing mechanism shows an unreadiness to take on this next step of definition and penetration.

"Skeletal" or fixating mechanism is in control; "visceral" or focusing system is loose. It will take another year for this sharp precision mechanism to develop. It is no wonder that, in their thinking, Tens appear to memorize better than to achieve keen insights. They prefer status quo, here and now. They don't want to reach out into new lands and especially don't want to wear glasses. Boy or girl will wear them if required to, but would prefer not to.

Tens function better binocularly than monocularly, having neither the refinement nor direction that a differentiated monocular pattern would give. Nor does the visual mechanism allow the freedom to project out widely into space. This may have some bearing on their tendency to stay close to home and to play with neighborhood groups. It may also be why they want the stimulation of movement, of bike riding and running, which thrust them bodily "out in space" when the visual mechanism can't accomplish this act as well as it will soon come to do.

Physical Development and Sex Awareness—Girls Girls at the tenth birthday appear to be about even with ten-year-old boys in size and sexual maturity. But, unlike the boys, the majority of girls will show the first slight but unmistakable signs of approaching adolescence during their tenth to eleventh year. Their childish body forms now undergo a slight softening and rounding, especially in the hip region.

There is a softer padding of the whole chest area and often slight projection of the nipples. The waist is more accented, the arms rounder, less modeled in contour. Even with the slimmer girls, who may not show softening of the body, there is a filling out of the face, which gives it a more oval shape. The features, especially the chin, seem a little less sharp and pointed, less elfin than at nine.

The majority of girls are on the brink of starting their more rapid height growth within this year, and some light, downy pubic hair appears on a number of girls. Most know about menstruation, and in some a noticeable vaginal discharge may begin. It is a normal prelude to menstruation unless it has a heavy odor or is painful or very itchy. Very few have begun to menstruate before eleven.

Partly because of their more rapid sexual (and social) development, girls are much more sex-aware than boys —though less outspoken about it. Girls are less prone to tell dirty jokes, with sex and elimination connotations. They are aware enough to have become reticent about talking of sex, even with their mothers. Yet they may be curious enough about their father and mother's relationship to ask rather personal questions—such as did their father really "do that" to their mother. The more aware girls are embarrassed when their brothers peek in on them, or when they see their fathers in the process of dressing or undressing.

Ten- to eleven-year-old girls are very much aware of their own breast development, and may be disturbed if there is no evidence of this. Often they complain of soreness and tingling in their nipples. Those who are advanced in breast development may feel unsure of themselves and not know whether they want to put their shoulders back or hunch forward to hide their changing contours.

Girls more than boys are apt to be embarrassed about receiving sex information. Some seem to have forgotten the knowledge they acquired at a younger age. But they are very interested in reading books about sex and babies. Sixty percent, when asked, claim that they think they have adequate information about sex.

Girls accept the knowledge about menstruation in different ways. Some are casual about it. Others look forward to it and indicate that they will be proud when it arrives. But there are also those who are horrified at the thought and will accept the idea only when they realize that they can't have babies unless they menstruate. Girls often ask about tampons and sanitary napkins.

Physical Development and Sex Awareness—Boys Boys and girls are of comparable height, but the rate of boys' growth is slower. The boys appear not to have changed much in their physique. But on closer inspection and in comparison with his nine-year-old self, each ten-year-old boy shows subtle changes. There is a more solid look to Ten, even though this is not necessarily reflected in his weight. There is a slight rounding off and softening of body contours, especially around the chin and neck and in the chest area. No visible traces of sexual maturing appear, except in a very small proportion of boys who may show some genital enlargement.

The ten-year-old boy's sex awareness is not much ahead of his physical maturity. He questions very little and when he does it is apt to be an offhand question—often asked at an inopportune time. Nearly half (forty-five percent), when questioned, say they think they have adequate information about sex.

Though sex information is taken rather casually, most boys are interested in reading books with simple text describing the starting, growth, and birth of a baby. Most boys already know about intercourse. They are interested in the father's role, though they may comment, "I should think that would be embarrassing." They recognize the possibility that they too will become fathers some day. They casually refer to their future children, mentioning what they might wish to tell them or save for them.

A few boys are more self-aware, more self-conscious than most. They want the door closed when they take a bath. They will no longer dress before a mother or sister, but curiosity leads them to peek at their sisters whenever they can. These are often the boys who pick up the slang words referring to sex and elimination, and who enjoy dirty jokes. They are quick to hear "dirty" words spoken by older boys and to notice them written on the bathroom walls at school. The boys who use these words may do so without understanding their meaning. They like to memorize limericks about sex or elimination. The more knowing boys begin to differentiate which ones can be said before their mothers or women in general.

2. Self-Care and Routines
Eating
APPETITE: Even poor eaters are eating more than they used to. With some, appetite may fluctuate from not so good to very good. But with others, it is affected by the food that is being served. Many can eat at any time of the day. Just the mention of a food produces a

strong response either for or against. A few are not hungry for breakfast but may make up for this with a snack at bedtime. Appetite rises during the day, and many Tens like to know ahead of time what is for supper.

PREFERENCES AND REFUSALS: Ten likes more food than he dislikes; in fact may like almost everything. Some have not only favorite foods but favorite meals. Meats such as steak, roast beef, hamburgers and hot dogs head the list, with potatoes a close second. Most enjoy pizza. A few Tens are branching out into more adult tastes for lobster and other seafoods. Raw vegetables such as carrots, celery, and tomatoes are liked better than cooked vegetables.

Ice cream and cake are the preferred desserts. There are those who crave sweets, and others who rarely touch them. Those who have a sweet tooth are ready to beg, borrow, or steal candy.

Refusals are dramatically expressed by an "I just hate . . ." or by feigning to vomit. Though Ten is adaptable and ready to try new things, most are very definite about real refusals. Liver, onions, fish, asparagus, spinach, and cooked tomatoes are all disliked. Gravy is now accepted, but "mixed-up things like stews" are still off the ten-year-old's acceptance list.

SNACKS: Between-meal snacking is indulged in by the majority of ten-year-olds. Cookies, "junk food," and fruit are preferred, with a drink of soda. Milk is drunk by some.

TABLE BEHAVIOR: There is much less complaint about Ten's table manners. As one child of this age reported, "I wouldn't say they were bad, and I wouldn't say they were good." The chief specific complaints are poor posture, elbows on the table, and the fork being held with a fisted grasp. There is a tendency to encroach on a neighbor with a lifted elbow. The napkin may still be forgotten temporarily but can be brought to mind. One reason there is less talk about table manners is that Ten has proved himself up to acceptable standards away from home or when there are guests. A goal has been reached, which allows for relaxation when the family is alone.

Sleep

BEDTIME: Tens are not yet aware of when they are tired and ready for bed. They still need to be reminded. And as always with Ten, alternatives are possible. "Mostly I go quite well; sometimes not." "If I'm tired I go right away, or if not I hang around." In general, bedtime is from eight-thirty to nine-thirty, with perhaps a majority going to bed at nine after a strong parental push.

Boys go to bed more easily and fall asleep more rapidly than girls.

They are, however, more ritualistic in their preparations and like to be tucked in by their mothers. Girls more often have difficulty in falling asleep. Listening to the radio, reading, or just lying awake thinking are common presleep activities. Most are asleep by nine-thirty, with boys usually asleep earlier.

On the whole, Ten sleeps through the night. The child of this age has the sense of sleeping well and is now reducing the time of sleeping to ten and a half or nine and a half hours, boys usually sleeping longer than girls.

NIGHT: Tens still may have nightmares, though they report a marked reduction or even disappearance. In fact, Ten reports as many pleasant dreams as unpleasant ones. Boy or girl notes that the bad ones are more apt to come during the flu or a cold, after an operation, or when frightened by something in a book or movie.

MORNING: Waking and getting up are usually not a problem for Ten. Many are even early risers, especially boys. Seven A.M. is a common waking hour. Ten can go about his business—dressing, taking out the dog, making breakfast—with much less reminding than is needed for going to bed. Some girls, usually the ones who resisted going to bed, may resist getting up. They sleep late and may need to be dragged out of bed.

Bathing and Care of Hair There is something about soap and water and being a ten-year-old that does not mix. The otherwise nice and cooperative Ten stands his ground when it comes to taking a bath. Girl or boy seems positively to dislike water. They especially dislike washing their faces.

There are, however, some ten-year-olds who have always been neat and meticulous. And there are those who wouldn't think of skipping their daily bath. Others already give glimpses of a future time when cleanliness acquires social significance. If parents recognize Ten's antipathy to washing, they may more readily adopt suitable measures. They will appreciate that Ten needs to be reminded to bathe, even driven to the bathroom. Mother may need to run the bath, empty and wash out the tub.

At times Ten will accept a bathing schedule if it doesn't interfere with other activities, especially radio or television programs. If left to his own devices, a boy might slip through three or four weeks without ever thinking of bathing. However, though Ten may resist strongly, he often enjoys his bath once he is in it and plays in the tub for as much as an hour. Many prefer a tub bath to a shower, though a shower often facilitates the shampoo with girls, who need help with rinsing their hair.

As for other grooming—combing hair, brushing teeth, and care of nails—all are in the hinterland as far as Ten is concerned. Short hair may solve the girls' problem. Chewing carrots and celery may be as important to the care of teeth as brushing.

Clothing and Care of Room Choice of clothes, especially school clothes, is of interest to most ten-year-olds. A few mothers continue to lay out the child's clothes, but if Tens don't approve they will change the selection. Though Tens are fairly good at choosing, they may not have considered the weather, and are also apt to put on the same outfit several days in a row. Therefore they need to be checked. Fortunately most respond fairly well to suggestion.

Love of old clothes predominates, and dress clothes may be so distasteful that a ten-year-old boy will refuse to go to Sunday school because he has to wear a white shirt.

Tens do not wish to draw attention to themselves either by dress clothes or bright colors. Some Tens hate new clothes so intensely that they will not wear them at all. Mothers regretfully report that "new clothes are handed on unworn."

The treatment of clothes is now fairly dismal. As one girl reports, "We sling our things down somewhere, but"—she adds with ten-year-old cooperativeness—"we do have to hang them up afterward." Dropping clothes "just where he stepped out of them" is all too commonly reported by parents. Some parents settle for the use of a single chair as a repository for clothes, plus a weekly cleaning of their child's room to ensure a periodic fresh start toward neatness.

BUYING CLOTHES: Ten is beginning to help in the selection and purchase of new clothes. Girls more than boys enjoy shopping with their mother. Boys are more apt to dislike both trying on new clothes and wearing them. Whether or not the child goes to the store with mother, she needs to consult him about his taste. Some sort of a compromise can usually be reached. The mother is usually granted the final decision.

Hand-me-downs are not as a rule scorned; in fact they may be cherished because they have that well-worn feeling.

CARE OF ROOM: With Ten's interest in the old, the tried, the casual in clothes, you could not expect him to live in extreme order in his room. Girl or boy says, "My room's a mess. If it was neat I couldn't tell where anything was. Books piled on top of things. More *friendly*, more natural that way." Messiness may alternate with neatness, but

Ten never finds enough places for storing treasures or hoarding useless odds and ends.

Ten needs a room of his own where he can come to terms with untidiness and achieve a fuller sense of self through specially chosen possessions and accustomed surroundings. Order will be created in time. Even at ten, pennants, banners, or pictures (football and baseball heroes for boys, and horses or perhaps Olympic gymnasts for girls) are beginning to embellish the walls. A bed may be left unmade, but a pennant is fastidiously placed at just the right angle.

Money Most depend on an allowance for money, though some supplement this with earnings. The weekly allowance ranges in amount from twenty-five or fifty cents to two dollars or more. (Inflation will undoubtedly cause all allowance figures given in this book to increase as time goes by.) The actual amount varies widely from family to family.

Many are very casual about money at this age—they forget to ask for it, leave it in a pocket, or lose it. Many parents say, "Irresponsible." Some save a little; others save nothing. Some worry that the family's money will not last.

Spending shows a wide range. Many Tens squander their allowance on worthless objects. Many like to "treat all the kids." But some plan quite carefully when buying presents, and most are aware of Christmas obligations.

Work Ten is not what you would call a worker. Even when paid for a job, such as emptying the wastebaskets, his response the first week may be splendid, but then comes the inevitable petering out. Tens can dabble at many tasks—burning papers, mowing the lawn, shoveling snow, baby-sitting at home—but they have no sense of continuation. Some days Tens are good about doing a job and some days not. Under pressure, nice qualities may be overshadowed by feelings of fatigue and resentment. Parents need to be quite flexible in their demands on Ten, and to realize that a boy or girl works best along with a congenial adult.

3. Emotions

What complimentary adjectives pop into the heads of friends or parents of the ten-year-old as they describe girl or boy! Nice, happy, casual, sincere, relaxed, companionable, poised, terribly friendly, frank and open—all tell the same tale.

With many, the change from nine to ten years is imperceptible. It comes so gradually that it is only through reviewing the past that the quality of the present can be discovered. But sometimes the shift comes suddenly. "She suddenly snapped out of many difficulties; it was like a metamorphosis." Or, "He's on the happy side this year. He was on the other side last year." It is almost as though there were a real divide between nine and ten years and that Ten has come into the foothills of a new terrain, of the whole new cycle of growth from ten to fourteen. Some Tens have a very precarious footing in this new terrain; they may be preparing to enter but have not yet done so.

On the whole, life is good for the ten-year-old, so good that he doesn't even have to think about it, and may be quite taken aback when asked specific questions about his emotional state. The child frequently answers that he doesn't know, can't say, has never thought about it. Statements are often qualified or include a range of possibilities with a "Well, it depends . . ." or "Sometimes I do, and sometimes I don't."

On the whole, life is better at ten than it was at nine, especially since the child can "do a lot more things." Ten is a person of action rather than of thought. Simple occasions give great happiness: playtime outdoors after supper, no homework, a visit to an amusement park. Good luck is pretty much on his side, though bad luck may have its occasional days, but "it all depends."

Fears are at a low ebb. Former fears of dogs and of the dark may show their beginning resolution by the fact that Ten reports spontaneously that he does not fear them now. Both boys and girls tend to be afraid of snakes; also, they tell us that they might not like to meet up with a lion in the dark or be all alone in an old castle. Ten worries nearly as much as he fears. There are always lessons and homework to worry about, and getting to school on time. But worries are, on the whole, rather specific and individual. One boy may worry that he might lose his wallet; a girl might be afraid that there isn't enough gas in the family car.

The most common emotional expression at ten is, surprisingly enough, anger. The contented, cooperative, nice little ten-year-old suddenly explodes in unmistakable rage; is quick to strike out, kick, or even bite. If more controlled, he boils over verbally, may cry, or go to his room in a furor of name-calling and foot-stamping. But Ten is selective about expressions of anger: "Depends who I'm angry at. If I'm angry at my sister, I shoot paper clips and rubber bands at her. And if one of my parents punishes me and I don't think it's fair, I just go in my room and boil over. At school you just take it—

sometimes I feel it's unfair at school. And I talk about it to my friends." Some outlet for anger can usually be found, even if it's only telling the dog about it, or planning some revenge which is never carried out. It is the short-livedness, the hot-point quality of anger which distinguishes Ten. It's all over in no time. The child of this age usually has an efficient exhaust system.

Though Tens may cry when angry, on the whole they feel "too old for that." This is one of the least tearful ages. A boy stoically says he wouldn't cry if he "got cut or couldn't go someplace," but might if his father died. The very children who formerly burst into tears now collect themselves and speak calmly. Sadness is occasionally at the basis of tears, but not very often. Anger is a more potent cause.

Ten's feelings may get hurt but usually not deeply. If they are hurt, many "cry and go home," but some can pretend that whatever it was didn't happen. Tens restabilize quickly and in general cover up any difficulties.

As with expressions of anger or happiness, Tens have sudden bursts of affection for their parents and give physical expressions of warmth, such as hugging and kissing. They say very naturally that they like their parents best of anything in the world, and can often accept demands or suggestions without conflict. Most are happy and contented in their family and their homes, and would seldom wish to change their lot with others, even though the others might have more possessions than they. But still they may have a hankering for a bicycle like that of some friend or the radio of another. Some boys covet the strength of other boys. A girl might like to be prettier.

Perhaps Ten's greatest difficulties are in relation to siblings—the eternal problem of close comparison. But fortunately their own busy lives allow them to give more latitude toward brothers and sisters than they did formerly.

In marked contrast to feelings toward siblings are feelings about competition and contemporaries. Though Ten likes the pull and tug of combat, he doesn't like to be best, feels funny if singled out from all the others for praise, and thinks about how "all the other kids might feel." Most want to do their best and would prefer to be as good as the others but not necessarily to win.

The average ten-year-old is not very skilled at high-class humor, but is watchful for possible puns and has a ready stock of corny jokes. He especially likes practical jokes that are often not funny to the adult. The child pounces on words with a possible double meaning—"Virginia, you must be a state." Telling a joke is a finer art than Ten can often master. He may tell the point too soon, or even worse there may be no point to tell. And yet he hopefully asks, "Get it?" His humor will have to change a great deal before it is appreciated by the adult.

4. The Growing Self

Ten has reached the happy state of being casually sure of himself. He can branch out into a wide range of interests, yet can concentrate on each interest of the moment. Ten likes to complete a task but doesn't wish to enlarge or elaborate upon it, preferring to cover the whole terrain with little rootlets. This is no time for deep growing. This is the time for expanding, for experiencing. Boy or girl wishes to try everything.

Tens move through the quicker, sharper, more superficial world of thought rather than that of deeper feelings, though they do have a general feeling of well-being. Ten may say that his self is "the way you think inside, not what you say." He relates these thoughts to his head, his brain, or his mind, which are where he is most apt to say his self is. Though aware of his heart, he is not yet ready to delve into its depths.

Girls and boys have some idea of their own greatest assets and their greatest faults. Some specific ability—such as reading, spelling, or ice skating—may be, according to them, their greatest asset, though a sense of fairness and being a good sport are uppermost in many a Ten's mind. Faults are recalled more specifically than assets —that he sticks out his tongue while practicing the piano; that he forgets to brush his teeth; that she picks frosting off the cake or writes 1987 when it's 1988.

Tens are, on the whole, content with themselves, their age, their parents, and their homes. The best time is "now," that is, ten years of age, because "you're not too young and not too old." A few, less well-grounded in the present, might wish to be much younger or much older. And as is often true with Ten, the reasons are very specific—for wanting to be younger, it is because "little children's clothes are nice and cute"; for older, "Then you can buy your own things." One ten-year-old girl managed to take in the whole gamut of past and future in one sweep: "The best time is from when you're a baby to eight years old and from twenty-one to thirty. From one to eight, you can do almost anything you feel like and don't have to go by the rules. And from twenty-one to thirty, you go out places and stay out longer; and you aren't going to college and you don't have to work for your money till you're about thirty. Between twenty-one and thirty, you get money from your mother."

Ten's wishes are like the rest of him. He thinks either in broad, general terms of peace on earth, good health, and happiness, or in specific terms related to material possessions, such as having a bicycle or a tractor. The joys of living on a farm with dogs and horses all their own may entice many ten-year-olds. A desire to have babies or to care for them is one of the strong wishes of girls.

Many Tens have thought about college (eighty-four percent of our girls, seventy percent of our boys say they plan to go to college), career, and marriage, and have some rather definite ideas about their choices. But these choices are strongly influenced by their parents—not through the parents' persuasion, but because Ten often identifies with them, admires them, and wishes to copy them. Therefore the college chosen is often the college of mother or father; the husband preferred should be "like Daddy" or just fatherly, and should be of the same profession as Ten's father. Boys are generally less articulate on the subject, especially about their future wives, whom they may not even have thought about.

As for a career, again Ten may choose the profession or occupation of his mother or father. However, it is often difficult for Ten to choose one profession out of the many possibilities that come to mind. But with both sexes there is a drive to help people and animals. Teacher or veterinarian are the leading career choices for the girls we interviewed; doctor, carpenter, or athlete for the boys. And the tendency for Ten to be inclusive makes the girls want to have both a career and marriage. As one Ten explained, "I wouldn't want just to be married and be a wife." Eighty-seven percent of the girls say they want to be married, approximately the same number as in 1950. But now eighty-two percent of the boys as compared with only fifty percent in 1950 say they wish to marry. Now eighty-four percent of the girls and seventy-nine percent of the boys expect to have children.

5. Interpersonal Relationships

If ever the word *family* acquires its true meaning, it is when the child is ten years of age. Not only home, but father and mother are just about right in Ten's eyes. Even his siblings, if they are not too close in age and don't needle him all the time, become family assets.

This is the last age for some time to come when the child enters happily into a family excursion.

Mother has again become the center of the universe, as she was for Five's. Both boys and girls get on well with her. They not only depend on her, but look up to her and admire her. Girls especially confide in her, confess to her. They may tell her so much that they are accused of tattling. They want to feel that their mother is their friend and that they can trust her.

Ten-year-olds especially like to have mother available when they get home from school. If she is not at home and available to chat with them about school when *they* are ready, Tens may have little enthusiasm for a chat later on.

They accept the fact that she wants them to do better, and they try to respond casually. In their turn, they are spontaneously helpful and may especially like to surprise their mother with some thoughtful gesture, such as bringing her a breakfast tray. Both boys and girls are very demonstrative in their affection for their mothers and like to be tucked in at night.

Fathers, in their own way, are also very important. In fact, father may even surpass mother in Ten's eyes and frequently is adored and idolized. Girls especially have strong feelings for their fathers and may be cut to the quick by any reprimand from them.

It's the companionship with father that has now become such fun. And father may enjoy it as much as does the ten-year-old. Going on trips, hikes, playing ball or watching ballgames, swimming, skating, or just palling around—these are the activities Ten enjoys most with father.

Tens not only respect their parents but also respect their role as parents. Their oft-repeated quotations of "Mommy says . . ." show that they accept their mother's word as law. They believe that parents should love their children, but disapprove of overindulgence. "As long as they're fair." That's all Ten wants—"not too strict and not too easy." They may attempt to test their parents, but if they aren't going to yield, Ten accepts their demands and is really glad not to be allowed to go too far.

As nice as Tens are, they still don't, as a rule, have the stamina or perspective to get on with younger siblings, especially with those between ages six and nine. Most have no real desire to be an only child, but they are guilty at times of wishing the troublesome sibling would "just disappear" or "go live somewhere else for a while."

Ask a ten-year-old boy how he gets on with brothers and sisters and he will tell you, "Well, sometimes we get along, and sometimes we don't." It's usually the younger sibling who taunts and pesters till Ten is forced, as it were, to retaliate physically. When the parent steps in to stop the fight, poor Ten usually gets the blame because he is older. Ten often feels that decisions are not fair.

Ten gets on best with much younger siblings, is good about caring for and helping with those under five. These younger ones are often reported to "adore" the ten-year-old. Ten especially enjoys reading to them.

Tens get on a little better with older siblings than they used to, and better than they will again until the older one has gained the broader outlook of fifteen years of age. Older siblings may play with ten-year-olds and take them places, but often they consider Ten a nuisance, especially when he tattles on them.

Friends, friends—how Tens love their friends. They want to bring one home from school every day, but most of all they like their neighborhood pals. They want the friend who is available at all times. And there is always so much to talk about with them. It's surprising to hear how much Ten knows about his friends, from their birthdays and bedtime hour, to their fathers' or mothers' occupation. One of the qualities Ten likes best in friends is that they can be trusted.

There is more "getting mad" or "not playing" among girls than boys, though the expression of this anger by "not speaking" doesn't last very long. Some Tens report that they used to fight with their friends, but that they haven't even had an argument for a long time. Ten can be quite diplomatic. One ten-year-old girl was known to add a note to the bottom of her birthday card invitation: "Please don't tell anybody. I couldn't ask everybody, and I don't want to lose any friends."

Boys are more apt to form large play groups than are girls. Certain sports, such as baseball, demand grouping. Groups are usually fluid, and a child may move freely from one group to another according to his interests. Tens also eagerly participate in formal organizations, such as the Scouts. In his own spontaneous grouping, Ten usually tries not to exclude others who he knows would wish to join. He doesn't want to keep them out by building up a wall of secrecy (as will be the case at Eleven.) In his casual way, he simply doesn't let the others know about the existence of the club.

It is true that the majority of girls are "not interested in boys yet," or as the boys say, "We haven't gotten to girls yet." When asked if he would like to date, one boy replied, "No way!" Both sexes, however, by their use of the word *yet* are quite aware that a future of boy-girl relationships lies ahead of them. Some girls are still included in the boys' play, but only if they are good at sports. Boys do "act rough," chase girls, pull their hair, push them down.

6. Activities and Interests

Play is paramount in the lives of many ten-year-olds. School and routines are even considered interruptions of the more important life of play. Tens are happily busy in whatever they do, and now have the skill and stamina needed in gross motor activities. Their days and their activities almost seem to plan themselves. There seems to be a happy meeting ground as enjoyment of the same activity draws Tens together. Boys like to organize for baseball, and even welcome available girls to make up a sizable team. Bicycling is more often enjoyed in groups of two or more. Now that they are quite safe on their bikes and can cycle without fatigue, they take longer trips. They even pick out rough roads in order to enjoy "that bumpy feeling."

Tens also enjoy sliding, ice and roller skating, swimming, climbing, rowing, and, above all, running. Some ten-year-old girls are known to be the fastest runners in their school. Racing is fun either on foot or on a bike.

Boys and girls mostly separate in their choice of other outdoor activities. The girls are busy at jacks, hopscotch, jump rope, and roller-skating. The boys may join in at times, but they prefer to hunt or fish if they have the opportunity. Even as early as ten, girls are competitive with boys and may establish their own softball team. Boys and girls share an interest in horseback riding, but the girls often show a far greater desire, and even passion, for this activity. As one ten-year-old girl expressed it, "I'd rather have a colt than a baby."

Animals and pets are of great interest to most ten-year-olds. Many show capacity and interest in caring for a dog or cat, but they can scarcely be expected to be fully responsible.

The ten-year-old is recognizing the growing-up process, feels on the verge of more mature interests, and is ready to give up earlier, more childish activities. This shift is so recent that he often feels a little superior about it; may say, "I just don't think those boys (nine-year-olds) will ever get over playing with guns." His mother felt the same way about him only six months ago. Or the very girls who enjoyed doll play may now classify it as "babyish."

However, there are still many boys who persist in playing cowboys, Wild West, or whatever the current gun game may be. And there are girls who may have given up paper dolls but who love to play house with real dolls, dressing them up and putting them through play activities similar to their own ten-year-old experiences.

Though indoor play is usually second best to outdoor play, Tens can occupy themselves happily indoors, especially with friends. Boys and girls enjoy playing the usual table games together. A great deal of time and effort goes into Ten's collections. Girl or boy will collect almost anything and may have a number of collections. When asked if she had collections, one girl exclaimed, "Do I have collections! Well—stamps, postcards, books, horseshoes, and just odd things." Added to these, Ten might collect coins, shells, storybook dolls, china animals, boxes (Ten loves boxes), stones, pictures of stones, birds' nests, snakeskins, airplane models, model soldiers, or just candy and gum wrappers. Most are not particularly selective, nor are they ready to classify or display. Mostly they just want more of what they are collecting.

Girls are busy writing plays, dressing up, and performing their plays. Some sew, either for their dolls or occasionally for themselves. A few may knit.

Some boys who are skillful with their hands draw gadgets, architectural plans, jet planes, and rockets. Others draw elaborate pictures of battles, violence, or cars and trains, with running commentaries. Ten likes to construct, making model planes or boats or rocket ships, or creating his own forms through carpentry. Boys need a place in the basement or a workshop where they can have a tool bench. They also need a place for a chemistry set if interest in chemistry goes beyond the concoction of explosives.

Clubs of all kinds are strong. Of all ages, Ten is one of the readiest to respond to the call of the group. Tens are enthusiastic Scouts. They also like to make up clubs of their own—secret clubs, mystery clubs. Such clubs demand high standards from their members. For one club of boys the motto was "No sulking." For a club of girls it was "Have will power" and "Share hardships together." Ten may show his age, however, by choosing as a club password "potatoes."

But clubs are fluid—here today and gone tomorrow. Some even remain in the planning stage. Usually the hut or tree house hasn't yet become the clubhouse, though there is a dawning sense of wanting a place to meet.

As for summer camp, reaction is highly variable. Some like it; some don't. Within reason, the child's preference should be considered.

Sedentary Looking and Listening Activities Ten's relatively active life comes to a standstill at times. Children of this age are blessed with a wide provision of entertainment, information, and thought-provoking media—television, radio, books, and movies. They most often take them in this order of preference, though at times they repudiate all in favor of outdoor active play.

Television is strong. Some girls watch as much as forty or fifty hours a week, though according to their own reporting, fifty percent watch twenty hours or fewer. On the whole, the passion for television shown at nine may be diminishing slightly. It is "no longer a matter of life and death," according to one mother. "He's tapering off—thank goodness!" says another.

Cartoons and comedies are the favorite kinds of program. Some girls and boys know they may have nightmares if they watch mysteries and thus avoid them. During a convalescence there may be a marked rise of interest in soap operas and game shows, which may be watched all day long.

Video games, which are often hooked up to the television, become increasingly popular. Stereo is now also a major interest and is played loud and long.

Reading shows as wide a variation of interest as television and radio, though more Tens are interested than are not. The avid readers have been avid since seven years of age, and the uninterested readers may never read more than they have to.

Besides horse and dog stories, even "sad ones that are going to come out good in the end," Ten likes biographies of famous people, adventure, and mysteries. Some restrict themselves to stories about children of their own age and time. Others like to experience children of their own age growing up to become famous people. Historical books are interesting, but sometimes they lack sufficient adventure.

The newspaper still receives only a glance from Tens. They may pick up the headline and look for pictures of accidents or war pictures. They do keep up with the funnies, though. Comic books, happily for many parents, are losing their hold on Tens.

It is rather surprising to find that Tens are not too interested in movies. They don't especially care what they see, and may prefer not to go at all unless they think it will be a good movie. Most Tens go only occasionally. Cartoons, Westerns, family comedies and slapstick comedies are favorites, with murder mysteries showing a rise.

7. School Life

Given the chance, Ten can really like school. Girl or boy likes the teacher and likes to learn. But, more than liking to be taught, he wants to be kept interested and motivated. You may hear a girl say to her teacher, "Gee, I've learned an awful lot from you!" Both sexes hate to miss school because they feel so much will be taught that they "won't be able to catch up."

Teacher is important to them even though they are not teacher-centered. Tens usually respect the teacher and often accept her word as law even more than that of their parents. They are most aware of the teacher's outward physical appearance and report about her size, her shape, her hair. Girls often comment to the teacher herself about how nice her hair looks. Tens especially do not want a partial teacher. They want her to like all the children, to be their friend. Tens also like their teacher to schedule time and activities for them. Then boy or girl will be the first to remind her if she has forgotten something in the schedule. Rather than starting the day in a more formal way, they may like to start it with stories.

Tens not only like to listen to stories but like to tell their own about something they have seen or heard or read about. Both boys and girls can talk on and on, and may run what they are talking about "into the ground," as one mother put it. Talking can indeed be one of Ten's favorite activities.

Their interest span tends to be short. They need a certain amount of liberty in moving around the classroom and can move quietly. They may want to get up to sharpen a pencil, go to another child, or go to the library. They handle these excursions well, without the need for permission. There is some note-passing, especially between girls. These notes are often about their schoolwork or what they are going to do at recess.

Tens take their studies in stride, but have specific preferences. They love geography, may know the fifty states and their capitals, adore to place states, rivers, mountains, cities on a map.

Ten loves to take dictation, though handwriting is often sloppy. Many have lost the precision they had at nine. When Ten writes a book report, he combines ideas in short, choppy sentences but with enough punch to catch the reader's interest.

And how the child of this age loves to memorize! Girl or boy masters long poems like "Paul Revere's Ride," and recites them with good expression. Ideally, since they enjoy it so much, more time might be spent on memorizing and less on penetration in thinking. Ten has difficulty in combining or connecting two facts and prefers to take things simply as they are. His catalogue of memorized material will stand him in good stead later—for penetration will come.

And toward the end of the fifth grade, boy or girl loves the challenge of oral arithmetic, has arithmetic facts well in hand and enjoys the exercise of putting these to use in a long, strung-out arithmetic problem of a fluid, step-to-step movement ($5 + 6 - 2 + 3 \times 5 =$?). They also like pictorial material. This is an excellent age for educational TV and computer instruction. Ten sees and listens well and wants to discuss. Sometimes curiosity is so great and listening so facile that the child becomes more interested in an adjoining group's activity than in his own.

Sufficient time needs to be spent out-of-doors or in a gym, for Tens want to exercise their muscles. Boys more than girls want organized sports.

Because Ten's interest span is short, a teacher needs to plan for timely shifts, especially to break into the more sedentary demands. Singing is a favorite "break-in" activity. Ten loves to sing and joins well with a group. But don't give boys any "sissy" songs. Dislike of such songs may well be a strong indication that ten-year-old boys are becoming aware of their manliness.

8. Ethical Sense

Many parents report that their ten-year-olds have a rather strict ethical sense. They are concerned when little children are pushed around. They might not accept an honor if they do not feel worthy of it. About half feel that they can tell right from wrong, though "I'm not always so hot at it." Most say they distinguish right from wrong by what their mothers tell them, what they learn in Sunday school and by their own conscience: "If you wanted to chop down a tree, the first thing you do is use a saw and not an ax if great bunches of people are around."

Though Tens may sound very ethical, as they tell it, when it comes right down to actual practice, they do not always come up to the mark. On the whole they are truthful, especially about big things, but most steer a course between real truthfulness and down-right lying by just not saying anything. Or they can alibi or fudge a bit. And sometimes white lies are, according to them, necessary to save other people's feelings or to get what they want. But when mother is present, and the relationship is good, Ten usually tells the truth. And it's easier to confess the truth when alone with mother—and after the crime is slightly distant in time.

As for taking the blame, that's not so easy. Ten's mother is blamed less than earlier, but any sibling near at hand is likely to be blamed automatically.

Tens are definitely concerned about fairness, particularly in their parents' treatment of them and their siblings. Tens are polite and obedient, for the most part, but when they feel that certain demands are not fair, they are ready to argue it out with their parents. Sometimes, however, what is fair and what the child wants are not clearly separated. Happily, Ten judges both cheating and stealing as "awful" and is rarely motivated toward either.

Boys and girls of this age have rather definite ideas about swearing. They think it is "awful" for their parents to swear. They are a bit more permissive about drinking. They don't mind grownups drinking, as long as they don't drink "too much." (Except for those puritanical Tens who declare that their mothers and fathers never touch liquor—though this may be quite untrue.)

About three-quarters of both sexes are satisfied that we as a society are doing enough about integration. Fewer than half think most politicians are dishonest. About half think that they themselves might one day do something to improve social conditions.

chapter five

THE ELEVEN-YEAR-OLD

MATURITY PROFILE

The typical eleven-year-old—what a change from friendly Ten! Just as your lovely five-year-old changed at six to a young person who found it as easy to object as to agree, as comfortable to reject your suggestions as to cooperate with them, now Ten's easy ways are replaced with often highly contrary and oppositional behavior. Though not yet a teenager, Eleven very often behaves like a beginning adolescent.

Perhaps the two adjectives which describe him best are egocentric and energetic. He is constantly on the go—eating, talking, moving about. It is hard for Eleven to sit quietly. He seems almost constantly in motion.

Egocentric to a supreme degree, the child of this age makes little or no effort to cooperate in even the most minor ways, let alone smooth things out for other people. He is slow to respond and very quick to criticize. If mother's behavior displeases in any way, girl or boy will insist, "No decent mother would do such a thing!"

Meager as the child's requirements of self are, he requires and expects perfection from others, especially from mother. "You lied! You lied!" he will scream at her. "You tell me to tell the truth, and now you lied!" (This, if she deviates in the slightest degree from total consistency of word or act.)

Help around the house? Forget it. A typical Eleven will say, as mother drives into the yard with her station wagon full of groceries, "Don't think I'm going to help you put those away!" As one mother puts it, "Tasks the child has done willingly for years—now it's easier to do them myself."

Another mother expressed it very succinctly when she commented, "Your best bet is to run the house like a hotel. You provide the meals and the service, and expect nothing back."

One eleven-year-old girl, quite typical, insisted that she was adopted. Her mother suggested that she look at her father's profile and then at her own and see how it seemed to her. "Okay," the girl replied. "I may be yours. But if you *had* been adopting, you wouldn't have adopted me."

Yes, Eleven is indeed a very different person from his ten-year-old self. Is this big change, seemingly for the worse, something that parents should be worried about? Not at all. The experienced parent understands that one of the main tasks of childhood is to become strong and independent. To do this, the child must get free of his parents, at least to some extent. And if she has a good memory, a mother will know that this kind of rebellion has been seen before, though perhaps in a less vigorous way.

She will remember the way in which her good little two-year-old turned into a "terrible" two-and-a-half, a child who lived at opposite extremes. Whatever mother offered, he wanted the opposite, and "No" was his most frequently used word.

She will remember that, even more recently, her docile, lovable, and eager-to-please five-year-old turned six, and became, briefly, an almost impossible person to live with. "No, I won't," was the child's favorite phrase. Tears and tantrums marked her days. And "I hate you" was an all-too-common response to any kind of parental discipline.

For it seems to be the way of Nature that any age of balanced equilibrium in the child's life needs to be followed by an age of marked disequilibrium. And Eleven is a prize example of a period of very definite disequilibrium. On his behalf, we should note that much of Eleven's inept behavior can be ascribed to sheer inexperience in making interpersonal adjustments within a culture which is changing as he himself changes. His quarreling with siblings, rebelliousness against parents, and resistance to imposed tasks and proprieties are largely manifestations of early preadolescent self-assertiveness and self-absorption.

Eleven-year-olds tend to be at their very worst with their mother. It is, unfortunately, quite natural to take things out on that all-important person at the center of one's life when things go wrong. This is true to such an extent that when father finds Eleven and mother in a terrible tangle, he is all too likely to make matters worse by complaining, "Are you two at it again?"

They are indeed likely to be "at it." For no matter how understanding a mother may be, no matter how much she loves her child and appreciates the difficulties of growing up, it is hard to be calm and collected with someone who baits and criticizes at every turn. "Just wait till I've had my coffee in the morning before you start criticizing," one mother told her eleven-year-old daughter. "The rest of the day is yours." "Resistant" and "rebellious" are the adjectives used most by others in talking about their child at this difficult age.

Eleven's criticism of mother, his challenge to her rules and restrictions, suggest correctly that the child of this age is more adept at rebellion than response. As he matures he will bring the two into improved balance. But at his present stage of development he tends to set up challenging resistances in order to evoke responses which provide a leverage to work against. This is not malice aforethought or simple obstinacy. It is a developing expedient which he uses, often very clumsily, to define his own status and that of others.

What then can we say that is good about the typical Eleven? A great deal, actually, if we can overlook his almost totally uncooperative and critical manner when it comes to mother. Even the fact that the child of this age is always eating, and his stomach sometimes seems like a bottomless pit may give satisfaction to the parent who earlier complained that son or daughter "never eats a bite."

One of Eleven's most engaging attributes is that away from home and family he can be mannerly, helpful, and outgoing. We have often suggested—and only partly in jest—that if all parents of eleven-year-olds could just swap their children around, life would be more comfortable for all concerned.

As much trouble as many children of this age make in the family, they themselves relish family life. They may state, "I'm a free person. Why do I have to do what my family tells me?" But at the same time they love the things the family does together. A girl may compliment her mother, "You're wonderful this year, Mommy. You're so active."

Teachers will tell you that eleven-year-olds are not the cooperative, accepting students that ten-year-olds tend to be. Not as bad as they can be at home, they still give quite a lot of trouble at school so far as conduct goes. But they are, nevertheless, keenly interested in their relative standing in the class, work hard for good grades, and are pleased when they do well. Though Eleven may tell you that he hates school, actually much of the time girl or boy behaves reasonably well.

Eleven loves to argue, but as one mother explained, "It is all one way. *You* cannot argue with *him*!"

Emotionally, Eleven does not have things too well in hand, though most boys and girls of this age seem quite unaware of the turmoil they cause. "What do you mean my 'rude outburst'?" a girl may ask innocently after a typical eleven-year-old explosion.

However, they themselves do admit that when really angry they "blow up," "blow their fuse," "blow their top." Physical violence is even more prominent than at ten, and is the most common response when angry. Elevens fight, hit, kick, slam doors. But violent verbal retorts are also common. They yell, swear, talk back, say mean and sarcastic things.

Fortunately, moods come and go, and things do not always look black. Eleven may burst into laughter as suddenly as he bursts into rage. In fact, Eleven literally blows hot and cold—first he feels too hot, and then he feels too cold. His body, as well as his emotions, tends to be at one extreme or the other.

No longer the balanced "Sometimes I do, sometimes I don't," of Ten, Eleven either loves or hates, and admittedly may seem to hate more than he loves. It may be another year before most reach a comparatively middle ground in their reactions to living.

Humor, though not always attractive since it all too often verges on the smutty, is less clumsy than it was a year earlier. An eleven-year-old can actually be mildly amusing, especially when insulting classmates: "Say it, don't spray it."

Though Eleven's typical emotional reactions to others are not always pleasing, in their own egocentric way children of this age are usually quite pleased with themselves. "I'm usually pretty happy," or "I'm a pretty happy person," boy or girl will tell you. That they often make mother unhappy does not seriously interfere with their own enjoyment of living.

They really do enjoy life and take great interest in all that goes on. In fact, many are regular gossips. In response to the questions which we, the examiners, ask when we interview them, they will tell us anything, often far more about family and family problems and activities than we had bargained for. As one teacher of eleven-year-olds commented, "When I get through teaching this class, I'm going to retire and live on blackmail."

Eleven will tell you, all unwittingly, "As my father said to my mother, 'I just can't stand for all your extravagance.' " Or "At breakfast we all scream and eat, but mostly we just scream."

For better or worse, Eleven is always on the go, always active, ready for anything. Even when sitting in a chair he twists and turns, waves his arms, wiggles his feet. In fact, the eleven-year-old is bursting with energy and enthusiasm for the things he likes to do, which are many. Outdoors, girl or boy may enjoy almost anything that involves physical activity—and the more active, the better. Girls, of course, love horses, to the extent that many plan to be veterinarians when they grow up.

Indoors, Elevens love to collect anything that takes their fancy: stones, stamps, postcards, china or wooden animals, boxes, matchbox cars, baseball cards. They also enjoy card games, table games, puzzles. Secret clubs or Boy or Girl Scouts, Campfire Girls, Rainbow Girls, 4-H, take up many happy hours. Eleven is not an age when boy or girl characteristically complains that "there's nothing to do." For Eleven, there is almost always something to do.

Friendships, as throughout all these years, are very important. Some children have just one or two best friends, others a whole gang. Girls, as earlier, tend to have rather intense and strong friendships, with much quarreling and making up. And boys do more quarreling with friends than they used to.

For most, it is still too early for dating, though some make such statements as "We girls each know somebody we sort of like," or "We boys don't mind girls, but we don't usually play with them. I guess we would if we had to."

However, when asked about possible girlfriends or boyfriends, some give a little half-smile even while denying the possibility that they could stand a person of the opposite sex, suggesting that heterosexual friendships may be not too far in the future. In fact, for all the negative comments which many make, more than half the eleven-year-olds questioned by us about dating said they would *like to start*.

Looking to the far future, eighty-nine percent of girls questioned, seventy-two percent of boys, say they do plan to get married someday. Approximately the same number say they plan to have children. The future of the family as an institution in the minds of these children seems safe indeed.

More than half of our eleven-year-olds admit (or claim) that either they or their friends smoke cigarettes. Approximately one-fourth claim that either they or their friends on occasion take a drink and/or use drugs. (One may hope that such claims may at least represent a slight exaggeration.)

An eleven-year-old at his best can be a delightful person—alert, imaginative, outgoing, energetic, ready for anything. But there are deep-lying characteristics of the age—rebelling against mother, quarreling with friends, extreme egocentricity—which can make this a time when many parents become discouraged.

Fortunately, as so often, an age of rather marked disequilibrium is followed by a time of equilibrium and calm. Twelve predictably follows Eleven, and twelve years of age, in many, is a comfortable time for all concerned.

Eleven is an age at which parents sometimes consider a geographic cure. In applying this cure, one simply removes a troublesome or uncomfortable child from the situation which is giving difficulty and sends him to camp, boarding school, or perhaps for a visit to grandparents. Admittedly, one cannot expect or even wish to solve all problems in this possibly evasive manner. But there are times when this solution may be appropriate, and at Eleven it may be the path of wisdom to briefly separate the child from his family. Most Elevens are reported to be "wonderful" away from home, much enjoyed by almost any adult other than their parents. Thus it seems the path of reason to give everybody a treat: You a rest from your eleven-year-old; other people a chance to enjoy him or her.

Otherwise, your best bet may be to do what thousands of parents have already done: Let things go as much as you possibly can. Your child's character will not entirely deteriorate if for a few months you do not follow through on all your directives, do not make your children do their fair share of household chores, do not force them to complete every bit of their homework.

So enjoy their enthusiasm, their energy, their appetite for adventure. Do your best to appreciate that not all of the difficulties they cause you are intentional. Try to look on these difficulties as merely the nature of this age.

MATURITY TRAITS

1. Total Action System

The incessant bodily activity and expenditure of energy that are so evident and often hard to cope with at eleven are the outer manifestations of inner changes and an inner seething. Though some

Elevens maintain their ten-year-old poise, poise is not the hallmark of this age. Eleven tends to burst, to bounce, to throw self around. Activity, especially when the child is in any way confined (as when sitting in a chair during an interview), is so constant that one almost becomes seasick when watching. Girl or boy bounces up and down in the chair, rocks back and forth, pushes the chair around. Suddenly the child will jerk his head or whole body forward, tipping the chair with him, or wave his arms over his head and stretch. Hands seem to be in constant motion. If there is an object in hand, such as a ball or a glasses case, they repeatedly toss it up and down.

As they grow restless they stand, stretch, want to shift to another chair or lie on a couch. Legs are no less active than arms. Often the child holds knees wide apart and then bats them together or fiddles with a sock or shoe.

The face is as mobile as the rest of the body. There is a remarkable play of expression across it. Eyes sparkle as they shift from side to side, then suddenly dart toward the person they are talking to. The eyebrows may be raised and lowered. Lips are often pursued or the tongue protrudes, usually to one side.

Health Though Eleven's health may be quite good, there is a tendency toward an increasing number of colds, flu, ear infections, and occasionally even pneumonia. The tendency for an infection to spread, as into ears and lungs or even into the meninges as in mumps meningitis, is a quality of the age, as it was at the earlier stage of five and a half to six years.

Eleven's whole physical mechanism is very labile. All of a sudden a boy may feel intolerably hot and fling off his coat. With any overexertion or overexcitement allergic children may develop asthma. Fatigue is more pronounced than it has been and may be evident in an increased need for sleep. A fairly common complaint of Elevens is that their feet hurt.

Many of Eleven's somatic complaints are valid, especially those about headaches, eye pains and twitching, which are often temporarily relieved by Tylenol. But some Elevens tend to be rather hypochondriacal. They go to bed at the first sign of a cold or the slightest injury. They hear about others' illnesses and develop similar symptoms.

Tensional Outlets The tensional outlets of Eleven involve increased motor activity. There may be more specific blinking, sniffling, or grimacing. At times, a peculiar smile may appear when Eleven is self-conscious, or a child may return to an earlier stage of falling down and dropping or breaking things without meaning to do so.

Vision The visual picture has changed considerably at eleven, as has Eleven's awareness of his vision. He knows when his vision blurs, especially after a long period of reading. He often reports that he gets headaches and blurring when he looks from a near to a far object.

There is a general loosening up of the visual mechanism and an improvement in focusing ability. There is less danger of nearsightedness starting to develop at this age than there was at nine and ten years.

Eleven is now developing fairly good skills in ocular coordination, binocular fusion, depth vision, and visual discrimination. The more common difficulties are likely to occur in the "near field" of vision, with unsteady eye movements, variable fixation, suppression of vision in one eye, and reduction in depth perception. When such difficulties are present, Eleven is more likely to report visual symptoms than he was earlier.

With focusing difficulties and reporting of blurring, the help of contact lenses for near work is often indicated. Eleven does not want to wear glasses all the time, often thinks it would be "horrible," but may accept them for close work. Eleven might be helped by visual training, but children of this age are not always cooperative.

Physical Development and Sex Awareness—Girls In contrast to the eleven-year-old boys, who appear to be a relatively uniform group in their physical structure, the girls at eleven show marked individual variations. Similar extremes are also evident in their sexual development. Some show no trace of sexual development, retaining the less differentiated form of childhood, whereas a few physically advanced girls already show the rounded contours and the physiological functioning of full adolescence.

The middle group of girls, however, shows a fairly consistent picture. By the end of this year, all but a few have some pubic hair. The pelvic area broadens, both in underlying bone structure and in the tissue over this, thus showing, in many girls, a prominence at both the upper and lower corners of the pelvis, with a hollow between the two and a narrowed waist above, giving the classic feminine "vase shape."

The great majority of girls have started their period of faster height growth, and nearly a third have reached the most rapid phase of this cycle. Already the average has achieved about eighty percent of her adult stature and close to fifty percent of what she will weigh at age twenty-one.

Breast development continues as the area surrounding the nipples elevates to form a conelike projection on an otherwise flat chest. Often one breast develops faster than the other. Even the girls without definite breast enlargement usually show a greater fullness and softening of the pectoral region.

Girls show an absorbed interest in these developments—not only of their own but that of other girls their age. They experience sensitive breasts, especially around the nipples, and may complain of pain. They watch the changes in their breasts. They are aware when one breast is "ahead of" the other one. Many dream of the day when they will be advanced enough in their breast development to wear a brassiere. Such a time may seem sadly distant to the most flat-chested girls.

By mid-eleven to twelve, the tighter T-shirts may be replaced by blouses. Soon the coveted brassiere is worn. Not all girls are proud of their breast development, however. There are those who are embarrassed, who hunch their shoulders in a vain effort to hide the inescapable evidence of development, though most girls soon surmount this initial embarrassment. Underarm hair, though present in only a few girls, may cause similar embarrassment.

Knowledge about menstruation is now better comprehended than before, probably because of its very imminence. Eleven is generally looking forward to menstruation more than she was at ten, but there are still those who shun the thought. Eleven is interested in sanitary napkins or tampons and how to wear them. Only a small percentage of girls start to menstruate in the eleventh year. However, there may be momentary premonitory signs of a sudden, sharp abdominal pain or nausea in the morning.

Girls are not as interested in smutty stories or in observing animal intercourse as boys. They are interested in knowing more about human intercourse, though they are becoming more reticent in talking about it with their mothers.

Fifty-seven percent of girls interviewed by us say they think they have adequate information about sex.

Physical Development and Sex Awareness—Boys Eleven-year-old boys make up a far more uniform group in their physical development than do the girls because so few show outward signs of sexual maturation. In this year pubertal changes appear in only the most advanced group of boys. About a quarter of the boys have started on their rapid acceleration of height growth, though even for most of these it is not yet far enough along to be very noticeable. Still, the average boy has achieved a little more than eighty percent of his adult height, though less than half the weight he will have at age twenty-one.

A definite "fat period" occurs in some boys, with an accumulation of adipose tissue giving them a "blown-up" look. The accumulation of adipose tissue over the hips and chest, especially in the breast area, is quite embarrassing to some boys. These boys tend to avoid tight-fitting T-shirts, wearing a looser shirt to cover up. When they are in swimming trunks they may try to mask their chest contour by assuming rather unnatural-looking postures, such as stretching their arms up and out.

Even in this well-padded group, a striking feature shown by Elevens is an apparent increase in bone size. This is not a fragile "boniness" but a seemingly heavy growth of bone which brings the skeletal structure into prominence. Even where overlying tissue obscures a sharp outline, one senses an increase in the framework beneath. The chest area especially seems to reveal this growth, with shoulders, shoulder blades, collarbone, and rib cage more in evidence than at ten.

Genital size has started to advance more rapidly for the more accelerated quarter of boys. Some have developed short, downy pubic hair, and an occasional boy has already moved on to the next stage of longer, straight pubic hair.

Elevens are more interested in sex than at ten but most information is gathered from other boys. There is much interest in a variety of erotic stimuli—books, pictures, conversation, jokes (usually dealing with elimination). Most boys have had some experience with masturbation.

Some boys are becoming more aware of girls as girls. They are more conscious of the girls' figures and may remark about "the way they walk—they wiggle their rears!" Boys respond to a pretty girl. They are curious about why girls sometimes don't go swimming. A few know about menstruation and are curious about sanitary napkins or tampons.

Some boys are curious about others who seem less masculine. Sometimes the more slender, immature, slow-growing boys or the chubby, broad-hipped, nonathletic ones may be called "fairies" or described as "gay."

Erections occur with some frequency among many eleven-year-olds. The sources of stimulation for such erections may seem almost haphazard to the adult: they include general excitement of any kind, not necessarily sexual, physical movements such as bike riding or rope climbing, conversations, pictures, literature, daydreams, and the individual's own body. Over the next few years, responsiveness becomes more selective and specific. Masturbation without ejaculation is a phenomenon known to many boys and experimented with, casually or purposefully, by perhaps half.

As at all ages, boys are more prone than girls to tell dirty jokes and to use special words referring to sex and elimination. They are now more aware of some of the implications involved, and many know that "the kids who laugh too loud don't necessarily know the meaning of the words."

Sixth graders are thinking less about the freakish side of reproduction (two-headed calves and Siamese twins) and now have a more wholesome interest in questions about their own bodies and personal development. A movie about menstruation is very helpful for girls. The sixth grader also asks many intelligent questions about heredity, about what makes blue eyes or red hair.

2. Self-Care and Routines
Eating
APPETITE: "She has two hobbies in her life," one mother reports, "eating and talking." This particular eleven-year-old can be joined by many other Elevens who "live to eat," who eat all day long, and who can be kept track of on their stealthy journeys for food by the sound of the opening and closing of the refrigerator door. Elevens often have fads and eat large quantities of one food: five bananas before dinner, the entire contents of a full cookie jar, a whole fried chicken, or three helpings of potatoes. Some parents feel it is impossible, almost indecent, for their children to be so hungry and uncontrolled. But likely as not with some Elevens, a ravenous appetite might be followed by a poor or finicky one. Fluctuations seem to come according to mood—"Some days I can't get a thing down—other days I'm hungry as a bear." The sight of a certain disliked food may also suddenly take away their appetite.

By eleven, a girl knows that there may be a relationship between how much she eats and how fat she is. She is also aware that no matter how much some other children eat, they will not put on weight. On the whole, however, weight gains are considerable and have a rather close relationship with intake of food. Dieting is discussed and planned for but is still mainly in the talking stage.

PREFERENCES AND REFUSALS: Eleven's emotionality is expressed even in his responses to certain foods. The child *adores* this food and *despises* that one. A boy dramatically throws himself into his reporting by grimacing about his dislikes, licking his lips about his likes, spreading imaginary sauces as he reports about his favorite meat. He bolsters up his own hates by including "a lot of kids" who feel as he does.

Though preferences and refusals are strong, they can change. The food liked today may be refused tomorrow. Often these shifts are hard to fathom. Eggs may be refused after the child learns that a baby chick grows from the yolk. A scrambled egg, however, may remove this association. Parents need to have respect for some of these seemingly irrational refusals until the child works out these new associations.

Even the finicky accept a certain social responsibility when eating away from home or when guests are present. A child will tell you he's pretty good at eating things he doesn't like. He at least makes a gesture of accepting. "Sometimes to be a good sport I take one pea" —he gestures—"and put it on my plate."

Sleep

BEDTIME: Bedtime and Elevens are not congenial. The child can be surrounded by clocks and watches but never see them. Nine may be the theoretical bedtime, but it is more often nine-thirty or even ten. There is more dissatisfaction with a too early bedtime, and Eleven is ready to fight a battle for his eleven-year-old rights, being fully informed as to when "the other kids" go to bed. Bedtime may vary according to the things he has to do, e.g., homework, a special TV program, a book being read. Elevens use any excuse to delay.

Many Elevens should go to bed earlier than they think desirable. When they are allowed to stay up later, they wilt the next day. But there are others who could seemingly stay up all night without being too tired the next day. They are usually the readers, and if not caught will read until midnight or later. Eleven should be allowed a certain amount of latitude as to bedtime, especially over the weekend, but there usually comes a time when parents have to crack down. Greater latitude during vacations allows Eleven to assert his need to feel grown-up.

Most Elevens stay awake for at least a half hour before they drop off to sleep. Some are anxious when they are in a room alone. They often would like to share a room with a sibling. Things they don't want to talk about, such as burglars, may come to mind. But on the whole Eleven daydreams—about much more pleasant things.

SLEEP: Once Elevens are asleep, however, they can sleep through thunder and lightning. You could blow horns in their ears without waking some of them. They themselves may say that not even an atom bomb could awaken them.

MORNING: The ten-year-old ease of getting up in the morning is no longer so common. Some mornings Eleven may feel like getting up, but other mornings feels "kinda dead about it." Often boy or girl is cranky on awakening. Even the early risers like to relax in bed for a while. More often than not, Eleven has to be awakened twice or more and finally dragged out of bed. Even the most cooperative may not fully wake up until they've splashed water on their faces. Average waking hour is seven; time of getting up, seven-fifteen.

Bathing and Care of Hair With so much of Eleven's behavior growing more difficult, it is both surprising and gratifying to see a decreased resistance to bathing. Eleven still finds bathing a bother, however, and wishes to bathe only if there is plenty of time. Though less often actually dragged to the bathroom, some still need to be reminded, urged, prodded, or poked.

Eleven bathes for a special reason; may bathe for two or three nights in a row and then not again for many days. Some prefer showers because of their ease and speed. Others are beginning to enjoy the physical sensation and warmth of the bath. Some Elevens scrub vigorously, but may restrict this excess to the legs, forgetting their ears, face, and neck.

But Eleven is by no means independent in bathing and often needs help drawing the tub. Girls still need help rinsing their hair, though the use of the shower facilitates this process.

This is the age when the dawning awareness of a new social self seems to be centered on hair and teeth. Teeth, earlier neglected, are now brushed more often. Some are said to be good about their teeth, a few even proud of them, and an occasional Eleven might feel guilty if he has not brushed. This new awareness of self may extend to the fingernails. At least there is an awareness of their being dirty, though usually not sufficient to clean and groom them.

Clothing and Care of Room Along with a certain sporadic improvement in bathing and combing of hair, Eleven shows a greater interest in clothes. The more immature boys dislike dressing up and may cling to the same old blue shirt which they would like to wear day after day. At the other extreme are the clothes-conscious boys, those who love to dress up and who are already beginning to wear flashy clothes, bright-colored shirts and socks. These are often the bigger, most robust boys, the social ones who date early.

In general it is the eleven-year-old girl who is most aware of clothes, though most nowadays wear jeans except for dress-up. The girl of eleven often has a definite idea of what she wants and what she will wear. The scales are tipped in her favor when she goes on a shopping trip with her mother, who realizes there is no sense in buying clothes that her daughter will not wear.

Favorite clothes may be hung up and cared for by Elevens, but otherwise their clothes are still slung around the room. Shoe trouble may return at eleven: Often they cannot remember where they left their shoes the night before.

Elevens are more likely than earlier to change their clothes from day to day, especially underwear and socks, but some mothers find that they need to be on hand to snatch the dirty clothes before they can be put on again.

Elevens' care of their persons, though spotty, is far better than their care of their rooms. But they are beginning to slick these up a bit with banners, pictures of rock stars, horses, or athletes.

The child is not quite so deep in collections as earlier. But most do need major cleanup sessions when they will be forced to release cartons of "junk"—at least to the attic or storeroom.

Bedmaking is a chore for Elevens. The child of this age seems unable to make a bed simply, but gives it his own personal touch, which tends to be a bit sloppy.

Parents would do well to keep Eleven's door shut so as not to be disturbed by the mess. They can then stage a glorious cleanup campaign at intervals.

Money Ten's casual attitude toward money may be developing into a real interest at eleven. We have the extremes of those who are "money mad" and those who care nothing about money.

An allowance becomes very important to many Elevens, who often speak up if it has not been increased. Allowances range from one to three dollars, or even more, depending on what friends are getting. Some Elevens are given the opportunity to budget a larger sum. This larger sum, however, imposes quite a demand on scatterbrained Eleven, and the arrangement should be given up if it is found to be unsuccessful.

Though some Elevens can't hold on to money, it is surprising to see how many are tightwads. Bank accounts may reach the high levels of thirty to fifty dollars. Saving is not usually this successful, but most Elevens do save some of their money. Those who are best at saving their own money, however, may be quite good at spending other people's. Counterbalancing the hoarding eleven-year-olds are those who are generous, even too generous. They treat their friends; they love to give big gifts for special occasions.

But spending, on the whole, is becoming a thought-out process. Eleven is beginning to save for a purpose. Boys are more apt to think of their own desires and needs, saving their money for a model plane, a guitar, or bicycle. Girls are more likely to think of other people and will often save their money to buy presents.

Money can be used to motivate achieving goals such as improvement in spelling. The opposite may also be tried; that is, deducting from an allowance when certain jobs are not carried out. This also is only a temporary solution. One method that can sometimes be used effectively to encourage saving is to offer to match Eleven's savings when they have reached a given amount. Children can then start toward goals ordinarily beyond their means and can possibly reach them before interest wanes.

Work Eleven not only hates work but resists doing it and acts badly when required to help. Energy is often spent in seeing what can be gotten away with, trying to trick mother into thinking something has been done which has not. Children report that they are *supposed* to clean their rooms or take out trash but really postpone these chores as long as possible. By his unpleasant response, a boy may force his parents into the unpleasant necessity of having to command. Eleven may then report that she *has* to do the dishes, or *has* to take out the trash. The child's often unwilling and unreasonable attitude is not pleasant to live with or work against. Parents may well question the wisdom of their own demands at this age and often wonder how they might alter their techniques or demands so that Eleven could become a less disquieting member of the household. But even compromise or bargaining may not work well with Eleven.

When children of this age do carry out a task, they are apt to give it their own truculent or unreasonable twist. Thus they may find it difficult to set the table as prescribed, but instead select "the dishes that are most out of reach." Or making a bed may become a tussle with ingenuity as the child refuses to make it in a simple way.

Whatever is demanded, a parent almost always needs to give reminders.

There are times, however, when Eleven does things for fun and spontaneously carries out tasks very nicely. The child of this age needs to be motivated from within rather than demanded of from without. This is especially true when mother is the demander. But many readily accept the challenge of tasks when away from home. Elevens become surprisingly cooperative under the stimulus of the new and distant, and may especially enjoy baby-sitting in the afternoon in other people's houses.

Eleven might act better in his own home if allowed a little more choice. One mother solved her problem by listing a number of small jobs—"sweep the walk," "water the plants," "empty the baskets"—from which Eleven might choose two or three.

3. Emotions

There may well be a vague feeling of wariness in the minds of parents of eleven-year-olds. It is as though some force of nature were grabbing hold of their offspring—as though they were acting under some influence quite apart from those of the tangible environment in which they live. A further disquieting factor is that parents often sense that they have been in this same place before. They recognize the feeling of sudden drops, high peaks, and junglelike confusion. The change in terrain comes gradually and imperceptibly. It is not until they turn a sudden corner and face it squarely that they recognize, in retrospect, that time when their now-approaching-the-teens child was entering a similar phase at five and a half to six years of age. The feeling is the same in memory—that sudden sweep from high to low, the unaccountable shift in mood, the same rudeness, the same devilish unreasonableness.

But there are differences too. The once-small child has now become big and strong, and now sets self on an equal footing with the adult. Though children may again act like untamed lions, they are influenced by a new complexity of emotions.

The sympathetic parent, who has been able to grow through each stage with her child, knows that this should be a time of diminuendo, of backpedaling. The time when the child was more receptive to direct influence and help from the adult is, for many, past. This is a time when the parent must hope that the child can find himself.

This does not mean that the parent should step aside and lose contact with the child. Rather, she needs to recognize the fuller dimensions of the parental role, to see herself as the caretaker of growth forces which need a steady but responding environment to grow in, one that can control but will not force.

As child specialists, we can see Eleven a little differently at a distance. The home cannot help but lose its sense of perspective when Eleven shows that sudden blaze of emotions out of all proportion to the thing at hand. How differently we speak of the eleven-year-old than we did the ten-year-old. Words come into our minds to describe the boy or girl—"fidgety," "disagreeable," "resentful," "argumentative," "insolent," "sulky." We also recognize their states of confusion and uncertainty. We see the child "flub-dubbing" around without knowing what he is doing. We feel Eleven's harum-scarum personality darting first this way and then that.

We may be so caught up in an awareness of the disruptive forces now at work that we too often overlook the positive forces—forces which may not have a chance to express themselves if the negative tendencies take over too completely and are allowed too free a rein, as can often happen.

If we think of eleven-year-olds only in terms of their difficulties, we will do them a real injustice. Give them the gay atmosphere of a lively living room and they will rise to the occasion.

But it is away from home that they can act most positively. During a personal interview (or just chatting with a good listener), boy or girl laughs gayly, is confiding and alert, tells you about "waves of happiness." Eleven knows what it is to be overwhelmed by some simple kindness expressed by a friend.

Eleven is aware of having a special disposition, knows how he feels, but often doesn't know why he feels this way. Children of this age know that they sometimes wake up in the morning feeling cross, peevish, and mopey. They also know that they may brighten up and feel more cheery as the day progresses, especially if something nice happens.

Some Elevens can explain this peevish feeling. They feel they have too much to do, no time to play, and that they wake up tired. If only they could get more sleep. This is more easily said than done, but Eleven's life might be improved if it were tailored more to his needs and capacities. Boy or girl needs a simplified program, especially more time for play and sports.

When Elevens work, they work intensively and sometimes to the point of exhaustion. They give generously of time and effort if it is their own idea. Theirs is the law of immediacy, whether in carrying out a project, wearing some new garment, or going on a trip. Eleven is so spontaneous in expression that there is no doubt about what he feels. A grimace of distaste is expressed before words are found. Children of this age can be so spontaneous that they are often unaware of the havoc they are producing and may report that life is better now because they have more privileges—even though parents may be certain that things are worse.

Though most Elevens often feel "real happy" over some specific event, ranging from the arrival of a new little sister to the eating of an ice-cream sundae, or for no special reason at all, many are beginning to feel times of unaccustomed sadness. A father's speaking crossly or a mother's sadness may inspire unhappiness in the child. A feeling of unpopularity may bring on dejection.

A far commoner emotion, however, is that of anger—sudden, furious outbursts uncontrolled, especially when directed toward younger siblings. Though many strike out physically at a sibling or a peer, others are beginning to try to control themselves, though if an opponent tempts them too much they're apt to hit him. Still others, in the midst of their anger and planning what they will do, may forget what they were angry about by the time they are ready for action. The violence of their anger is often expressed through yelling or saying mean things.

Eleven can become red in the face from anger which may be out of proportion to the cause; or it may be righteous anger when actions seem unfair and adult promises are broken. Nor is anger so easily spent as at Ten. Eleven is more deeply involved and needs to find ways to come back to equilibrium. A child of this age is more apt to carry out a planned revenge, to say mean things that hurt, to hold a grudge, to pout and sulk.

Eleven is more apt to cry when angry than Ten. In fact, eleven is one of the most tearful ages. Bursting into tears is often over some trivial happening or when the child is tired. Maybe a favored cover of a magazine was torn, or mother "looked cross-eyed" at him. Disappointments and hurt feelings bring on tears. Boys are just as apt to cry as girls. Eleven may even refer to self as a crybaby.

Relatively fearless Ten has become more fearful at eleven. Children of this age seem afraid to be alone. This may account for their constant presence in the family circle and may be the reason they spend so little time in their own rooms. They don't talk about this fear but may ask to have the light on in the hall and the door open. They look in closets or under the bed. When mother asks what they are doing, they reply nonchalantly, "Just checkin', Mom." A child may keep a flashlight by his bed. Some are afraid of being kidnapped.

Girls are more fearful of physical pain or infections or that something will happen to their mothers. Girls more than boys fear that no one likes them—and considering the turmoil of their social interplay, it is no wonder. They may also be afraid when boys gang up that they will be the target of teasing.

Elevens aren't as nonchalant about hurt feelings as at ten. They are more vulnerable than they wish to be and often go off by themselves to cry it out. Girls are especially sensitive to any criticism from their fathers. A few may want to retaliate for their hurt feelings, but on the whole they contain these feelings within themselves.

It seems natural for Elevens to reach out for physical love when we realize the extent of their emotional turmoil. They need a mast to hold on to, someone who will accept them as they are. But the approach must be theirs, not mother's. Boys especially are embarrassed by any public expressions of affection from their mothers, and girls may freeze up. But in private they snuggle close, can't go to sleep without that good-night kiss, and even act so "mushy" that it may be the mother who is embarrassed.

Though Elevens are usually happy with their lot, their family, and their possessions, they may covet some possessions of others, such as a dog or a TV set. But more important, Elevens may be envious of others' physical attributes, beauty, or strength. Girls are often jealous when their friends of the moment pay more attention to another friend. And all eleven-year-olds seem to be jealous of younger siblings, feeling that they get all the breaks and attention. Elevens are very aware of their friends' privileges and may be envious of a later bedtime hour and the chance of going out at night.

Elevens are competitive. They say, "I'm in there fighting" or "Competitive—who wouldn't be?" Some strive to be best in grades, others in sports.

Eleven's humor is expanding. They are good punsters and like slapstick humor, especially when things are so impossible they couldn't be true. A boy becomes the clown and has a ready audience in his eleven-year-old friends.

Elevens can be very silly over almost anything. Some slight remark about a girl will make a group of boys roll their eyes and laugh hysterically. The awareness of sex is also expressed in smutty jokes, so natural to this age, though "dirty" humor still deals primarily with elimination rather than sex. A group may roar with laughter at another child's expense (teacher told a boy to zip his fly), then later be indignant, feeling she was grossly unfair to humiliate him before the whole group. Eleven moves widely and freely within the realm of humor and may fluctuate from uproarious laughter to a deadpan look. Children of this age are quick to catch the point and have their own way of quipping and making light of serious things. "Temper, temper," a girl may say to herself when she is angry.

4. The Growing Self

"Oh where, oh where has my delightful ten-year-old gone?" may be the refrain sung by many a parent of an eleven-year-old girl or boy. There is a loss of ease, of responsiveness, of getting on with others (parents especially), which characterized the ten-year-old. Now parents may well ask, "What do I have on my hands?"

It is not always easy to understand this particular stage of development, for so many of its manifestations appear to be inconsistent. The eleven-year-old is full of paradoxes, very "good" for a spell and then very "bad." A child can be terrible at home, yet suave, giving, and charming away from home.

As we blame our Elevens less and try to understand them more, we realize how strongly the typically unpleasant qualities of Eleven —belligerence, selfishness, unapproachableness—are expressions of a search for self, a self which is trying to emerge.

Understanding on the part of parents doesn't mean that a parent can smooth things over entirely. The child must do his own growing. But the parent can provide the atmosphere which is conducive to good growth. When the wobbly eleven-year-old self seeks affection to restabilize itself, may the parent be there to give whatever expression of affection is needed! When rebellion is expressed by extreme rudeness, thoughtlessness, and selfishness, may the parent ask, "Is Eleven rebelling against me personally, or is he rebelling against the complexity and uncertainty of his own inner depths?"

It is important for the parent not to stir up these uncertain depths. Better not try too hard to point out the child's extreme rudeness and discourtesy toward elders (and contemporaries too) but rather to work out ways and means to bridge over difficulties of interrelationships. Eleven can more readily pull together on a businesslike, bargaining basis. You can say, "If you do this as your part in the family, then I will do that as my part in the family." Such bargaining may involve, for example, the child's helping to wash dishes in exchange for the mother's help with homework.

Eleven complains, all too accurately, "Now everything I do seems wrong. Ever since I turned eleven." Girl or boy says the wrong thing when company is present, pushes too hard and breaks a gadget, falls down and gets messy. And more often than not, they don't realize what they have done, even when their acts and words are brought to their attention.

Elevens seem to gather strength by an "against" response: They strike out, hardly realizing what they are doing. This striking out— in action, words, and feelings—is all the more apparent to us because it is against people. Elevens are especially interested in constant interaction (positive or negative) with other people.

Eleven is far more aware of his or others' faults than assets. But it may be difficult to pin the child down to the acknowledgment of a special fault. "I guess I have a million. Everyone has. I don't know exactly which is the worst." In general, the faults recognized are those which imply friction with others. Eleven may admit that he talks back, contradicts, gets angry, and tries to get away with things. Those few Elevens who recognize their own assets refer to their kindness or friendliness to others—again, evidence of their responsiveness to people.

Eleven, like Ten, pretty much likes being this age, but also likes the idea of being in the process of growing up. A few are very eager to grow up. Very few resist the idea. The best age is judged by the majority of Elevens to be from fifteen to seventeen years because of parties and dances. Those girls who are interested in dating are more apt to project to college as the best time.

Though Elevens may still be influenced in choosing a career by their own parents' profession or occupation, they are beginning to show a capacity to choose on their own. Girls and boys have a certain awareness of themselves, of their capabilities, their feelings, giving them a better basis for choice than earlier. They even know that they may change later on. Elevens are quite articulate about what they want to be. Many have settled down from the multiple possibilities they envisioned at ten to two alternatives: "a farmer or a doctor," "a model or a designer," "a nurse or a ballet dancer." Eleven shows a specificity of interest—"a *commercial* artist," "a *dress* designer," a *nightclub* singer."

Teacher leads as a career choice for girls; doctor or some kind of athlete for boys.

At Eleven, a boy or girl often dreams of becoming the center of the stage, a dancer, author, designer. He or she dreams of fame, wants to be at the top. Thus if a boy chooses law, he wants to become a Chief Justice. If he chooses professional baseball, he wants to become the captain of the team. If he persists in his interest in farming, he wants to own his own farm. A girl may want to be a prima ballerina or an astronaut.

Those Elevens who plan to go to college (eighty-two percent of girls, seventy percent of our boys) are less influenced than earlier by their parents' choices. Some are not quite sure whether they want to go and may even fear that they won't be accepted. But Eleven recognizes that training is needed for a future career. Some are already thinking of graduate school.

Eighty-nine percent of our girls, seventy-two percent of our boys say they plan to get married. This is about the same number of girls as in 1950 but many more boys, since only fifty-two percent of our earlier group of boys said they intended to marry. A few more articulate boys have thought about the appearance of their future wife—"blond, pretty," "smart and rich."

The eleven-year-old girl, on the other hand, is thinking as much about the qualities she desires in a husband as about her future profession. She has thought the problem through carefully and has relegated good looks and wealth to second place. She wants her husband to be kind, honest, understanding, to have a nice disposition, and a sense of humor. She wants him to make enough money so that they can live and eat. (Trust Eleven to think of eating!) She also wants him to be reasonably intelligent and nice-looking. But most of all, she wants him to be someone to whom she can relate.

Most eleven-year-olds, both boys and girls, want a family. A few still think in terms of a very large number of children, but the majority are thinking of two. Elevens want both boys and girls.

5. Interpersonal Relationships

Eleven, like Ten, is firmly placed within the family unit—but for a very different reason! Now boys and girls are right in the midst of any family activity, working at the dining room table, responding to everything that is going on around them, fearful that they will miss something. In fact, some spend very little time in their rooms. But even with the family group, Eleven is fidgety and restless and is constantly punctuating the conversation with "What are we going to do now?"

Once-adored parents have lost their halo and have tumbled down to earth. References to his formerly adored "mommy" have changed to "she." Fathers, who may be stricter with their all-too-demanding eleven-year-olds, may be dubbed "old so-and-so." Both boys and girls are less enthusiastic about discussing their parents with others and are more cagey for fear they are revealing too much. Though they quote their mother, they disagree almost at once with her opinion. They are aware that mother doesn't know as much as they thought she did; they are aware of father's temper; they are increasingly aware of people's motives. This awareness affords new ammunition for them either to produce conflict or avoid it, or to wangle out of their parents what they most desire.

The first-thing-in-the-morning conflicts are the hardest on parents. Eleven argues about everything. As one parent reported, "She is exuberantly defensive." It is no wonder that the parent is often forced to resort to yelling.

It might be wise for parents of eleven-year-olds to list the kinds of behavior they would like from the child and then to make another list of how the child thinks he or she might comply. The parents' list may be quite long:

1. Be a little faster.
2. Work more around the house.
3. Take better care of room.
4. Help with animals.
5. Be neater.
6. Have better table manners.
7. Get on better with siblings.
8. Be better about going to bed and getting up.

The child's answering list is quite short in comparison and not too well defined:

1. Be helpful when in the mood.
2. Do most anything except wash the dishes.
3. Don't yell at him.
4. Don't tell father.
5. Stop criticizing.

Eleven doesn't appear from this list to be very capable of answering his parents' demands. Girl or boy has again acquired the raw texture of the beginning of a new cycle of growth.

But life isn't all terrible for Elevens and their parents, although most get on better with one parent than the other. Both sexes have fun with their fathers—going together on walks, to the beach, to the zoo, or to the movies. They especially enjoy going fishing, boating, swimming, or to ball games.

Mothers also have their special place—they are always there to be confided in. They are good about talking things over. And they are wonderful to be affectionate with.

Perhaps no other age gets on as badly as Eleven does with siblings. Boy or girl may control physical expressions of anger, but they frankly admit, "I'd like to hit him over the head with a baseball bat, but mother won't let me" or "I'd like to give vent to my emotions and grab his hair. I feel like pulling it out by the roots." A younger sibling, knowing that Eleven will respond this way, deliberately tries to get a rise out of him by needling him, teasing him, joking with him, or getting into Eleven's things. Then the parent has to step in to save the younger sibling from destruction.

But in spite of all Eleven's difficulties with siblings at close range, there is no stauncher friend if a sibling gets into trouble. Eleven also thinks of himself (or, more often, herself) as a friend, almost a parent, when trying to improve a younger sibling, but would, alas, "murder him trying to get him to do the right thing."

Eleven gets on a little better with an older sibling, but, unfortunately, the older sibling is apt to call Eleven names such as "big fat slob" or "stubborn mule." Such names can fit almost too well, which is perhaps the reason Eleven responds so violently. An older sibling, knowing of Eleven's perceptive nature and drive to talk, would be wise not to bring a date around where Eleven could get at him or her. Some things are better left unsaid, especially in the midst of a budding romance.

Friendships are not as casual as they were at ten. Eleven does not just choose friends because they are nearby and like to do the same things, but may choose some even though they are at a distance and must be corresponded with to keep up the friendship. They like friends who have "the same temperament" or who are "reasonable." That's probably why they get on so well (most of the time) with their best friends. This is truer of boys than of girls. In general, boys are more apt to have one good friend and to go around with a lot of others. Their main purpose in life is to have fun together. A tree house may be the preferred place for the gang. And their interest in baseball and bike riding is never-ending. Two friends alone are more apt to play games, read comics, or just sit around and talk. Boys often spend the night at each other's houses. Throwing pillows may be the extent of their exuberance.

Girls have neither the strong, single, best friendship nor the grouping in gangs that boys do. They are more apt to have a fair number of good friends, three to five, among whom they shift. Girls are more influenced by their friends, are more apt to be one of the pack, and may actually be under the sway of a friend as though they were under a spell. They take it for granted that there will be stages of quarreling and stages of "not caring for anything." One Eleven defined the situation well: "We have to quarrel to break up the smoothness, and then we have to make up about four hours after we quarrel." Eleven can't stand not speaking for too long. Her drive to talk is too great. Girls also like to spend the night at each other's houses and are apt to do this in groups of three or four.

Whereas a ten-year-old may report that he hasn't "become friendly with" the opposite sex yet, Eleven is more apt to report that he's almost there or beginning to move in this direction; thirty percent of the girls, forty-two of boys, claim that they do some dating. Girls are apt to do a great deal of talking about boys with their girlfriends. They can be quite aware of the qualities of boys and may paint a verbal picture that is quite frightening. One girl described an admirer—"a shrimp: he weighs only fifty-nine pounds, and he's terribly skinny. He has a flat face with freckles and a pale, dirty complexion. Just horrible all over." Boys do not usually have this type of perception, but they are aware of girls' ability to talk. One eleven-year-old boy reported that "you really have to keep away from that one. The talk of the town will spread to the talk of the city."

Girls enjoy the joking, teasing attitude boys have toward them. "It's neat fun," they will say. They even enjoy the spitball and snowball fights and, as one boy said about girls, "There's not a better target around."

Interest in birthday parties has worn off, although a few girls have parties for girls. There is a definite transition at this age away from what is classed as a "babyish" party, though they still act like babies at their cook-outs and their Halloween parties unless the party is well planned and supervised. In mixed parties, which girls most often organize, they "play games and eat" or "dance and talk." It becomes an unfortunate occasion when a spontaneous game of boys throwing food at the girls arises.

6. Activities and Interests

Play is no longer paramount in the lives of eleven-year-olds as it was when they were ten. Play can be included in their relationships with people, but the people are now actually more important than the play. Elevens rarely choose to be alone and are forever in the midst of the family circle, even though they may get on badly with both parents and siblings. If forced to be alone, Eleven might imaginatively become two people to play both sides of a chess or a baseball game so that he can experience that feeling of interplay which is enjoyed so much.

Eleven's relationship with people is often far from positive. Sometimes the child's main effort is directed against a certain contemporary. No one can be more cruel than an eleven-year-old girl who doesn't quite realize what she is doing. And if her poor victim responds to her chastisement, this girl is inspired to double or triple the dose.

The interests of Eleven are quite similar to Ten's. Eleven, however, doesn't have the strong urge to be out of doors and constantly exercising that he had at ten. Eleven is in constant motion and loves gross motor activities, but is also a watcher, explorer, and, above all, a conversationalist. Eleven is a great age for building tree houses which may require months of elaborate planning.

Though an eleven-year-old may seem clumsy and bumbling in motor acts around the house, on a ski slope or at a skating rink you may wonder how this child has acquired such agility.

Both boys and girls like to go on walks and romp around with their dog and a companion. Everything can be of interest to Elevens. They watch animals and birds. They observe insects and discuss their habits. They visit cemeteries and read the poems on the stones. They are far more apt to walk than to ride their bikes because you can't romp on a bike the way you can on foot. Collections are still going strong, and Elevens may be most interested in trading things in their collections.

There are definite differences between male and female interests, as previously seen at ten. Some interests can become very intense with the added emotional force that Eleven brings, though the child of eleven is apt to drop an interest suddenly. Girls may still be interested in dress-up and may like to rifle their mother's closets, especially for shoes, though some will have outgrown this interest. Some are unusually adept at mimicry. Some like to play theater. Some still like games of being a secretary or librarian.

Many girls are becoming interested in sewing clothes for their dolls (and occasionally for themselves) and may be ready for an inexpensive sewing machine. Some maternal help should be available for unsnarling mistakes, or the child will tire very quickly. Knitting may be of less interest than it was earlier.

Boys are more apt to use their creative imagination in games and inventions. They can think of all sorts of variations for war play and ball games. A few play Ping-Pong or tennis. Others like target shooting with cork guns. Boys like to play with electric trains or chemistry sets.

Organized clubs are strong with most, though a few of the more mature may dub them "boring." If Elevens were consulted more and the activities were planned around the child's interests, which shift rather frequently, girl or boy might enjoy organized clubs more. Many join and continue to belong because they think they should, but more often than not their hearts aren't in it. Their own private clubs don't carry far either. Somebody's always absent or forgets to pay dues. Paying dues may be far more important than electing officers.

Eleven has lost the idealized approach to clubs that was characteristic at ten. At eleven clubs are for fun, for eating, "to be private from the boys," or just for play. They no longer involve "improving" oneself.

Sedentary Looking and Listening Activities Eleven continues strong with both television and stereo. Children of this age keep their radio on while doing homework, if permitted, and also while going to sleep. Favorite television programs for girls are comedies or situation comedies; for boys, comedies and sports. Most girls have given up cartoons; boys still enjoy them.

Though there is interest in music on the radio, there is much greater interest in listening to records. Eleven is swinging into the teenage interest in rock and roll.

Reading depends a great deal on basic personality. If the child read a great deal at ten, he may read even more at eleven and may sneak in extra time after going to bed at night. Sometimes electric light bulbs have to be removed to break this habit, though if they are, boy or girl may use a flashlight under the covers. Even those who formerly read very little are reading a bit more at eleven. Their taste in books is similar to Ten's, with a greater interest in animal, insect, or nature stories. Eleven's interests in pets are extending to guinea pigs, hamsters, turtles, and fish.

Eleven often thumbs through the current newsmagazines to keep abreast of the times. Comic book interest is diminishing; if it continues, the child is more selective than earlier.

Many Elevens go to movies more than they did at ten. A fair proportion may go every two or three weeks, and most go at least occasionally. Many are still accompanied by their parents, but an increasing number are going with friends.

7. School Life

The casual, adjustable, eager-to-learn ten-year-old has turned into a critical, demanding, sharp-seeing and talking Eleven. When this child is on your side, he is all for you; but when he's against you, you have to watch out or, better yet, see if you can put things right.

Though many Elevens are school enthusiasts, liking school even better than they did when they were ten because "it goes faster," all too many Elevens are speaking of school as one of their "problems." They make such remarks as "I disagree with school" or "school is disgraceful."

It is very evident that Eleven comes to school chiefly because of the "kids." The need for contemporaries, even when the child gets along badly with them, is insatiable. They tease, chase, push, grab, or hit classmates, sometimes not realizing how much this may hurt, at times with actual intent to hurt. But Eleven also nudges or pokes with an elbow in a friendly way to get a neighbor's attention. They are often seen walking down the corridor with an arm draped around a friend of the same sex.

Elevens cluster into small groups. There is nothing casual here. They may come together with intent as much for evil as for good. The group may suddenly dissolve to exclude certain unwanted members. Then the nucleus re-forms and may or may not allow the excluded one or ones to reenter its confines.

The teacher is probably the single most important factor in the school life of any eleven-year-old. Eleven doesn't want to be held with an "ironclad hand," but really prefers a "tough" teacher, one who provides challenges. Eleven especially doesn't want a teacher who "treats us like babies." However, the same teacher may be criticized at other times for being "way up above our heads." Probably one of the most endearing qualities of a teacher to Eleven is that he or she "cracks jokes," or tells funny stories. Saying that "horse sense" means "horses have sense because they don't bet on men" throws Eleven into stitches of laughter. Eleven likes to be teased by the teacher on a personal basis at an opportune moment. But a teacher always has to balance in her mind whether her joking will upset Eleven or spur the child on to action.

When Eleven's teacher can be described as patient, fair, humorous, not too strict, understanding, someone who "makes things interesting" and doesn't yell, there is every reason to expect that Elevens will become very fond of her and will not be afraid to show or speak of their affection. Eleven often has a crush on the teacher. Boys express their affection more readily by doing things for the teacher—bringing her presents, staying after school to help.

The atmosphere of a sixth-grade schoolroom is very different when the teacher is spoken of as a "real crab." "Ooh, she's terrible," "she yells and is too strict." Eleven can give us a fairly clear idea about what's wrong with a teacher if we will listen. Here is the report of one eleven-year-old girl:

"You know what I'd like to be? Not when I grow up but for just one day. I'd like to be the teacher and give my teacher a taste of her own medicine. I'd make her sit in a seat that she's cramped in. And then I'd give her work up to the sky. And then I wouldn't let her talk for one minute. Well, that's what she does to us. And I'd say, 'Oh, no, you shouldn't do this, children.' And then I'd make her go up to the map and show every little city. And make her spell very hard words. And then do around twenty-five arithmetic problems. And before school I'd make her do twenty, and then I'd call her marks right out loud before the class. And then I'd make her stay after school and clean up everything and do all the dirty work, and then she could go home."

If a teacher or a school would right all these wrongs (if such they are), then the positive side of Eleven would have a chance to grow in a healthier atmosphere. Not that life would become entirely smooth in the schoolroom, but it could at least be fitted to Eleven's growth characteristics.

We might analyze Elevens' school behavior to see how it reveals them more fully. When Eleven's teacher knows that the usually peaceful atmosphere reminiscent of fifth grade may suddenly explode in her face, then she is on her toes, ready for anything that may come. She can be assured of one thing—that Eleven is still excited about learning, that children have not yet become "blasé" as they may be when thirteen and older.

With Elevens' difficulty in getting up in the morning and their tendency to cause friction in whatever they do, the child sometimes comes to school in mental and physical disarray without having eaten breakfast. Without food, girl or boy is worse than usual. It is to be hoped that the school might provide at least a midmorning snack.

A wise teacher knows that when she can't get an idea across to an eleven-year-old, sometimes another child can explain things. There is less friction, less foolishness, and less giggling if boys and girls are separated.

Restlessness and wriggling are very common in sixth grade. Elevens need to be allowed to move around the room and to talk, though they shouldn't be allowed to disrupt others' work. With a certain amount of freedom there might be less note passing, fewer vituperative remarks, such as "Donnie stinks" or "he's a dope."

Most of all, Eleven enjoys gym and sports. Baseball is a favorite, but soccer, kickball, volleyball, and football are close seconds. Boys and girls prefer to separate in gym and in ball games. Boys have a hard enough time putting up with poor players of their own sex, but they won't tolerate poor players of the opposite sex.

When teams are chosen, the best players are chosen first and friends second. Games need to be supervised, for Eleven is a hard and critical taskmaster. A boy calls out, "You damn fool" when a comrade misses a ball; and may further threaten, "You didn't even *try* to get that ball. If you can't *try*, you're not going to be on my team." Parents may sometimes be ashamed of their eleven-year-olds at home; but teachers too can be ashamed of eleven-year-olds. Boys may get into a fistfight, apparently without reason, and sometimes have to be separated. Or they will get even with another boy by excluding him. Eleven is not a fully socialized animal and needs help from a teacher or leader both to point out what he is doing and help him find a better way to settle differences.

Classroom teaching of eleven-year-olds can be exciting or exhausting, sometimes both. If a teacher is warm and enthusiastic, if she can share the group's interests, then, as one told us, she can "swing them ahead without allowing them to drag." She soon realizes that Elevens thrive on a certain amount of routine, that they like to know what is expected of them, and what changes in assignments and scheduling occur from day to day.

Eleven is keen on competition of any sort. He will "work his head off to beat his best friend." A favorite method of competition is for one sex to be against the other. Not only spelling and arithmetic can be used for competitive games but history and other subjects as well.

In arithmetic, problems may be too complex, though Eleven enjoys the mechanics of arithmetic—delights in adding, subtracting, and, above all, in showing his knowledge of multiplication tables. Definition of words may be quite as hard for Elevens as problems in arithmetic. They want to use words in sentences, in context, and like to separate them into syllables, but hate to define them.

There's nothing Elevens like better than a good story—whether of adventure or nonsense. They are better at oral than at written book reports, but are apt to go on too long in the telling. Therefore it is wise to restrict them to one incident. They tend to prefer current events to past history and like to locate places mentioned in the newspaper on the map. At all times, Eleven wants his schoolwork to be related to reality.

Elevens like drawing too, especially as it relates to stories and projects. They like to make long, continuous friezes, preferring to project their thoughts imaginatively rather than copy someone else's ideas. Give Eleven a project and he will enthusiastically gather information, make exhibits, and do the artwork.

But even with the best of teaching and planning, Elevens tire rapidly and, as a result, tend to show an inconsistent learning pattern. One day the child does remarkably well, the next day appears to be not so bright. Elevens may be out with illnesses periodically, more than at any time for the next three years. Body temperature varies widely. Elevens keep busy putting the windows up and down according to the way they feel. By the end of the afternoon at school, Eleven shows fatigue by becoming very scrambly, and when finally let loose may run wild.

These fatigue patterns are similar to those shown at the earlier age of five and a half to six. If half-day sessions cannot be arranged (and they probably cannot), it would be wise for Eleven's mother to give him a half day off every now and then.

8. Ethical Sense

Eleven is not only emerging from the child world, but is truly out in the midstream of the adult world, shifting this way and that in an effort to determine his course. The child wants to cut loose from the established authorities of home, school, and church; wants to figure things out for himself. Most are less strict in their moral code than at ten (or at least their code is changing). They like to have more freedom to make decisions.

More often than not, Eleven makes a good attempt to do things right. Girl or boy "tries to tell the truth," "tries to do right," "tries not to swear." They often *know* what is right even though they do not always *do* what is right. Children tend to be puzzled about right and wrong and are apt to go by their feelings, by common sense, or by what their parents tell them. Those Elevens who are ruled too much by what their parents say may be dubbed "yellow" or "chicken" by their contemporaries. Elevens are conscious of the problem of choice between being accepted by their peers and holding to their own ethical standards.

Eleven does have pretty good controls through conscience, which may bother children of this age if they do wrong. Eleven's chief ethical concern may be about fairness. Most Elevens are not good about listening to reason, however: "I'd rather do what I plan; I'm not easily convinced." Or, "It's hard to persuade me. I stick to my own way." Still, Elevens tend to keep thinking about something they have done wrong. This concern may produce the opposite extremes of either retribution or confession to one's mother.

The truth is not sacred to Elevens. They are more concerned with self-protection and are apt to tell things in a way that favors themselves. Not that they mean to lie. It is just that they want to get out of doing certain things. If Elevens are ashamed of something they have done, they may deny it when asked but protect themselves by crossing their fingers as they lie. Some Elevens almost automatically blame others when they do wrong, but more often they alibi or cover up by criticizing others. On the whole, though, Elevens are good about telling the truth about big things.

Eleven is more tolerant of swearing and drinking than at ten. Girls still don't like swearing, but they might swear just to remind their parents how bad it sounds. Some might swear sometimes because "it sounds real grown-up." Boys may also be critical of others' swearing but might swear themselves when they get mad. Drinking in adults is condoned if the adults don't drink too much. Eleven doesn't mind when adults drink cocktails, but thinks it's very bad when they take a bottle of whiskey and drink a great deal.

Where Eleven really rises up in indignation is in relation to cheating and stealing. Maybe the heat of the child's indignation is fanned by guilt feelings over his own cheating or sore temptation to do so. At any rate, these acts are on the child's mind, and he often reports the misdemeanors of others to mother.

Boys may cheat more often, but girls are more apt to steal, especially in stores where the merchandise is out on counters. Sometimes they go in groups of three or four for the express purpose of shoplifting. There is usually one girl who is the leader and who has an undeveloped or nonconforming ethical sense. Many girls refuse to accompany the group, considering the plan "horrible." Others want to experience the excitement of such a jaunt. One experience like this, especially if Eleven is caught, is usually enough to cure shoplifting. If stores, schools, and parents realized the prevalence of this tendency at eleven and twelve, they might help nip it in the bud. If the young stealers are caught right in the store, the impact is the strongest and the whole incident can be handled in a serious but humane fashion. The parents should be notified; the law should be brought in. The children should experience the fright that comes when one is close to the edge of something terrible and yet have the assurance of being within the protection of those who love and wish to help them. But at the same time they must learn the necessity of becoming responsible, worthy of the respect and the privileges given to them. It is unfortunate when an offense like this is successful and leads to further exploits and successes.

As to politics, just half of each sex believe that most politicians are dishonest. Slightly more than half think that they themselves may do something to improve conditions in this country. Just over half are satisfied with our efforts at integration.

chapter six
THE TWELVE-YEAR-OLD

MATURITY PROFILE

Calm Twelve follows picky, quarrelsome, objecting Eleven as sunshine follows storm. Girl or boy is in many ways a dream come true.
The most beautiful thing about typical twelve-year-olds, from a
parent's point of view, is that they are comfortable and secure
enough within themselves that they can allow other people to be
less than perfect. Twelve will even allow mother to make a mistake
or to display a less-than-even temper. "Oh, you know you when
you have a headache, Mom," a girl will say if her mother should at
times seem cross and irritable. In fact, the typical mother of the
typical Twelve will correctly describe her son or daughter as tolerant, sympathetic, and friendly.

Some mothers tell us it is almost as if the eleven-year-old child
had been climbing a very steep and difficult incline, which left him
breathless and uncomfortable, concerned only with the troublesome
task at hand—no breath or energy left for any but his own concerns.
Life was indeed a struggle.

Suddenly the child comes to the top of the hill, the struggle over,
looks around, and the view is good. Thus it is as if Twelve, following Eleven, has suddenly emerged at a whole new level of comfort,
achievement, and security. His relations with immediate family
members (except sometimes siblings) tend for the most part to be
smooth indeed.

The typical twelve-year-old is friendly and somewhat objectively
detached from mother. This is one of the things that add harmony
to family living. No longer does the child watch her like a hawk,
ready to pounce on her slightest error or inconsistency. Thus a girl
shopping with her mother and her mother's friend may comment,
calmly, "Children have to laugh when their mothers say 'Yes, dear'

and don't even look at what they're showing them." Eleven would have snapped, "You didn't look. You don't care. You're not interested."

To a large extent, Twelve is willing for adults to live their own lives. Father too enjoys the friendly comfortableness of Twelve's attitude toward him, though since most Elevens are nowhere near as difficult with father as with mother, the change from eleven is neither as much noticed nor as much appreciated.

To mother, it is indeed a marked relief that son or daughter is now less embroiled with family than just earlier. To father, it may bring at least a slight twinge of regret. When a twelve-year-old tells you, "I like to spend time with my family, but I also like to spend time with my friends," a mother thinks "Great!" A father may tell you, "We're a sailing family, and all of us always sailed together. Now that Sandy is twelve, sometimes she doesn't want to go out with the rest of us, and it kind of spoils the fun."

At all too many ages, notably two and a half, six years, and eleven, the child's quite normal and necessary effort to separate himself from his mother and family is accompanied by rather painful tug and pull. It is the beauty of the twelve-year-old that he can merely step back, rather gently, view parents tolerantly and somewhat objectively, merely prefer to stay at home on Sunday when the rest of the family goes out for a ride.

To a large extent, this increased smoothness can be seen at school as well as at home. Twelve, secure, calm, expansive, is often quite emotionally well suited to the complexity and turmoil of junior high school's changing rooms and many teachers. School will be difficult for the overplaced eleven-year-old who still needs a single main classroom and his own personal teacher, but who is thrown too early into the complexity of junior high.

The majority of twelve-year-olds are said to be "nicer" in class, more cooperative, not as lazy, aggressive, and rebellious as they were just a year earlier. However, many teachers do comment that although easier as individuals, as a group their behavior may leave something to be desired. Twelves do sometimes egg each other on.

Relationships with siblings are improving, though only very slightly. Most get on reasonably well with brothers and sisters under four or over sixteen. With others, Twelves vary from no more than one quarrel a day to "constant fighting." "Guess I have to say I like them" is about as far as some will go. "I like my dog just as well," another will tell you.

Friends are something else again—a source of both support and pleasure. Most Twelves are branching out to a larger group of friends, and most relationships can be described as relatively harmonious. A certain amount of criticism or evaluation is natural: "He brags," "She's silly." Also, a certain amount of "telling him off" occurs.

But when friendships break up it may be more as a gentle drifting apart than because of an explosive quarrel, as earlier. Even at this young age, some find that their own tastes and interests are changing more rapidly than those of their friends. "She's too much of a goody-goody. I used to be that way, but no longer."

As to relationships with the opposite sex, the more immature Twelves may still be strongly anti-boy or anti-girl: "Just drips," "Useless." Most, however, express a definite friendliness and interest: "Well, I have one boy I kind of like." "I got a girl to keep up with my friend, but he gave up his so I gave up mine."

In spite of the lukewarm attitude which some express, one third of our twelve-year-olds claim that they are dating or have dated; and thirty-four percent of the girls, eighty percent of the boys say they would like to start.

As to the relative behavior of the two sexes at parties, party-time gives an excellent example of the maturity of girls and the immaturity of boys at this age. Most girls of twelve attend parties rather hoping that something romantic may happen. Boys, as a rule, go in order to horse around, eat, drink, and throw food. Many describe the girls' attentions and interest in them as "stupid and bothersome."

A certain social smoothness with adults outside the family is shown in the twelve-year-old's response to our interview procedures: "This is fun!" "Just see all the attention I'm getting!" Or, generously, "Quite a nice place you have here." "Tell me, is it interesting to work with children?" Eleven, admittedly, was as friendly as could be in an interview. But *he* told you about *himself*. Twelve is interested in you.

One especially attractive sign of maturity in twelve-year-olds is that they seem quite as much interested in their friends' responses as in their own. In an interview with an examiner they often ask, "What did the other kids say?" They may also show an interest in their own past: "What did I say about that last year?"

Many girls mature sexually, as evidenced by their first menstruation, sometime during their twelfth year. There is a wider range of differences in rate of physical growth among twelve-year-old boys, but the middle group now show definite traces of beginning puberty. Sex is really interesting to Twelve, and they tend less to think of it as dirty than earlier. Boy or girl wants information and wants to be set straight.

Plans for the future definitely include the opposite sex. Three fourths of both boys and girls tell us that they not only plan to get married but to have children. (And thinking of the future, though the last one thousand boys and girls whom we interviewed came from a very wide variety of home backgrounds, three quarters of our girls and two thirds of our boys said that they plan or hope to go to college.)

How sophisticated is the typical twelve-year-old today in some of those worldly ways which most grown-ups are rather reluctant to think about? School and family background, combined with varying personalities, make this evaluation somewhat difficult. But according to our own current data, approximately three quarters of the boys and girls interviewed by us claim that they, or at least some of their friends, do smoke cigarettes. Just over half say that they or friends drink alcoholic beverages. And close to one third claim that they or their friends use drugs.

Ethically, as in so many other respects, the typical twelve-year-old seems to have moved light-years beyond his just-earlier ways of responding. Twelves will tell you with rather excellent perception of their classmates' reactions, "I'm not bad, though I'm not too good either. If you're too good, kids don't like you." It is probably the wish to get on with the other kids that leads some Twelves to be as rowdy and ill-behaved as many of them are in group situations, including school and Sunday school.

Many admit that even without group influence they sometimes do things that are wrong. Many admit to having "big" consciences, which often bother them, but are more likely than earlier to try to figure out for themselves what would be right and wrong; also, they do not depend as much as earlier on what their mothers would say. And a big step in moral development is that Twelves may now take the blame when they have done wrong "because people wouldn't like me if I didn't."

However, attitudes toward cheating and stealing are not as rigorous as formerly. Many say about cheating, "all the kids do." Only a few admit to stealing "for the fun of it," but the majority claim to know boys and girls who do. (Our group does not include outright muggers.)

This would seem to be an age of real concern about race relations, if responses represent Twelve's true feelings. Twelve is a low point for girls, *the* low point for boys, who feel that we are not doing enough about integration. More children than earlier (sixty-one percent of girls, fifty-nine percent of boys) believe that most politicians are dishonest. A rather touching fifty-five percent of girls, sixty-one percent of boys, believe that they themselves, when they are older, might do something to improve social and political conditions.

If one were to choose a single word to characterize the emotional reactions of the typical twelve-year-old, it would be *enthusiasm*. Much of the time boy or girl seems to be just bursting with energy. Boy just LOVES this or that; girl just HATES something else. There is little middle ground. In spite of the energy which most have at their command, there is less boiling over or exploding when angry. This is the last age for many for actual physical violence. Many just "sit and seethe" or more likely make some verbal response—"Just tell him off," "Talk nasty." If angry at a teacher, Twelve usually just mutters mean things under his breath.

Boy or girl of this age tends to have a reasonably good sense of humor. Though Twelve's sense of humor is by no means adult yet, they do become increasingly humorous from an adult's point of view. Much humor is in the form of insulting remarks addressed to friends. Smutty humor is now more likely to relate to sex than to elimination as earlier.

Putting all this together, how and what do twelve-year-olds think about themselves? Probably most are quite comfortable with their own personalities if we can judge by the fact that they now say they know they are not perfect themselves and don't expect perfection of others. Most have not yet begun those probing comparisons with others and downgradings of self which can, for many, make the next few years so uncomfortable. Twelve is a pretty nice age to be— a satisfactory, comfortable time not only for growing boy and girl but for those around them as well.

MATURITY TRAITS

1. Total Action System

The seething, spilling-over, talkative, "bursting with energy" eleven-year-old is beginning to calm down at twelve. Twelves are more capable of organizing their energy, though they express this in seemingly opposite extremes: Intense activity that pushes through to achieve a goal may alternate with leisurely, noncommittal "hanging around." Enthusiasm is a prime characteristic of Twelve. With boys, this enthusiasm is especially given to sports—baseball in particular. Even among those who lack the ability to play the game well, an interest in it may pervade everything they think or do. Girls are often especially ardent in their interest in and desire to care for young children.

Some Twelves, after intense activity, collapse hard and do not recover easily. As they did at eleven, they suddenly feel very tired, may develop a cold, and need to rest up for a day or two. Others seem to have a safety valve for more frequent, more gradual releasing of tension. The ones who take it easy and "fool around" aimlessly manage this release process rather well. Too frequent attempts by others to goad them into more productive use of time seem to throw their revitalizing mechanisms out of kilter and actually retard the return to energetic pursuits.

The changed behavior of Twelve is very evident in a personal interview. Children of this age do not throw themselves into the situation as much as they did at eleven. They become enthusiastic and may frequently interject such remarks as, "This is fun," but now they have the calmer demeanor of a co-participant capable of give-and-take. They are now more likely to remain seated in a chair, though that does not mean that they are not wiggling around in the chair. Their hands tend to be busy, reaching out to investigate objects and fiddling with such attached ones as telephone cords. Boy or girl has less need than at eleven to get up to investigate a room. Instead, they now make comments or ask pertinent questions about things they see. This calming down of "motor drivenness," this reduction of the need to contact the things he is looking at, shows a new capacity for abstract perception which gives more scope and flexibility to actions. Girl or boy is less controlled by the object, more in control of it.

Twelve is more aware of what he says in our interviews and may groan—with delight, really—when realizing that the interviewer is taking down even his initial exclamations ("Well . . . ," "Ugh . . . ," "Heh-heh . . ."). Though Twelve answers promptly, he is more thoughtful than Eleven. Answers are clear, spontaneous, and interesting. There is less clowning, dramatizing, and making faces than at eleven.

Twelves enjoy the interview, like to talk, like the interplay with the interviewer. Sometimes their eyes grow big and they regard the interviewer intensely, caught up in their own enthusiasm of reporting.

Health Though general health is excellent in some, and illnesses such as colds and bronchitis are less frequent, Twelve may not possess consistent good health. He tires less frequently than Eleven, but periods of extreme fatigue can occur when girl or boy hates everything and everybody that demands anything. This is the time when the child would profit by a day off from school. The school needs to be aware of this kind of fatigue and to be ready to cooperate with the home, allowing an absence if it seems desirable.

Twelve, like Eleven, may still have sudden, unexpected, sharp, but short-lived pains in various parts of the body, localized most often in head or abdomen. These probably portend the coming of puberty and are more common in girls. Twelve's feet hurt, as they did at eleven, but now the pain is often localized in the heels. A change of shoes may alleviate this pain. But greater care needs to be exercised in the choice of shoes.

Colds are most likely to develop when Twelve is overtaxed with too many activities. If the child does develop one, he wants to get well as soon as possible and is not so apt to pretend illness as was likely to be the case at eleven.

At twelve, eighty percent of our girls, sixty-eight percent of the boys say that "some of the kids" they know smoke cigarettes, and *for the first time, more than half (fifty-two percent) drink alcoholic beverages.* (Or so they say.)

About one third claim that at least some of their friends use drugs. But those who report drug use still can't say how often the supposed users use drugs. Nor can they say what kind of drugs are used. Thus some of this reporting may be less than reliable.

Tensional Outlets The very reduction in the intensity of Twelve's tensional outlets suggests that the child is on a more even keel. There are still those who, under tension, clear their throats, blink their eyes, show a nervous stutter. But nail biting may be restricted to one thumb, and stuttering may occur only in a particular, restricted situation, such as in the presence of the father. It is when Twelve is tired that nervous mannerisms most often occur, and they are no longer accompanied by that odd or confused look that was prevalent at eleven.

Vision Twelve is both aware of and concerned about his vision. During a visual examination he keeps asking if something is wrong with his eyes. Those who have had visual symptoms, such as blurring or aching eyes along with headaches, are even more concerned than most, and the visual examination usually reveals an underlying cause.

Twelve, visually, now has a better combination of the ability to fixate (which was dominant at ten years) and to focus (which was dominant at eleven). Difficulty in achieving this combination may produce a reduced power in focusing or a difficulty in discriminating, so that responses to some focus tests may be vague. Each eye tends to respond differently in its focusing ability, but it is expected that the eyes will regain their stability in working together and responding more similarly by fourteen.

The Twelves who show difficulties in their combination of focus and fixation without being aware of any symptoms may be expected to develop symptoms by fourteen, and should then also be more ready to accept and profit by visual help (glasses or visual training).

The question of having visual help to improve visual coordination and efficiency at twelve is still as difficult to answer as it was at ten or eleven. Twelves will usually cooperate, especially if their family feels they should, but it isn't their own idea. They may dislike the idea of having to wear glasses all the time; they feel it would interfere with their activities. They will cooperate in wearing them to study or read, though carrying them around is a nuisance. There is less danger of the child's starting to become nearsighted than there was between nine and eleven.

Physical Development and Sex Awareness—Girls Twelve is the age when the middle group of girls start to take their biggest steps toward achieving the form and functions of young women. This is the usual period of most rapid adolescent growth in both height and weight. (By the end of this year, the average girl has achieved more than ninety-five percent of her mature height.) Thus, despite an increased weight, many girls look less "chunky" than they did at eleven.

There is now a definite filling out of the breasts, a darkening of the nipples, and some growth of underarm hair. Menarche occurs most often toward the end of this year. And one event less often remarked on, but common among both boys and girls, is the sprouting of a fine crop of freckles. (It is significant that freckles were especially evident once before—at six years, an age which has characteristics similar to twelve.) This is more evident in some children than in others.

The intense interest girls had in their breast development at eleven is calming down somewhat at twelve. Their self-consciousness may now be expressed by their choosing to wear tight sweaters, flaunting their development.

A stronger interest is now centered in menstruation. A few girls are still having real difficulty in becoming emotionally ready for this new biological event, which they see as a threat and disruption of their lives. However, a majority nowadays are looking forward to menarche. They have been prepared for its coming, and, though naturally uncertain as to just when it will arrive, they are ready in their attitudes and ready with the necessary equipment.

The initial periods are generally light and irregular. Usually girls have very little premenstrual warning and are surprised to discover a few stains on their pants. There may be a very heavy flow following a long lull of two or three months, even after menstruation has begun.

These early periods are usually not accompanied by such premenstrual changes in disposition as may occur in the next few years, though some girls are "a little crabby" before and during their periods.

As to sex information, girls are much more likely than boys to turn to their mother now—to tell her of their thoughts and experiences, to ask her for information and guidance. Sixty-eight of our twelve-year-old girls say they think they have adequate information about sex.

It is for the mother to answer questions as best she can. She can, without laboring her point, help the twelve-year-old to view sex in its fuller perspective. Above all, she can help her daughter come to recognize that these feelings she has are natural to her new development, that physical sex acts she may have heard of, observed, or performed are also understandable as part of the growing-up process.

Physical Development and Sex Awareness—Boys There is a wider range of differences in rate of physical growth among twelve-year-old boys than among ten- or eleven-year-olds. Both highs and lows stand out. The advanced group is far more advanced at twelve, while the less advanced group hardly shows any changes since eleven. The middle group, however, now shows definite traces, of one kind or another, of beginning puberty. An increased growth of both penis and scrotum is noticeable in many. Long, downy hair generally starts to sprout near the base of the penis and a few darker, coarser hairs are intermixed. But even within this middle group of boys, there are sharp differences in the way incipient puberty is shown. Some boys show genital size increase but no trace of pubic hair. The situation is reversed in others, while some show both. Within an individual physique, similar discrepancy appears, some parts appearing more, some less developed. The blossom of the pubertal fat period may come into full flower only at twelve. Many of the boys experiencing this could endure it better if they knew it was only a temporary phenomenon.

Boys are becoming more interested in sex than they were. Some still allow their mothers to come into the bathroom when they are there and may show her any evidence of pubic hair with pride and amusement. Many appear to be embarrassed by sex talk and information from parents, however, and an occasional boy gets "red as a beet" at the very mention of the word *sexy*.

Two thirds of our twelve-year-old boys say they think they have enough information about sex.

Twelve is relatively less interested in the sexual activity of grown-ups and more absorbed in his own sexual interests. He has usually learned about (though not experienced) ejaculation. He is beginning to realize more fully that sexual activity occurs quite apart from the conception of babies and may, if he is a younger child, ask his mother if she has had intercourse with his father since he was born.

Some interest in girls is almost inevitable for the majority of twelve-year-old boys, even though it may be as short-lived as it is sudden. Twelve is fond of attending school gatherings. He shows a change in his care in dressing for an occasion and may still be wound up two days later. But in general, Twelve enjoys group activity most, and many would not try to kiss a girl except under the sanctioned ritual of kissing games, preferably with the lights out.

Erections often occur—both spontaneously, without apparent external cause, and under various kinds of stimulation. Mothers are now apt to find pictures of nude girls in their sons' pockets. Conversations and horseplay with other boys can be a potent source of arousal. And excitement of many kinds other than sexual, especially fear and rage, can induce erections. (This phenomenon is usually already forgotten by late adolescence, but it can be a puzzling one to Elevens and Twelves.) Masturbation is engaged in with frequency by many. It may occur alone or in groups. Some boys are beginning to go to their rooms and lock the door, though this does not always indicate masturbatory practices, by any means. A few may have one homosexual experience with an older boy in experimental sex play or out of curiosity. Or an older man may lead Twelve on without his knowing at first what the man wants. Twelve should be warned about this (realistically rather than dramatically) and protected from it, if possible.

Sex is really interesting to the twelve-year-old boy and he tends to think of it as "dirty" less than he did earlier. He wants information, and he wants to be set straight. Many boys would willingly go to a counselor with whom they could really talk freely and have their questions answered in a straightforward way. Twelve may prefer to seek information from such a friendly but detached source rather than from his parents, however frank and confidence-inspiring they may be. If he does turn to a parent, it is more likely to be his mother than his father.

Mother, indeed, may be the best person to give information, since a boy will not feel with her, as he might with his father, that he will have to live up to the model set by father's memories of his own childhood. Mother may say "This is the way I understand it. Is this happening to you—or is it the way you feel?" Girls, quite naturally, talk these matters over, if at all, with their mothers.

As to the facts of reproduction, some Twelves may feel awkward about discussing them. If parent or counselor does not help, Twelve seeks out information elsewhere—searching magazines, newspapers, and dictionaries for sex words and stories; swapping information (and misinformation) with friends. Twelve-year-old boys often have bull sessions to discuss matters rather freely, at least as far as the pooled knowledge of the group will permit. There is also a folklore of sex jokes that they tell only to each other. Yet somehow the same jokes crop up afresh with each new generation.

2. Self-Care and Routines
Eating
APPETITE: In the realm of eating, Twelve's stomach is described as a "bottomless pit." No matter how much he eats, the child never seems to feel full. Twelve can go directly to the kitchen after a large meal of two to three helpings of everything, to rummage around for cookies or other standbys. Children of this age may neither think as much nor talk as much about food as they did, but they eat with real appetite at meals or snack time.

Many girls and some boys have a very small appetite for breakfast but are starved by midmorning at school. Twelve would relish the planning and purchase of food for this important break in the morning and would even raise the necessary funds. Educators might be amazed by the change in the atmosphere and rise in energy and motivation in a seventh grade when Twelve's hunger pangs are quelled.

Twelve more often than not has a big snack on arriving home from school in the afternoon. This snack seems in no way to interfere with the evening meal, when appetite is enormous. Again at bedtime, a large majority of Twelves feel unmistakable pangs of hunger that can only be quieted with a big snack. It is a pleasure to watch Twelve "rustle up" a meal in the kitchen. Many are competent in cooking hot dogs or hamburgers and in making double- or triple-decker sandwiches. Unless they have been indoctrinated about proper eating, they will pour on the jam and ladle out peanut butter in thick layers until the contents are spilling and dripping from the edges of the sandwich.

Though Twelves' appetite is enormous, they may be beginning to restrict eating to meals and snack time. They may also be aware of restricting the quantity of food they eat if overweight. They may cut out desserts and foods they don't like. Girls are more aware of their waistlines, and may be making a valiant effort to diet, though they often fool themselves by pulling their belts very tight. Twelve also may control his appetite by thoughtfulness for others and leaving something for them. Whereas the child might have eaten a whole pie at eleven, he now leaves at least one piece for someone else to enjoy.

PREFERENCES AND REFUSALS: Surprisingly few Twelves have finicky appetites. Nor do their appetites fluctuate the way they may have at eleven. Many Twelves speak of their "ideal meal," in which mashed potatoes and gravy figure strongly. Any form of meat and sweets of all sorts are favored. Certain foods are still refused, especially root vegetables, fish, and creamed dishes. But Twelve isn't entirely averse to eating disliked foods and may adaptively camouflage their taste with a piece of bread or wash the food down with a swig of milk. Some are branching out in new directions with new favorites such as mushrooms, artichokes, fried apples.

TABLE MANNERS: Parents complain less about Twelve's table manners than previously. At least manners aren't as grossly disturbing as they were. However, desire to converse and eat simultaneously forces some to talk with mouth full. Or as they converse, they poise their knife or fork at an odd angle in midair. Twelve is still tempted to eat with his fingers and needs to be reminded about passing things or not reaching for things.

PREPARATION OF FOOD: Twelve can be interested not only in cooking or baking special, well-tried accomplishments, but may even be interested in the general preparation of food. Boys as well as girls like to "hang around" in the kitchen watching mother cook and may even be inspired to cook a whole meal themselves, though they may have to call to mother frequently to make sure they're doing the right thing.

Sleep

BEDTIME: Twelve has, in large part, given up the eleven-year-old fight about bedtime. To be sure, boy or girl still needs to be reminded more often than not, but on the whole doesn't object. There are still a few who resist, who need stronger pressures. But there are also those who go to their rooms earlier than necessary and enjoy the slow preparation for bed as they read, listen to the radio, or finish their homework. With less resistance and better cooperation, Twelve proves that he has earned a shift in bedtime, which is around nine-thirty with a flexible extension to ten or even eleven for special occasions or over the weekend. Boy or girl can now "take" these exceptions and reduction in sleep without having to pay the price of exhaustion and illness.

SLEEP: Twelves are happy to slip into bed, but that does not mean that they fall right off to sleep. Though they don't mention any fears of the dark or of being alone, they often keep a trusty flashlight handy. Or the radio may keep them company. Thoughts before sleep may range into the fantasy realm of heroic exploits. But the child also mulls over the happenings of the day and the things left undone.

Sleep is not as deep as it was at eleven. At twelve they seem more restless and may talk in their sleep. Dreams are of nice experiences near home or of a future time when they may be getting married. But troubled dreams, though fewer, still occur. At times they awake so frightened from a dream that they are riveted to the spot. They cannot move or even turn over.

MORNING: Twelves have fortunately lost the disagreeable disposition with which many awoke at eleven. They may lie in bed for a while before getting up, but often they wish to rise to read, draw, or to complete the homework they may have been too tired to do the night before. Average waking hour is around seven.

Bathing and Care of Hair The improvement in bathing that began at eleven continues at twelve. The idea that one *needs* to take a bath has entered the thoughts of the twelve-year-old, especially when girl or boy is obviously dirty. A child might even experience shame on seeing that his feet are dirty.

But Twelves do not restrict bathing only to times when obvious need is present. They prevent this state of affairs by bathing quite frequently, even as often as once a day. But with the majority, every two or three days is often enough. Showers are definitely preferred, but girls are apt to take tub baths, often indulge in a little soaking, though on the whole the bath can be accomplished with dispatch. Not that ears are always washed. These may still be the special province of the mother.

Some girls still need the help of their mothers to shampoo or rinse their hair, but those with nimble fingers are quite capable of grooming their own hair.

Though bathing may be under good control, a reminder may still be needed for hand washing. The very girl who has beautifully combed hair and may be wearing lipstick may have to be sent from the table to wash her hands. Fewer reminders are needed for brushing teeth. This is pretty much under Twelve's control, though he may brush them only once a day before going to bed.

Clothing and Care of Room Twelves are becoming much more aware of their appearance than earlier. They are especially aware of what the crowd wears and almost never go against it. If scarves are the style of the day, girls want scarves. If slacks or jeans are the style, girls will not wear skirts. If corduroy pants are in vogue, these are the only kind boys will wear. They all want to wear what they consider "suitable." Twelve is particular about what matches and goes together—unless unmatched outfits are "in."

The fit of clothes is also important to Twelve. Sometimes a whole new wardrobe is needed because of Twelve's rapid growth. All too often, an expanded waistline dictates a certain expansiveness in clothes. Twelves may try to pull a belt so tight that it restricts their breathing.

Some girls may try to look glamorous. They want to wear lipstick. Even if it is not needed, many wish to wear a bra, though there are others who do not wish to progress so rapidly.

Their choice of jewelry is usually reasonably tasteful. But however elegant they look, however long they may have preened before the mirror, many give unmistakable evidence of their age by a dirty neck or dirty fingernails.

Boys are most concerned about not wearing "sissy" clothes. They are not yet ready for the flashier sports clothes but may love bright plaid shirts or like to concentrate their new love of color and daring in a tie. They may, however, be all dressed up for an occasion but still wear their sneakers—even to church or a party.

Buying clothes is not the chore it has been. There are fewer issues about clothes between parent and child. Twelves know more what they want, both because of growing good taste and of bowing to style and what others wear. Twelve usually buys clothes with mother. Girls especially feel the need to try things on to see how they look. If the mother brings home clothes she has picked out herself, she knows that she needs the leeway to return them if the child does not like her choice. But Twelves are adjustable and, as they say, "We work it out if we have different ideas."

Beginnings, with Twelve, tend to be better than endings. Choice of clothes is better than care of clothes. There are sporadic moments when the latter improves, but on the whole it is the unusual Twelve who is neat and careful about hanging up clothes, changing into clean clothes as needed, and disposing of dirty ones. Twelve has a way of letting clothes pile up to get wrinkled and "bent over." One mother of a twelve-year-old boy in her exasperation pressed her son's bent-over trousers in their bent-over position and made him wear them. This didn't change things much, but he did "sort of hang things up" after that.

Not only do clothes clutter up the room but also collections, systematized or otherwise. And a new type of collecting is arising: mementoes such as ticket stubs, clippings, pictures of school teams.

Twelve needs a bulletin board so that he can plaster it with all these bits and any other special interest of the moment. With some, it is pictures of dogs; with others, horses. Pennants, football pictures, rock or movie stars' photos are finding their place on Twelve's walls. Fortunate is the Twelve whose walls readily receive the anchoring force of a thumbtack. Unhappy is the Twelve who needs to spend his allowance on Scotch tape to display treasures on the wall. "It costs so much," he says.

Twelves spend more time on fixing up their room than in keeping it in order, but do keep it nice when they think about it. However, with boys especially, mothers have to step in to clear up the room, at least once in a while.

Money An allowance is still the main source of income for most, though an increasing number supplement allowance with earnings. Some earn several dollars a week.

Allowances vary vastly from family to family. A middle value is three dollars or slightly more, depending on how much it has to cover. A good many Twelves budget. An allowance might be divided as follows: savings, Christmas club, comic books, movie candy, Sunday school, school supplies, emergencies. Some have to pay their own bus fare or pay for school lunches.

Twelve does not accumulate money as much as at eleven. It is more often saved for a special purpose—perhaps a baseball mitt, a guitar, or some records. The Twelves who handle money well always have money on hand. They are generous in lending and are especially delighted when mother needs some money. They not only like others to pay them back but are rather scrupulous in transactions as to paying back their own debts. These careful Twelves do not as a rule spend money foolishly, though this is not true of all Twelves.

In fact, quite a few are reckless squanderers with a burning desire to spend whatever money they have on hand. As one mother put it, "He can't stand prosperity." These are the children who are in terrible money trouble all the time. Money goes through their fingers like water. They are generous when they have money but are more often broke and in need of an advance or of borrowing.

Work Twelves are losing their earlier unpleasant, almost automatic, resistance to work. They are now recognizing the fact that they have to do it and therefore had better get at it. They may not volunteer and may still need to be reminded, but they are often reasonably good about helping. They have, however, worked out with mother the chores they *don't* have to do, such as making their beds, helping with the dishes, or setting the table. Mothers may realize that most help best over the weekend.

Most mean to carry out a request or chore "in a couple of minutes," though mother may feel they delay longer than this. Often Twelve does his best work when mother is pressed for time or when she is away.

Twelve is now not only helping with accustomed household and outdoor tasks but is spreading out into more difficult work. Twelves are dusting, cooking, even ironing, washing the car, cleaning the garage, or doing rough carpentry.

Earning money is part of Twelve's motivation. He prefers to be paid by the job rather than the hour. More boys and some girls are taking on a paper route, and both boys and girls are baby-sitting away from home, even in the evening. A few enterprising Twelves establish their own small-scale businesses, with wares for sale that they have made themselves. Through such projects Twelve may accumulate quite a sum of money, which often provides capital for further ventures or helps pay for his active social life.

3. Emotions

What a happy respite year Twelve can bring! Gone are the harum-scarum ways of Eleven. Gone are the belligerent, disagreeable, argumentative, and moody expressions of Eleven. Not that these more negative aspects of behavior are gone *entirely*. But the good periods have steadily grown until they last longer and longer. The same child who at eleven had sudden flares of emotion at the least provocation may be good-natured, warm, and adaptable at twelve, with the ability to take a ribbing. Twelve stands out even more as "a delight" or "a joy" when compared with his eleven-year-old self. Girl or boy may still show the extremes of behavior—a "black and white" response—but these are better defined and not in constant conflict with each other. When Twelve loves, he loves wholeheartedly. A more exuberant girl may sign her letters to her mother with "Love, Love, Love (multiplied by 10,000)." Twelve's abounding enthusiasm may be equally expressed for pretzels, parents, or religion. And hatred, alas, can be quite as strong. More often than not, it is directed toward school. Twelve's extremes may be expressed in caution or daring, in uproarious laughter or complete absence of humor.

In spite of these extremes, Twelve shows a "miraculous smoothing out" compared with his earlier self; seems to want to keep things in balance, to level forces of disagreement, to smooth over rough places. The child may at times be spunky and impatient, but on the whole is good-natured, pleasant, and willing to listen to reason. Twelves show a healthy caution in the midst of enthusiasms and anticipatory eagerness. This caution keeps them from jumping into situations too soon and saves them from the sometimes disastrous results experienced at eleven. On the whole, the twelve-year-old feels that good luck is on his side. But at other times luck is considered to be "about even," "in between," or it "balances." Most are ready to take the bad with the good.

Though Twelve recognizes that growth brings more responsibilities, he also feels that more fun is added too. Along with Twelve's more even-tempered disposition, a girl or boy often sustains a mood of happiness. A boy may be spoken of as "merry" or may be heard singing because of happiness. At times there are sharp peaks of wild exuberance, especially over some future event such as going on a ski weekend. Twelves are especially happy over success in schoolwork and seem unusually capable of enjoying vacation periods. They are quick to see the beauty of nature walks, and this perception produces added happiness.

Life can be terrible as well as wonderful. Most "terrible" is homework over the weekend. But in the end, Twelve usually overcomes resistance, buckles down, and completes assignments. Twelve-year-olds are sad on occasion, especially when the death of an animal or a person comes within their personal experience. They also respond to a sad book.

Anger is still not under control at twelve, though it is moving in that direction. More often than not, it is aroused by a younger or slightly older sibling. Attack by hitting, chasing, saying mean things, or throwing something is more common than withdrawing. But an increased number are responding with silence, saying something under their breath or going off by themselves, especially to their rooms to "think it over." A sophisticated Twelve may say herself, "I'm beginning to suppress my emotions" or (more likely), "Haven't been really mad lately."

Twelve might cry, especially if angry or moved to sadness, but on the whole this is not a tearful age. A boy may be just on the verge of tears. They may brim up in his eyes, but he stoically holds them back. Even when suffering pain, as from a bee sting, a boy sets his jaw and is determined not to cry. Twelves are more apt to cry at home than away, and if asked if they cry at school may say, "Don't be ridiculous."

On the whole, twelve is not quite such a fearing age as eleven, but Twelves often do not feel too comfortable alone in the dark, either on the street or in the house. They hear creaking noises at night and fear an intruder; think of criminals and killers and men bothering them on the street. Most Twelves will not tolerate a baby-sitter at night because they themselves feel capable of baby-sitting, but there are those who still need an adult near at hand.

Twelve's biggest worry may be about schoolwork, exams, report cards, and not being promoted to the next grade.

Twelves are not immune to hurt feelings, but try to avoid showing it. They may ignore an unfriendly comment, walk away, blush, laugh it off, or try to figure out the reason for the remark. Not all Twelves are successful at this; some strike out with a sarcastic remark—"I'm glad you think so!"—slam a door, or hold a grudge.

Children of this age have their own feelings enough in hand to be more aware of other people's feelings. They are often said to read mother's emotions clearly. They watch her face to see how she feels. Twelve respects other people's feelings and is cautious not to tread on any toes.

Most Twelves are not as demonstrative in their affections for parents as at eleven. They restrict expressions of physical affection mainly to kissing, and this they definitely enjoy. They kiss goodbye. They kiss goodnight. Twelves may talk about whether they are for kissing or against it. No twelve-year-old party can be guaranteed safe from some form of kissing game.

There is little jealousy or envy in Twelve, except where siblings are concerned. Girls who desire dates may be jealous of an older sister who already is dating. Twelves who haven't yet shaken off their eleven-year-old ways may feel that parents pay more attention to a sibling than to them.

Twelves recognize that other people may have more and better possessions than they have but still consider themselves lucky and ready to accept their lot. They become quite philosophical in their judgments: "Everybody has some bad and some good" or "It evens up."

In the desire to hold things in balance, Twelves have lost the sharp edge of competition so conspicuous at eleven, preferring to be even with peers, no better, no worse. They want to do their best, have a good time, and give others a chance. Those who are good in athletics or studies like to excel in their special lines of ability.

Parents of twelve-year-olds not only enjoy them in general but enjoy their sense of humor in particular. Feelings of irritability toward a parent can be voiced under the guise of humor at twelve. Rather than criticizing a father for being overweight, Twelve may remark, "What a physique!"

Twelve adores double meanings and seems to spot them with or without the least provocation. A teacher needs to be ready for Twelve's humorous thrusts. Thus, when she decides against letting a boy and girl sit next to each other and says she is going to separate them, some Twelve is sure to retort, "I didn't know they were married."

Dirty jokes are greatly enjoyed by Twelve, who not only understands them but tells them with great relish and laughs uproariously. Though elimination jokes, especially ones relating to bowel movements, are still prevalent, sex jokes are most in vogue.

4. The Growing Self

Eleven was searching for self. Twelve is beginning to find it. Parents speak of the child of this age as self-contained, self-competent, self-reliant. Twelves can't quite grasp this change in themselves but know that they feel different, that the reexperiencing of special occasions such as Christmas and birthday seems different from what it used to be.

And Twelve's actions do indeed proclaim a change. There is a return of joie de vivre, according to parents, which is reminiscent of the child when he was six and a half years old. At twelve he has become thoughtful, humorous, and a good companion, even though there are times when he is nasty and cross and may become "hipped on one subject." Initiative is high, which helps the boy or girl to plan ahead and have life more under control. Young people are now able to take over the responsibility of more and more of their own lives, not only in relation to home and family but also to the outside world.

All of these manifestations of positive behavior bespeak a new awareness of self, a total self in action. Some Twelves may still, as at eleven, identify their self as being in particular parts of their body, such as their feet because they like to climb mountains or dance. But most Twelves refer their self more to their total body, which is alive and functioning. They say of their self, "It's all me." Or they will say that their self is in their brain because it "regulates the rest of me" or "controls everything." Sometimes they divide the self equally between the brain and the heart "because you can't live without them both." Or the mind is referred to as "the center of everything."

Twelve is concerned with his similarity to others both in body and experience; may find it difficult to locate self because, as one girl put it, "Each part is like someone else's. No part is yours and yours alone. It may belong to you, but it's like someone else's." This feeling of similarity to others may well come from a closer identification with the group. One twelve-year-old boy held the misconception that he alone made mistakes until he began to have common experiences of error with other twelve-year-olds. Some Twelves feel this loss of the sense of uniqueness rather acutely. When they are baby-sitting, for example, and are treated merely as "the baby-sitter," they miss the feeling of individual uniqueness which they have at home. At the same time, Twelve doesn't like the sense of feeling "peculiar" or "funny" when alone. This feeling is most apt to come on after some sudden change—turning off the radio or awaking in the night.

On the whole, Twelves don't delve deeply or want things very different. They are satisfied with their lot and feel that "everyone is best the way they are." "Better off to be what you are 'cause everyone has their own difficulties," they say.

Twelves do not wish to hasten the growth process because they like "what happens along the way." And they think that "people should do what is suitable to their age." Most do not see that there is any reason to wish to be older because "you are going to get older anyway." There is a certain amount of time it will take, they recognize. They may appear excited and expectant about what is going to happen in the near future, but most are well rooted in the present as it unfolds from day to day. They can wait to grow up.

Twelves are nicely aware of their assets. They seem able to pick the very ones which best characterize their age—"being good-natured," "having a good disposition," "being kind," and "getting along with people." Likewise, they know their own shortcomings, the most outstanding of which are becoming angry, fighting with siblings, or getting mad at others. The biggest problem of many is homework.

When Twelve is allowed three wishes, a dog or horse is still desired by some. A boy may wish to move to some far-off place or at least to move into a new, big house. Or he wishes he could have a bigger room of his own, a gym, or a swimming pool. He may be thinking of vacations and travel. And with Twelve's increase in intellectual interests, he often wishes for better grades or to be smarter.

Twelve's wishes are not only for self but for others. Girl or boy wants to help the family or to take them on a trip. Girls especially wish for their father's success and health and that he wouldn't have to work so hard. Those who are without siblings wish for them. Twelve not only desires peace in the world but would eradicate diseases, famine, and the threat of nuclear war.

Twelve is less sure of his future career than in the past; is more apt to restrict himself to one possibility or may combine two instead of giving alternatives as at eleven. Boy or girl vehemently states the things he or she does not want to do. Twelves also recognize that what they would like to do now might not fit into their ability later and that they might not continue to want to do the same thing when they grow older. This recognition that there might be a change in choice shows Twelve's flexibility and scope. A few Twelves are still influenced by their parents' professions, but most have ideas of their own. Raising and caring for animals is less of an interest than it was. Besides the usual desire to be a teacher, doctor or dentist, or veterinarian, girls are now interested in writing, and especially in writing and illustrating children's books. Both sexes are interested in art and painting. Boys lean toward becoming athletes, carpenters, lawyers, doctors, and businessmen.

Some Twelves have a fair idea of which college they want to go to, though many haven't thought that far ahead.

A few boys now think they will be bachelors, though they realize they might change their minds. Actually eighty-three percent plan to marry—more than in 1950, when only fifty-five percent so planned. A few contemplate marrying their present girlfriends (with whom they may have only a speaking acquaintance), but again, they might change their minds.

This is one of the low points in girls for planning matrimony (seventy-four percent as opposed to our 1950 figure of eighty-five percent). This is also a low point in career planning for girls, with only sixty-six percent planning to work after marriage.

One of the main concerns of girls is that they have something in common with their future husbands. Their usual tendency to strike a middle way appears when they name the attributes desired in a husband. A husband should be "neither fat nor skinny," "not too intellectual but not too dumb." Twelve doesn't necessarily want her husband to be rich, but she also doesn't want him to be poor.

As for children, seventy-two percent of boys, eighty-one percent of girls, plan to have them. A few girls at twelve want many children, though two is the preferred number, as at most ages.

5. Interpersonal Relationships

It is difficult to catch hold of the subtle change that occurs at twelve, but there is an unmistakable clearing of the air. Not that Twelve has changed completely, but, as a mother may say, "He's over the hump." Twelve may first be aware of a change in his relationship with parents. Children now recognize that they get on better with parents than they did. They argue less. One twelve-year-old girl attributed this change to her belief that "father is less strict; he changed gradually." Then on second thought she added, "I think it was me."

Twelve's improvement occurs, in part, because children see themselves, as well as others, in a new light. They are now more selves in their own right, more congenial members of the household. Girl or boy can be with the family or away from them. They recognize the change for the worse in their own behavior when they are tired. They know it is no time to clash with a younger brother or sister just before the child's nap or before supper when everyone is fatigued.

Life is smoother, and Twelve is beginning to take some initiative. But in daily routines most are stimulated by the pressure of parental requirements rather than by forethought. Twelve rarely becomes angry with parents when demands are made and is less apt to argue back than before. Young people know ahead of time that they are going to act eventually, but they still need that strong push to get them started. They know that they will clean up their room after a long lecture; that they will "feel terrible" enough after criticism from parents to act.

Much parental criticism (there is less than at eleven) is accepted at face value. Twelve knows that parents think he is lazy, should take better care of his room, that table manners should be better. But the child has set up a camaraderie with parents so that fewer major battles arise. A boy is "insolent in a polite way" toward his father. A girl turns a scolding by her mother into laughter by her "amusing reception of it; not with indifference but just kind of pleasant and funny."

Twelve demands less of parents than earlier. Sometimes he wishes to be more appreciated by them, but does less with them than earlier. A boy may complain that his father is so busy that he has little time for him, but actually Twelve needs his father less. Girls are at times flirtatious with their fathers and are often said to be able to handle father better than any other member of the family does.

Fighting with younger siblings who are close to them in age (those in the six- to eleven-year range) is calming down. Twelves know that this is the main area where their parents wish they would improve. They also wish that their parents would improve by not spoiling younger siblings as much as they do. Those younger ones do bother him. They get into his things and are prone to tease him. However, neither boys nor girls are as vulnerable as they were at eleven and are less apt to explode when teased about liking certain members of the opposite sex.

Twelves do well with siblings in the preschool range. They seem to know how to play at their level and are often extremely fond of them.

Twelve is apt to admire or even idolize an older brother or sister. He or she may still squabble with those aged thirteen or fourteen, but the relationship with those who are fifteen and older is not only more neutral but often very positive. Twelve may confide in a sympathetic older sibling instead of in parents.

Twelves move easily and freely among their peers and rarely seem to be at a loss for friends when they want them. They may rotate among as many as eight to a dozen friends, first "going with one and then with another." Girls, especially, like to go in twosomes. Nearby, handy friends can be drawn upon, but school friends allow for wider choice and greater selectivity. Twelve is fairly observant about friends, knowing which ones still continue to quarrel, which ones don't seem as interesting because they are still "too good," and which ones are silly. Twelves visit back and forth with friends, including sleeping over.

Larger groups will form for athletic activities or possibly going to the movies, but on the whole Twelve likes a small group. The few informal, spontaneous clubs which continue may be on the verge of breaking up.

Twelve, for some, is an age of considerable boy-girl interest and activity. Some boys who were not interested in girls at eleven, and may not be again at thirteen, enjoy a short period of genuine interest at Twelve. Each sex professes interest in the opposite sex. Those more newly interested will speak of the members of the opposite sex as "okay" or "all right." But there are those who are more outspoken and speak of them as "darn nice." However, as one boy said, "I've been into girls for quite a while now, so I just left them, I quit." But he, along with many others, will be "in and out," first giving a good bit of his attention to girls, then not bothering about them and being too busy.

It's usually common knowledge among a group which boy likes which girl and vice versa, but girls don't expect a boy to come out and say that he likes them. Talking together at school may be the extent of the friendship.

Both boys and girls show a lot of shifting of interest from one friend to another. Boys get a girl in order to keep up with the other boys, and they may give her up as quickly as they got her. Few want to settle down to one friend of the opposite sex. Girls are the more talkative about the opposite sex among themselves. They may enjoy talking about boys as much as anything they actually do with boys. They may be "looking around," "keeping their eyes open," and they don't mind waiting until the boys come to them. "If they want us, they can have us," one threesome of girls declared.

Parties can be fun, but, alas, if they are not carefully planned for, if they are not held in check, the results are often disastrous. Girls often leave the parties unhappy and disconsolate because they haven't been picked by the boys to dance with. And boys can wreck the party by throwing any available food or beverage and breaking glasses and bottles.

If Twelves' parents aren't able to plan for a party with them, assist with the games and the fun, and provide the necessary controls when needed, then it would be better not to have the party. Twelve is an age when a party with both sexes invited is most desired.

Of course there must be one game such as "Hide-in-the-dark," which seems essential to Twelve's craving for close, accidental, and exciting contact with the opposite sex. In fact, a significant number claim that they "make out" at parties. Dancing is now popular with many.

Simple refreshments should be served at that magic moment when food alone satisfies the inner cravings of Twelve. Very few at this age admit to drinking alcoholic beverages.

Whatever the arranged activities may be, no time should be left unplanned, and parents should be on hand even if not right in the room.

6. Activities and Interests

Twelve has lost some of that insistent note characteristic of the child of eleven, when many were convinced that they had to have this or had to "do that" immediately. Twelve-year-olds want to be a part of the group and are heavily ruled by the group. But they can also enjoy themselves alone. Though they like organized activities, they enter readily into the shaplessness of "fooling around," "hanging around," "sitting around," "hacking around," or "walking around." They like to let life happen spontaneously at times and like to flow along with it.

Twelves don't get into conflict with others the way they did at eleven, when they insisted on having their own way and on having things done according to their dictates. Rather, they now want to hear what the other fellow thinks. Or they just want to enjoy life. They like variety and change. Twelve is not one to repeat, and lets you know about "the boring old schedule of doing the same thing over and over again." Twelves get sick of hearing the same record played over and over again by a fourteen- or fifteen-year-old brother or sister.

But they really aren't bored often because there isn't time to do all the things they want to do. They imply that they have little extra time with the phrase "when I'm free."

Both boys and girls can now be readily separated into the more athletic and the nonathletic groups. The one sport that holds up with all Twelves is swimming. Perhaps their extra weight insures the buoyancy and ease of swimming. They not only swim in the summer but choose to sign up for winter swimming in indoor pools. They dream of owning a pool of their own. "No water seems to be too cold for her," one mother reported. And there is indeed no better place to "fool around" than in the water. But Twelve likes to receive instructions and spends time and effort trying to perfect his stroke when this is demanded.

For the more athletic Twelves, basketball and hockey seasons are now being added to the football and baseball seasons. Both sexes participate in tennis, roller skating, and rope jumping. Some are becoming interested in sailing, golf, and fencing. Horseback riding persists as an interest, especially with a group of horse-loving girls.

Sports can be such a strong interest with some boys that little time is spent indoors. The less athletic boys, however, spend more time in the house busily making things. Their products include little cars made of tin and wood (often of their own design), model planes, cars, and even trains, photographs taken by themselves, radios, and puppets. Girls enjoy making puppets, putting on plays, hooking rugs, knitting scarves, along with sewing. With both sexes there may be some difficulty in completing these projects, but with a little help and encouragement from parents Twelve usually comes through to fair completion.

Both boys and girls have a wide range of interests. Some continue to collect all varieties of things, but this urge is reported to be "not too vicious at the moment." The collection of postcards, especially those which picture many different lands, is a favorite. Twelve spends much time looking over and talking about his postcard collection with friends. Both drawing and painting can be favorite activities at this age, and some try their hand at creative writing. This is the age when letter writing is less of a chore, and the interest in having a pen pal from a foreign land is strong. Some friendships flourish through this exchange, though they may bloom only a short time.

Twelves enjoy some form of organization. Perhaps this is why summer camp is so successful with Twelve. Perhaps the lack of organization in some Scout troops is the reason why so many Twelves drop out, often with the complaint that they "don't do anything" in Scouts. Likewise, spontaneous clubs of the same sex are often dissolved at twelve. They don't seem to have enough substance to keep them going.

Twelve's best organization comes through individual or twosome projects in which girl or boy is heavily motivated, especially if the goal is to earn money. One boy may deliver coffee and rolls to a neighboring construction crew. A girl may make plastic pins to sell. One project may provide money for another project, and that one for still another, in true businesslike fashion.

Sedentary Looking and Listening Activities Radio and television don't have the grip on Twelve that they have had. Some Twelves have their favorite programs, but they don't have to listen to or watch them every day and often restrict their watching to convenient times.

Fifty percent of the girls now watch fifteen hours a week or less; fifty percent of the boys, twenty hours or less. Comedies and situation comedies are still the favorite programs of girls; comedies, situation comedies, and police or detective programs the favorites of boys.

Mysteries don't scare the viewer the way they used to. That is probably why Twelve can take them or leave them. Though he would like to listen to the radio or watch TV while doing homework, if parents object he may desist. Radio and phonograph are well used by most. Twelve often keeps them on even after going to bed.

There is less time to read, and there may also be less desire to read. Most Twelves do not find time to read more than one or two books a week. Boy and girl are entering the adult sphere of interest and may use the library regularly. A few are aware of the authorship of books and may wish to read other books by the same author. Mysteries are a favorite type of book for both boys and girls, and adventures are a close second. Comic-book reading may persist, but without the avid concentration that demands rereading and hoarding. Twelves are less apt to spend their own money to buy comics but will read them if they are around.

Movies, along with the rest of Twelve's activities, have come into fairly good perspective. In fact, they may be as demanding of a movie before they choose to see it as they are about their demands of a teacher. They want first to know all about the movie, what it is, who is in it. Also, they want to know if it is put on well and if there is good acting in it. If the movie doesn't pass muster, if they haven't heard "good talk about it," they don't bother to go. Twelve usually goes with a friend of the same sex. A few boys go alone if they are interested in seeing the movie a second time or wish to see a favorite actress. If Twelve has a favorite actor or actress, this may determine in part why certain pictures are chosen.

7. School Life

If Twelve has one outstanding characteristic, it is enthusiasm. Enthusiasm can be so strong at this age that the child is carried away by it. Twelves will be in such a rush that they might literally even knock down anybody who is in their path. This same twelve-year-old enthusiasm can whip up a group to such a boisterous pitch of heated discussion that their teacher may need to step in to quiet them down.

The group is indeed very important to Twelves. Their own identity can become lost within the group. The extremes, of first being drawn toward others, then being as strongly repelled by them, so common at eleven, are less apparent at twelve. Girls, especially, have a way of flocking together. And how they chatter.

It is not so difficult for them to get ready for school in the morning as it was at eleven. If they have homework, they may finish it when they awake in the morning. They like to get to school early to finish any task left over from the previous day. After a weekend, girls especially will flock and chatter, telling each other about a dance or party, about what they bought on a shopping trip, or about the endlessly interesting topic of boys.

Twelve is not as dependent on the teacher as at eleven. Twelves don't gather around her the way they did, but will include her in discussions or activities if she wants to be included. There should be a good flow between teacher and pupil. Twelve tends to like his teacher, often speaks of her as "wonderful." They still like a teacher who tells good jokes and understands them. But more than anything else they want a teacher who can teach. They want her "to know her work better," and "not to teach more than she knows." They think she "should know what she is talking about." And if "she knows just about everything you can ask her" then she is truly "the wonderfullest teacher of all."

Twelves can be challenged by their teacher. They are ready to be held in line, to have demands made of them. If a teacher is not too sure of himself, is not too good on discipline, then Twelves lead him a merry pace. They throw spitballs, cough in unison at a prearranged time. The minute the teacher is out of the room they tell risqué jokes and laugh uproariously. But they act this way only with the teachers who do not hold a firm and challenging hand. They wouldn't think of acting this way with a teacher they think is "wonderful."

Each student is more on his own, more ready to buckle down than at eleven. But Twelve needs to be allowed to move around, to get up to get books, sharpen a pencil, or get some paper. Sometimes they just stand by their desks to relieve fatigue. If allowed a certain amount of freedom, Twelves wiggle less in their seats and talk less to their neighbors. Note passing can also be cut down to a minimum because the need has been absorbed by allowing more freedom of movement. The increased restlessness that may occur around eleven or eleven-thirty in the morning might be related to hunger and could be relieved by a snack.

Twelve shows a wide variety of interests in schoolwork (though boys still prefer sports). Arithmetic is often a favorite subject. They like the definiteness of arithmetic, and many especially enjoy decimals. They like to practice and enjoy the ease with which one can do arithmetic almost without thinking. If there is an arithmetic assignment on the board, many will choose to do that first.

Twelves don't like to be held to too rigid a schedule. They like to be allowed a block of time of more or less standard length which can be extended so that they can finish. Sometimes when the child is really interested, he likes to go on considerably longer than usual. Many are especially carried away by certain topics in social studies. A good example might be one related to the Spanish Armada, Francis Drake, and stealing gold and silver from the ships. Such tales of adventure and outlawry might stimulate debate, a favorite activity with Twelve. Enthusiasm may rise so rapidly that they may be ready to debate before they have built up a case. They are more concerned about carrying out their ideas right now than about how to proceed.

Twelve is quick to volunteer if a play is to be produced or read. Children of this age love to read their parts aloud. The use of a speaker's stand is especially congenial to Twelve.

Narrative and humorous poetry are enjoyed by both sexes, but a demand to memorize passages might spoil this enjoyment.

Boys are especially interested in astronomy and anything to do with outer space. And they especially enjoy any simple but real experiments in science.

The extra subjects of art, music, shop, and home economics are all favored. Twelve likes adequate provisions for these activities. In art, children often like group activity and might enjoy painting scenery for a play with the entire group. In music, they especially enjoy singing in harmony, and some like to play in an orchestra. In shop, Twelve shows good cooperation, but most do not do a very finished job. They are interested in accomplishing something in just a few sessions. Some fairly simple three-piece task like making a hamburger press would satisfy this desire for rapid accomplishment and also the interest in food and cooking.

Gym for many is the favorite period. The boys enjoy the usual baseball, basketball, and football. The girls continue to play softball, dodge ball, and volley ball. They are still apt to stop and chat in the midst of the game and may need someone to jostle them back into line. Twelve does a good job of selecting a team according to the ability of the individual, though he may occasionally be influenced by jealousy. Twelves are competitive, but not in the same ruthless way they were at eleven, when they wanted to win at all costs. Many are beginning to enjoy a game for its own sake.

Twelve is delightfully open and uninhibited in the classroom as well as at home and is especially outspoken about dislikes. Twelves speak up if they feel their rights are being infringed upon. They especially feel it is unfair to be held over in class just before gym.

Girls are very aware of their appearance. They primp before a mirror, combing their hair whenever they get a chance between periods. They flock together before a mirror. Twelves often follow fads of wearing charm bracelets, pendants, gadgety pins, or long strands of beads. Just where the knot should be placed in the strand of beads may involve important group discussions. It should be kept in mind that beads or any other decorations are now "in" and now "out." Fashions change with great rapidity.

Girls, on the whole, are more interested in boys than vice versa. In fact, the girls are often chasing the boys. They want to sit near them. The boys' interest rises as the year progresses. They express their initial interest by poking. Soon they are snatching a girl's wallet or pencil box and are off to hide it. Sometimes the teacher needs to be sought to use her authority to redeem the lost article.

Within a free-flowing, moving, but challenging school structure, Twelves can have a wonderful time in seventh grade. Enthusiasm carries them in many different directions, and they need help in channeling it and giving it expression. They need firmness and control. But when freedom is too curtailed, when they are forced to move on before they are ready, when they are asked to conform in spheres that have no meaning for them, then they become frustrated and the negative side of the age comes to the fore. Homework is a point at issue. Twelve wants to work, wants to complete a task. But as soon as it becomes a set pattern, as soon as it usurps free time when sociability is so important, then boy or girl rebels and comes to hate school at times.

8. Ethical Sense

Twelve takes a level-headed approach to ethics. Boy or girl seems to make decisions more through considered thinking, past experiences, and possible consequences, and less through immediate feeling than earlier. Children of this age seem to have spontaneous checks within themselves as through conscience. They give each problem that arises due consideration and weighing. They are basically diplomatic; not only tolerant toward others but also toward themselves. However, they still are not averse to seeing what they can get away with and are also lovers of fun. And, above all, they do not wish to veer too far from the dictates of their group.

To some Twelves, the decision and choice of right as against wrong is still arrived at almost spontaneously by how they feel, by common sense, or by the inner dictates of conscience. But, increasingly, it is thought of as a deliberate, weighed process. Twelves like to figure out how many good points there are for a certain decision and how many bad points there are *against* it. But, if necessary, they can always think up an extra point for or against, and their choice of points is made not so much on a moral basis as in terms of personal advantage. If they know that doing a certain thing would cause them to be kept after school, they are less apt to do it. They are less tempted to do the wrong thing than at eleven. And though some may think primarily about what advantages they will secure from a decision, they are also aware of what others—grown-ups or contemporaries—think. Above all, boy or girl does not wish to do anything to be classed as "too good" by peers, knowing that this might turn them against him or her.

Conscience stands guard at this age and can, at times, be quite demanding. But it doesn't, as it sometimes did at eleven, have that ruthless control that either dogged every footstep or, through defiance, made the child go to the opposite extreme of raising havoc. With this easier, looser control, the child may actually appear more conscientious than did alternately conscience-ridden and unrepentant Eleven. But, as some say, it's "half and half about getting away with things." Conscience can speak out clearly when the child has done something wrong, but what he does about it depends on his evaluation of the severity of the situation.

Twelves are much more casual about cheating than when younger: "All the kids do." Similarly, they are less critical of those who steal than formerly—some admit to occasional stealing for the "fun" of it.

Telling the truth is generally not too difficult for Twelve, who can be counted on to be truthful about big, important things, though not always about little ones. Girl or boy recognizes that there are times when you have to tell a lie, such as to protect another person. One can lie, according to Twelve, if there is a good reason.

Accepting blame, along with telling the truth, is a part of Twelve's more positive growth, though those who do this are not trying to acquire martyrdom by taking on extra burdens. They say that if a sibling or friend were being wrongly accused they wouldn't let them down, but if someone deserved the blame, they would "let them have it." Usually Twelves try to be fair.

Twelves no longer argue just for the sake of argument as was the case at eleven. At that age children are out to win and to prove mother wrong at any cost. Now they argue to make a point, especially when they feel they are in the right. But they can show a politeness toward parents even in the midst of argument. Twelves can be pretty fixed in their ideas and may not listen too well to reason. They can be convinced, though they still may feel that their parents are ordering them more than convincing them.

Twelves extend their tolerance to swearing and drinking. Everything has its place in moderation, they seem to feel. They aren't against swearing themselves when they get mad, but they don't think that parents should swear in front of their children. This is not setting a good example for children, who are easily influenced.

Skepticism about politics is high. Two thirds of our Twelves believe that most politicians are dishonest. Just under half think this country is doing enough to integrate the races.

chapter seven

THE THIRTEEN-YEAR-OLD

MATURITY PROFILE

Every now and then, in fact more or less at yearly intervals during the teenage years, Nature puts on the brakes and effects a sudden and sharp turn in the young person's behavior. So it is for many at thirteen.

All of a sudden, as we have observed earlier at three and a half and again at seven, there is a marked turn toward inwardizing, withdrawal, uncommunicativeness, uncertainty about self and other people and the world in general, almost a slowing down of metabolism.

Where, oh where, did my lovely, lively, enthusiastic, friendly son or daughter go, a parent may well ask as Twelve inexorably turns into Thirteen. In fact, where may he even be physically, one may ask. Very often, except at mealtimes, there will be no sign of girl or boy around the house. Or you may catch a brief glimpse as he withdraws into his own room for privacy's sake. Withdraws, and if you have been so bold as to ask the simplest question about where he has been or what he has been doing, mutters darkly, "Prying into a person's private affairs," "What's it to you?" or "Any business of yours?"

Twelve, though basically friendly, often had begun a slight withdrawal from participation in family affairs. Thirteen, unfriendly, withdraws physically as well as emotionally. Much of the time, so far as family is concerned, he just isn't there. Thirteens tend not only to keep their door closed but even locked. One boy we knew pushed a bureau against the door, just in case anybody tried to get in.

"Critical and withdrawn," a mother may tell you if asked to describe her boy or girl of this age. The sun most certainly has slipped behind a cloud, at least temporarily. Thirteen is sad. Thirteen is sour. Thirteen is suspicious, unfriendly, uncertain, unhappy.

Phyllis McGinley has described this age as well as anyone we know in her sympathetic poem, as follows:

Portrait Of Girl With Comic Book

Thirteen's no age at all. Thirteen is nothing.
It is not wit, or powder on the face,
Or Wednesday matinees, or misses' clothing,
Or intellect, or grace.
Twelve has its tribal customs. But thirteen
Is neither boys in battered cars nor dolls,
Not *Sara Crewe*, or movie magazine,
Or pennants on the walls.

Thirteen keeps diaries and tropical fish
(A month, at most); scorns jump ropes in the spring;
Could not, would fortune grant it, name its wish;
Wants nothing, everything;
Has secrets from itself, friends it despises;
Admits none to the terrors that it feels;
Owns half a hundred masks but no disguises;
And walks upon its heels.

Thirteen's anomalous—not that, not this:
Not folded bud, or wave that laps a shore,
Or moth proverbial from the chrysalis.
Is the one age defeats the metaphor.
Is not a town, like childhood, strongly walled
But easily surrounded; is no city.
Nor, quitted once, can it be quite recalled—
Not even with pity.

—Phyllis McGinley

The typical withdrawn and sensitive nature of the thirteen-year-old may seem to some entirely negative. We see it as something extremely positive and constructive. By withdrawing and refusing to share, Thirteen protects something far too fragile and half formed for others to see, his budding personality. This personality is not secure enough, at thirteen, to come under anyone else's scrutiny.

It is almost as though at twelve, boy or girl is trying self out against the world, and though things seem to be going well superficially, he or she realizes (even if not in so many words) that self is not ready for what the world requires.

So, back into himself to build up, by brooding and thoughtful rumination, a stronger self with which to meet the world when life forces, in their inevitable rotation, take him out of himself once more full force, at fourteen.

There is perhaps no age in this difficult teenage period at which boy or girl worries more about his or her body, features, and general personality than at thirteen. Sometimes almost nothing about him seems satisfactory. And the more Thirteen broods and wonders, the worse things may seem, with the result that many seem turned off completely about themselves. At other times one must assume that they rather enjoy trying on different personalities, moods, facial expressions. (Their mirrors at this time are very well used.)

Thirteen thinks about himself, and he thinks about the future; asks himself not only what he is like now, but what he will be like later on.

Rather touchingly, little as girls or boys may think of their family, more than eighty percent of both sexes plan not only to marry one day but also to have children.

One's emotional responses are of course closely connected with one's sense of self. When feeling positive about her thirteen-year-old, a mother may describe boy or girl as thoughtful, quiet, self-contained. When aggravated, discouraged, despondent, or anxious about the young person she has produced, her adjectives tend to be rather negative: morbid, morose, moody, indifferent, sullen, secretive, "in a minor key."

So it would be fair to say both from parental reporting and from our own observations that Thirteen is not, much of the time, a happy age.

Possibly one of the unhappiest aspects of this age is that still-vital relationship with parent, especially with mother. The specific and sharp criticism of mother as a total person, which will be even stronger at fourteen, has already begun. Many Thirteens consider everything mother does or says or is to be absolutely *ridiculous*. One mother of a Thirteen thanked us for warning her in advance of what things would be like between her and her daughter. "Otherwise," she confided, "I would have felt either that I had failed my daughter completely, or that I was just a natural-born mess."

Thirteen complains that people simply do not understand him. But if you give good evidence that actually you do, this makes him all the more dissatisfied because he does not really want to be understood. (At least not by you!) Thus you are in a double bind with the usual thirteen-year-old. He is not pleased either to be understood or not understood.

Most are still less rebellious with father than with mother. Of mother, a girl may say, "We yell at each other. Then sometimes we brush it off, but sometimes it's terrible." It helps that Thirteen spends so much time in his room and thus there is often not too much contact—unless mother goes into his room or perhaps *looks* in.

Thirteen is not particularly well satisfied with his family and their doings. One girl of this age, away on vacation when her family moved into a really beautiful house—she had not wanted to move in the first place—remarked only, on seeing the house, "Big, isn't it?"

Friends, we are happy to report, do give some pleasure—in fact may be the only bright spot in a rather dreary landscape. However, many Thirteens seem to have fewer friends than at surrounding ages. They are not entirely solitary, but neither are they entirely social.

Approximately one third of our subjects say that they date "quite a lot." In fact, forty percent of the girls and forty-four percent of the boys claim that they either have gone steady or are now going steady. A rather startling ninety percent of both sexes say that either they or their friends "make out." (We didn't ask this question of twelve-year-olds, but from the responses obtained at thirteen, we probably should have introduced it earlier.)

Parties can be a matter of considerable pleasure. They are slightly calmer than a year earlier, in most cases. Activities are chiefly playing games and dancing. Eating, talking, "having fun," and listening to records are also mentioned; and twenty-four percent of girls, twenty-eight percent of boys tell us that they also "make out" at parties.

Many at this age now rather enjoy school, perhaps because school doesn't pry. Some enjoy the increasing intellectual tug and pull. They especially enjoy independent and challenging projects. And many, in their increasing maturity, can recognize that a teacher is a good teacher even when they may not like him or her personally. In fact, in their typically self-protective way, even when they like a teacher they tend to be less involved with her than earlier.

Some principals, amusingly, comment that where thirteen-year-olds are concerned, they themselves might just as well be invisible so far as any recognition is concerned. Thirteen is not particularly sociable with any grown-ups.

Most Thirteens, though by no means happy, do tend at least to be rather ethical. They enjoy trying to figure out what is right and wrong. (Even this late in life they are helped in their figuring by what they think their mother would say.) But for many, their own conscience makes a rather good guide. In fact, some girls tell us that their conscience is *very firm*. Most are much concerned about *fairness*, and most now really try to take the blame when they have done wrong. Standards for others, as well as for themselves, tend to be high. Most consider that cheating is *really* wrong.

If one thinks of smoking, drinking, and drug use as ethical (as well as health-related) matters, there is much more of all three of these activities than most grown-ups would like to see. Of our own group, eighty-four percent of girls, sixty-eight percent of boys admit that they or their friends smoke cigarettes. Two thirds of each sex say that they or some of their friends drink. And very close to fifty percent of each claim that some of their friends use drugs, at least on occasion.

Thirteen-year-olds apparently have positive attitudes but not too much information about social issues in general. Girls more than boys think that they, when older, might personally do something about "conditions" in the world. Most think that politicians are dishonest.

Thirteen's relative withdrawal from close contact with adults is seen even at our Institute with a friendly and presumably somewhat neutral outsider like one of our staff, long familiar with each of our earlier group of subjects. "Oh, I'm not going to tell her too much," a boy may say to his mother before an interview. Most are polite, most relatively friendly, but most are not revealing. On the plus side, it is fair to say that most give thoughtful and accurate, even though brief, answers to questions asked. And with respect for their increased maturity—for now indeed they are true "teenagers"—an interviewer feels the need of phrasing her questions cautiously so that they will not seem babyish to the interviewee.

Most of what we have said so far in this chapter may seem a little on the negative side. We do not mean to downgrade boy or girl of this age. We respect their need for privacy. We empathize with their awareness that right at this time in their lives they are not particularly good with their parents. We sympathize with their many worries, as in the case of the boy who told us, "Most of the time I worry that people won't like me. I worry that I'm going to worry. I worry that I should stop worrying."

No, Thirteen is not an easy age to be. We're glad to report that, for most, living will be easier and sunnier when Fourteen brings a new burst of energy and enthusiasm.

But till it does, we strongly recommend that parents respect the need for privacy and isolation which the young person of this age displays. A healthy organism seems much of the time to know what it needs. This at thirteen may not be at a highly conscious level—it may be just an instinctive feeling that it's more comfortable to be by oneself.

It's altogether likely that the developing psyche, right at this point in its development, bruises very easily. The withdrawal from others, which often is so distressing to parents, in all likelihood is a healthy and necessary part of growing up. If this is true, it will make both you and your thirteen-year-old more comfortable if you can accept this withdrawal and not take it as a personal slight or an indication that you are failing as a parent.

It may indeed be a sign that boy or girl is growing away from you, but that is as it should be. It is, in fact, what growing up (at least to quite an extent) is all about.

MATURITY TRAITS

1. Total Action System

The change which takes place between twelve and thirteen can be very profound. At thirteen there seems to come an inner mobilization and organization of forces. The tendency is to pull things together, to inwardize, to think about things. This narrowing down and compressing produces a great deal of energy, but how this energy is expended depends upon the success of the organism.

Thirteens almost seem to know that they need to be more selective than they have been, that they need to concentrate and to discard in order to achieve further growth. When the child accomplishes this by withdrawing to his room, many parents are both worried about the behavior and hurt by the feelings of being left out. It is even harder to accept this change if Thirteen gives lavish time to a friend over the telephone. It is often wise for parents to take their cue from Thirteen, not only allowing children to withdraw but also withdrawing themselves, or at least standing by on the sidelines, ready to help as needed.

Though Thirteens appear more quiet and withdrawn than earlier, they can be very active in their thoughts, storing up ideas and energy to be expended at a later date. As one boy said, "What I hate to do is nothing." This same boy recognized his own change from twelve when he continued, "I remember last year I'd just sit around and get kind of sick of myself. This year I've too much to do."

This busyness can be so extreme that it may be hard for Thirteens to squeeze in even things they want to do, let alone household chores. But energy can be bountiful. One parent reports, "No physical feat is too hard for her to undertake"; another, "She's never tired, always anxious for more activity." This is by no means true of all Thirteens; many are well on toward fourteen before this phase occurs. But when Thirteen is both mobilizing and expending efforts in an organized fashion, especially on something that has aroused enthusiasm, it is amazing to watch the child in action. The death of a pet mouse might involve an entire evening as Thirteen fashions a beautiful little coffin, composes an epitaph or a poem to accompany the mouse to its grave, and finally buries it. The mouse's demise might have occurred in the first place because of the time and loving attention spent by Thirteen in handling it.

In an interview the poised, withdrawn side of Thirteens is most in evidence. They are usually friendly but not spontaneous and communicative. They sit quietly with little movement. Voice is often low and difficult to hear, and the child speaks more slowly than formerly. Boy or girl may answer with a shrug of the shoulders. Thirteen thinks hard before answering questions and may bite his lips as he cogitates. Answers are sincere and honest, but most tell no secrets. At times they look sad, but as interest is aroused begin to warm up. At times a boy may laugh while drawing in his breath. Everything about him is pulling in in his attempt to choose, to discriminate, and to define.

Health Thirteen's health is, in general, continuing to improve. Fatigue is less marked than it was at eleven and twelve. A few may still complain of stomach or chest pains. Skin sensitivity to wool, as evidenced by a rash on the inner surface of the arms, is present in some. Headaches are less frequent and have a definite relationship to specific cause, occurring after a great deal of physical exercise or prior to menstruation.

All too many young people now appear to smoke: eighty-four percent of the girls and sixty-eight percent of the boys say that they or their friends do smoke. Over sixty percent of each sex say that they or their friends drink. And now we are moving up to nearly half who admit that they or their friends use drugs.

Tensional Outlets There is a further reduction of tensional outlets. Fingernail biting, hand-to-face gestures, or scratching of scalp persist in some. There are some small ticlike movements and twitches, which may lessen by taking vitamin B. A dry and scaly skin and scalp may also respond to vitamin B complex and Evening Primrose oil.

Vision About a third of our Thirteens reported specific or nonspecific symptoms or complaints concerning their vision. About half of these were related to reading and occurred in those Thirteens who love to read and who read a great deal. The symptoms varied from individual to individual, with reports of feeling tired when reading, of print running together or blurring. Headaches were also reported after movies or television; discomfort also occurred when riding in a car. However, few Thirteens recognized these complaints as arising from their vision.

During a visual examination, Thirteen sits quietly and asks very few questions. The child can, however, view vision and its proper care with greater maturity than earlier. Girl or boy will wear glasses if it is necessary. Most can accept the advantages of wearing them for near work—reading and studying—though many think them a nuisance. Thirteens who wear their glasses all the time may dislike them for social affairs but know they might feel unsure of themselves if they went without them. By fourteen the girls especially will have a drive to be more free from their glasses and will work to secure this freedom. They will then be more ready to accept and cooperate with a visual training program. Contact lenses are popular.

Thirteen, in typical inwardizing process, is reducing functional farsightedness (or hyperopia). This trend, if continued, would result in a measurable nearsightedness, but fortunately Fourteen reverses the trend, and then farsightedness is increased slightly. Those children who showed no farsightedness at eleven are in definite danger of becoming nearsighted at thirteen. And those who are already nearsighted are likely to show a further increase in this same direction. If Thirteen is somewhat farsighted and finds it difficult to focus from near to far through reading glasses, he might profit by bifocals so that in school he can shift more rapidly from the near work at his desk to the far work of the blackboard.

Thirteen is showing a greater power to focus than at eleven and twelve. Though some may fixate beyond the testing target, the visual findings indicate a better functioning of the two eyes together as a team. Most Thirteens, except the nearsighted ones, show good mobility of their eyes as they follow a moving target, and they accomplish this with a high degree of accuracy and ease.

Physical Growth and Sex Awareness—Girls Thirteen is a period of continued ripening for most girls. Weight and height continue to increase, though at a slower rate. There is a general filling out of hollows for many girls, giving hips, for example, a smoother appearance as the dip between the outer crests fills in. Yet at the same time there can be an appearance of slimming in the very girls who are filling out. This is most noticeable around the face, neck, and shoulders. This slimming down in the more ordinarily visible areas together with the increased height of Thirteen can give a duality to a girl's appearance. Fully dressed, she appears to be slender. But in a more complete physical appraisal, her hips and thighs reveal her fuller development.

Most girls have menstruated before their fourteenth birthday, and the average thirteen-year-old has achieved ninety-five percent of her mature height. The secondary sex characteristics of breasts and body hair are developing steadily but slowly. But the main concern is menstruation if this hasn't occurred yet. In some ways, Thirteen is relieved when her periods finally appear. A few harbor some resentment for fear their periods will curtail their activities. But this resentment is usually a passing emotion, and most girls do not curtail their participation in sports.

There appears to be a relationship between onset of menstruation and a reduction in frequency of headaches. The menstrual periods themselves are not usually painful. Occurrence is still irregular, with a relatively long interval (as long as six months) between periods, but this interval tends to contract until, by fourteen, the periods assume more regularity.

Though Thirteen is not particularly reticent about letting her friends and family know that she is menstruating, she is often not ready to purchase her own sanitary napkins or tampons. The situation is too embarrassing, and Thirteen is not yet beyond blushing.

Physical Growth and Sex Awareness—Boys Where Twelve marked just the traces of physical maturity features in many boys, Thirteen brings more definite changes. For the middle group of boys, this is a period of rapid growth of genitalia. Pubic and axillary hair appear in about two thirds. The hair at the corners of the upper lip starts to darken. The nose may seem to jut out like a promontory in both boys and girls; it will appear to fit with the other proportions of the face within another year. The voice deepens perceptibly in many boys and cracks in some. However, there are those whose voices sound higher and clearer than at a younger age.

By the beginning of thirteen, most boys have started their sudden spurt of growth in height, but only a handful have reached the peak of this spurt. Boys are more concerned than girls with their height at this time. By the end of the thirteenth year, just about half of the boys will have reached their peak rates of growth, and thereafter they will grow more and more slowly.

Erections occur, not only with direct stimulation or erotic fantasy but often spontaneously or under other forms of excitement. Boys may wonder why this happens when they are neither with girls nor thinking about them. Because of the unpredictability of this function, many boys choose to wear an athletic support not just for athletics but all the time. Though only about half the boys have had ejaculations before their fourteenth birthday, most boys know about them.

As earlier, if the relationship between a boy and his mother is free and open, she may be one of his best sources of information about sexual matters. Perhaps the most important thing she can tell him is that the response of boys is quite different from that of girls. She can explain that girls like to be held and kissed and cuddled and that this "making out" may be all that a girl of this age may want. But, clearly, the same cuddles and kisses that satisfy a girl may arouse a very specific desire in a boy. This knowledge will not solve all problems, but both boys and girls should be aware of the facts.

2. Self-Care and Routines

Eating Thirteen's appetite has become well established, especially over the last two years. With some it is still as large as at twelve, but with others it is calming down somewhat. Whereas before they might have taken three to four helpings, some are now restricting themselves to one or two. They don't usually think about food except when they are eating; then they thoroughly enjoy it. Or if they hear some mention of food, they might start thinking about it.

Thirteen often snacks when returning home from school in the afternoon or just before bed. Some may be so hungry just before dinner that they can't wait and may eat a little something, which in no way takes away their appetite. But they are less apt to want the tremendous snacks they had at twelve, and are more apt to choose fruit or soft drinks. They may concentrate on one thing such as apples or oranges and consume large numbers of these. Some Thirteens are beginning to congregate after school or after a movie to purchase a soft drink or a soda. (Sundaes are usually too expensive.) But it all depends upon what the group does and what the home influences are, and a few are becoming aware that they should avoid sweets.

There is much less fuss at the table than there has been. Thirteen can now sit more quietly. There is no longer any battle about what girl or boy should eat. Most eat well, and they are usually allowed their refusals, which can be very strong. Thirteens seem to resent certain foods, especially vegetables, and may wish to have no part of them. Not even to taste them. But these total refusals are not many. There are the usual meat and vegetable preferences, and at thirteen there is an increased interest in fruits and salads. Desserts are more favored than they were at twelve. But candy is not craved the way it was. Some Thirteens are slimming down, but others remain overweight. There is some talk of dieting, but on the whole there is more controlled appetite, and this may solve the problem of being overweight.

Table manners are said to be vastly improved. "He doesn't gulp his food the way he used to." "She now sits up straighter and doesn't bow her head down to the dish as she had previously." Nor does Thirteen "monopolize the conversation," though he still likes to talk.

Sleep

BEDTIME: Bedtime remains close to nine-thirty if not ten P.M. As a boy may say himself, "My bedtime is nine-thirty, supposedly, but it depends on how long the supposedly is." Getting off to bed isn't usually too difficult, especially since many Thirteens go up to their room early. Their greatest need is to be checked on by their parents as to whether lights are off, radio turned off. To these demands most respond without too much resistance. Many even like bed, and muse on the curious shift that "the older you get, the more you like your bed." Some Thirteens go to sleep almost at once, but others listen to the radio or think to themselves for about a half hour. They are likely to plan ahead, to think of what they are going to do the next afternoon, or even the next summer. A few take unfair advantage of their parents and stay awake until one or two A.M., reading or listening to the radio. The majority, however, are asleep within half an hour and sleep soundly.

SLEEP: Many report that they dream even though they cannot remember their dreams afterward. Boys often dream of sports, and girls dream of boys and of dances. A dream that starts out nicely about ordinary things may later become quite confused. A distressing dream may recur. Parents often report that Thirteen talks or mutters while asleep.

MORNING: Awakening in the morning is not usually a problem for Thirteens. They are apt to awake on their own early enough so that they can lounge in bed and awaken slowly. If awaking at a certain hour is on their mind, they may awake too early. At times they will want to get up directly after awakening, and may manage to do so, considering that "it's just a matter of will power." Average waking hour is still seven.

Bathing and Care of Hair The whole problem of cleanliness is now being taken more for granted, and less time and energy are expended on it than earlier. Parents frequently report, "He doesn't object but has to be reminded" or "She has to be reminded, but no argument." Thirteen hasn't the same enjoyment of water as at twelve but has more the attitude of "let's get it over with as quickly as possible."

Thirteen bathes on an average of twice a week or every other day and is more apt to shower in the summer and take tub baths in the winter, though some prefer to shower in all seasons. You can always count on Thirteen to bathe before a dance. With increased perspiring (related both to athletic activities and to development of new sweat-gland structures with stronger characteristic odor), Thirteen recognizes the need to bathe.

Girls shampoo their hair once a week, or even more often, and may need some help in rinsing. Increased interest in hair on the part of both boys and girls makes the care of hair, both washing and grooming, rather easy. Some mothers are quite surprised, when they stop to think about it, at how much time their thirteen-year-old sons spend looking in the mirror as they comb their hair.

Fingernails are not given the same care as hair. Parental reminding is usually necessary to cut both finger- and toenails. Care of teeth is pretty well established, though reminders to brush are still necessary for some Thirteens.

Clothing and Care of Room A new kind of precision has come into the personal appearance of many Thirteens, both boys and girls. They are said to be "very particular," to "always look neat," or to be "very meticulous." Those who have previously been sloppy now look much better.

Group preferences will influence Thirteen's choice of clothes, but girl or boy isn't a slave to the group the way he or she was at twelve. Now they are surer of their own likes and dislikes, fully capable of buying all but major purchases by themselves. Even with a major purchase Thirteen is usually the one who makes the final decision, though it may be helpful to have a parent along. Frequently there is a good deal of argument between parent and child, and it is surprising to see how often there can be disagreement and yet still respect for the other's taste. But generally Thirteen holds firmly to his choice and persists until just the right clothes are found—driving mother almost crazy in the process. At the other extreme is a certain group of boys who think little of clothes, prefer to be dressed in jeans and T-shirts, and judge new clothes by their weight—the lighter the better. However, even with these boys, when it is time to dress up they usually comply without fussing. Girls are especially aware of the clothes of others. They can size up pretty well which clothes will bring compliments and which will not.

Even with this more precise interest in one's own appearance, Thirteens may not yet relate the care of clothes to the way they want to look; may still sling clothes down or throw them around. Some hang clothes on the back of a chair or on a doorknob. Good clothes are more apt to be hung up properly. A very few are aware of the way clothes wrinkle if they are not hung up properly and will even press their own clothes.

Thirteen has improved about putting dirty clothes in the hamper and is also quite reliable about changing into clean underwear. In fact, some mothers may even wish they wouldn't change so often. Many are also becoming aware of which clothes should be sent to the cleaners.

Their rooms are not only cluttered with clothes but with books and papers on the floor, along with dishes left from snacks. They recognize the need for picking up, but don't seem able to get around to it more than once a week or once in two weeks. Mother may need to mention it, but no major battles need to be fought because Thirteen usually can comply eventually.

Thirteens spend quite a lot of time in their own room. They may plaster their walls with pictures of rock groups or movie actors or actresses or with pennants. They spend a great deal of time lounging on their beds, reading, listening to the radio, or doing homework. A boy often has his door equipped with lock and chain to insure privacy, especially from younger siblings.

Money Though a few Thirteens are still down in the three dollar allowance class, the majority receive four dollars or considerably more, and even this can seem inadequate. Some allowances include lunches and bus fare, and Thirteens are allowed to budget a larger allowance of around five dollars a week. Some boys earn as much as ten to fifteen dollars a week, as from a paper route. Some boys at this age are said to be "money mad"—"they just earn in order to spend." Others may save their money for making specific purchases. These range from a camera to a power mower or a boat. These boys who earn may even pay for their own clothes.

Even the quieting down, thoughtful, inwardizing process of Thirteen doesn't resolve the financial difficulties of the spenders. With them "money just goes," "it disappears." If they don't spend their money at once, they are at least "broke" by the end of the week. Somehow they always seem to need more, no matter how much money they have to begin with. Still others who don't lack funds have difficulty in organizing their spending. They may have good intentions about budgeting but get all muddled about it. They leave money all over the house, in their pockets, or on the bedside table. Someone needs to collect it for them and to sit down and go over their budget with them.

Work Helping in the house is acquiring a certain pattern which parents can count on, and Thirteens often carry through with a certain amount of willingness. As they rattle off four or five chores that they are responsible for and allegedly carry out, it almost seems as if that long-desired millennium has arrived. With Thirteen's greater willingness and proficiency, demands can actually be relaxed. There are still the "just a minute" boys and girls, but on the whole Thirteen has worked out a routine, often taking turns in a job with a sibling, and carries out his or her fair share.

Boys especially enjoy handyman jobs, which include repair of simple electrical devices and fixtures. They enjoy running errands and are adding caddying to their outside jobs. A very few are beginning to assist in a store. Girls are beginning to clean other rooms in the house besides their own and enjoy cooking breakfast, especially over the weekend. Both sexes are doing considerable baby-sitting away from home and enjoying the earnings they secure.

3. Emotions

The changes that have occurred from twelve to thirteen, though definite, are rather subtle. Often boys and girls feel that, if anything, "things are a little better"—for horizons are widening both in the things they can do on their own and in their relationships with friends.

Thirteens admit that they are "not too good-natured," and often recognize that they are nicer away from home than at home. Other people may sense the changes in them more strongly than they do. Parents time and again report that the child shows a real quieting down, that a more serious note is creeping in, that periods of marked moodiness occur. The exuberance and enthusiasm so prevalent at twelve have definitely calmed down. Even compliments paid by mothers in the parent interview are given with caution and reserve: the child is said to be "fairly good," "quite cheerful," "pretty good." In many Thirteens the prevailing theme is a minor one, described variously as sullenness, moroseness, secretiveness, pessimism.

Thirteen, if his calming down hasn't gone too far into withdrawn behavior, usually has emotions in good control; may feel more independent and may act more independently. Boys or girls may separate from the family group and go to their own room because they like to be alone. They are reasonably content with themselves and seem happy to be by themselves. Very happy moments may come for no special reason, but these don't usually last very long.

Feelings of sadness are more intense than they have been. These feelings may be a part of a mood when the child feels "gray and dismal as if things weren't too good," without any apparent reason. More visible causes, such as people or pets dying, friends moving away, may be the basis of sadness. But the thing that makes them feel terrible is when their mother gets mad at them and has a big talk with them.

When angry, Thirteens seem to be able to control themselves better than formerly and don't often get really furious and explode the way they used to. Girl or boy is more likely to be annoyed or irritated than angry. Even when really enraged they are able to exert some conscious restraint. Some Thirteens, the less controlled ones, will immediately say mean things when angry. But many say or do nothing. Others walk out and go to their rooms to think things over and calm down. And now the response is often a deflected one. Seemingly restrained at the time, Thirteen may later take things out on someone else, especially on mother. Or, perhaps even more often, Thirteen turns anger back on self, "tells himself off." This seems to quiet things down gradually.

On the whole, Thirteens recognize that they "can't do anything" when mad at parents or teacher. They have also come to learn that their parents are often proved to be right later on. But the teacher often poses quite a problem for Thirteen. Some Thirteens get so mad at their teachers, justly or unjustly, that they feel like being "terribly bad." Those who don't have the courage to act aggressively may do the opposite of what the teacher demands of them. They will go so far as to depreciate a great person just because the teacher says he is great.

Thirteens are not often seen crying, but are at times found crying in their own room. Sometimes they cry in anger, but also often when "things are just too bad." Both boys and girls may cry because they haven't been asked to a party. Usually these are the young, brilliant Thirteens who are competing with well-seasoned Fourteens.

Thirteens are not especially fearful. They might say they have the "usual, normal" fears that everybody has. But they often have fearful thoughts on their minds, which they may try to belittle as they talk about them. You often hear Thirteens say they fear "nothing big like an atomic bomb" or that they are not "afraid to stay in the house alone, but just get awful lonesome." They say that they are not afraid of walking down a dark street at night but that they just "walk a little faster." Thirteens are trying to convince themselves that they are not afraid. There is one special fear that a number of Thirteens do have—the fear that comes when one is hemmed in, confined by a crowd or in a subway.

Though Thirteens may not be very fearful, they are great worriers. They say that they "worry about most everything" or that they "worry that they are going to worry." Each Thirteen seems to have something personal to fret about. A fair number worry about schoolwork—the poorer students about their passing arithmetic, the good ones about making the honor roll. Some worry about a sibling's popularity. Still others show concern about paying their debts or getting things done. A few go far afield and take on the burdens of international affairs. Thirteen's resolution of the state of world affairs can be quite simple. As one thirteen-year-old girl said—"If they used their heads they could settle it. They just want things. They never think about other people."

When faced with the question "What is your chief problem?", however, Thirteens are apt to say that they have no "major problems" or "all little problems that can be worked out easily." Girls are more concerned about popularity, attractiveness, and their future, whereas boys are more concerned about school or money matters. A few are held within the grip of the specific, such as staying up later on Friday night or concern over some physical inability or blemish. And there is still a fair number of Thirteens whose main problem is a brother or sister with whom they have now been fighting for years.

Thirteens, though they may seem so callous at times, have a very sensitive core. Feelings are easily hurt. It's not only what people say to them but also disappointments and failures, as in schoolwork, that hurt their feelings. A number don't do anything about hurt feelings. Others pointedly ignore or snub the person who produced them. And a few are able to laugh things off or try to crack a joke.

Thirteens, increasingly, are aware of their own feelings. Many show their feelings and don't care if others know how they feel. But many want to "hide" or "cover up" feelings, or will let people know when they are happy but not when they are sad. Often they will let only their intimate friends and, on occasion, their mothers, know how they feel.

Expressions of affection do not come easily to Thirteens. They are more standoffish. They seem to have pulled into themselves and are more inclined to think and resolve feelings within. They are not very jealous of those who are better endowed than themselves or who have more possessions. "Once in a while" they might be jealous of "just little things," but on the whole don't wish to change places with another.

Thirteens have reached the stage when they like to compete in "things that matter." They are quite selective about what they want to be best in. But they are not too disturbed if they don't win, even though they want to, and try to excel—at least they say, "It doesn't break my heart" if they lose.

Humor has become rather crisp and sardonic in some Thirteens. A few are especially good at sarcasm. They like to repeat in an exaggerated fashion something someone else has said. Thirteen's take-offs on a teacher's mannerisms are biting and can be very telling. Some of their sex jokes are quite advanced and often include at least a veiled mention of intercourse.

4. The Growing Self

What better way can an adolescent find himself than by pulling in all forces at intervals from the active scene of life and communing with self? How each individual utilizes what the growth forces provide may vary greatly, but the terrain is the same. The rapid, shifting, conflictual movement of eleven has settled down through twelve to an apparently almost quiescent point at thirteen. But the quiescence is dynamic with inner resources. With newfound intellectual powers, Thirteen is focusing perceptions into sharp, even piercing insights.

Thirteen is "willing to let time take its course." As one boy said, "I used to want to grow up fast, but now I would like to grow just slowly, just the natural way." That earlier hurry and eagerness for future experience which he wasn't ready for is now leaving him. He wants to live now, wants to exist more fully. Thirteen is a natural existentialist, giving to life what he has to give, taking from it what he can absorb.

Thirteens are not complimented by their elders the way they were at twelve. But they are appreciated and usually understood. How often a parent will say, "She definitely has a life of her own" or "He lives by himself." At times the parents feel hurt by this withdrawal, feeling that Thirteen is shutting them out. Or they are concerned and worried that they should do something about this withdrawal. Too often they don't realize that this is a time for withdrawing, for being alone.

Not all Thirteens withdraw physically in the home by going to their rooms. However, even those who are still a part of the family group are at times "lost" within the house. Or they do not wish to enter into the same group activities that they used to enjoy with the family. They are more independent from the family group. They are even more independent from their own contemporaries. They are not slaves to the group as they were earlier.

Thirteens are beginning to see themselves more clearly. First and foremost, it is their appearance that concerns them. This is their outward self. They are drawn to a mirror as to a magnet. Any stray lock must be combed into place. They are definitely interested in their clothes and may groom themselves with meticulous care.

As for inner self, that too receives scrutiny. A boy may be said to have good insight, to know what the other fellow means. Right in the middle of his own experience he can stand off at times and laugh at himself in an adult manner. His self-criticism is directed toward his inner self, his character. He recognizes his selfishness, his laziness, his too-rapid anger, his poor understanding of the other fellow. He may catch himself in what he later considers lies. He knows when he tells stories to make himself feel better. But he can be true to himself and will confess later, "I just hate myself when I try to get sympathy. I just told you that story so you would say I was right and Billy was wrong."

But Thirteens don't spend much time in criticizing themselves. They are more concerned with being themselves, getting on with themselves, pleasing themselves. Most are fairly quick to list their assets: good disposition, determination, brains, athletic ability.

Boy or girl of this age is becoming aware of a new focal point, the brain, that seems more than anything else to be the place which is the seat of the self. A girl will tell about the time when she thought her braids were part of her self, but now these external parts are not essential. They can change. Self may be expressed actively through thoughts, conscience, or critical ability. But the place where all this action goes on is in the brain, where "all conscious thought and all conscious movement go on." A boy may be so aware of the brain that he sizes up his classmates and calls a more intellectual one "the brain." Or this can be his form of salutation over the telephone with his friends, "Hello, brains."

The intellectual surety of Thirteen's self can be so strong that much interest and time are spent in verbal pursuits. An unabridged dictionary may become a treasured possession, and even the breakdown of words into syllables suggests an interest in word origins. Thirteen feels his intellectual powers.

With those Thirteens who are less secure in themselves, this age may be a very disquieting time. They may be hypersensitive to criticism. They may be so anxious, as when talking over the phone, that they first have to write down what they are going to say. They may be so uncomfortable in themselves that they take on an imaginary role to become someone else, to be someplace else. These are the ones who have to escape from themselves to find themselves.

Thirteen's awareness of his assets and faults most often concerns the matter of intellect. A typical boy may cite as assets his reasoning power, his brains, or getting good marks. He knows he has the ability "to stick to things" and he speaks of his determination. Those Thirteens who are more aware of other people speak of their friendliness, their thinking before they speak, or not wishing to hurt other people's feelings. The opposite is often true when Thirteens consider their faults, recognize that they sometimes don't try to understand the other fellow, that they get angry too quickly, and that they are selfish. They know when they are putting things off and when they are being lazy.

Thirteens may be so concerned with "right now" that it can be difficult for them to voice even one wish, let alone the three we traditionally ask for. Or if they can't be specific about their wishes, they might wish to have as many wishes as they want. Though many still wish for material things such as fishing tackle or a better home, some are now thinking of other people primarily and of themselves secondarily. One thirteen-year-old gave her wishes in order of preference. First she wished "that the people of the world would learn to live together." Second, "that I could design my own home with all the furnishings, materials, etc." And third, and perhaps most important, "that I had a boyfriend."

A feeling for others in trouble, especially in physical trouble, is typical of Thirteen. He or she wishes that there were no disease, no illness. Also the person of this age may, rather globally, want to "clean up communism," or "ban the Bomb."

Thirteens have thought a lot about their future careers and have often discussed this matter with their parents. They recollect the careers they have previously chosen and now given up. The earlier choices of being a nurse, veterinarian, or lawyer are frequently given up. Some Thirteens realize that they first need experience to find out what they would like to do. One of the most common choices of Thirteen, which undoubtedly is related to the child's intellectual drive, is to become a teacher. These Thirteens who choose the teaching profession know pretty well what specific age group they wish to teach, anywhere from nursery school to their own age. Some new professions on the horizon are those of psychologist and sports announcer. Girls are thinking both of marriage and career, and, though many would like to dovetail the two, the majority give marriage top priority.

Those Thirteens who plan to go to college (eighty-four percent of our girls, eighty-eight percent of the boys) have a fair idea of their choice, determined by what college has to offer them. Many are beginning to consider the advantages of a small college. The pull of coeducation is strong.

Marriage is definitely on Thirteen's mind. In fact, this is a high point for marriage plans. Eighty-six percent of the girls and eighty-eight percent of the boys plan to get married. Boys may not yet know what attributes they desire in a wife, though some boys would like their wives to be smart. Girls want their future mates to like things they like and also to be like them. They wish to feel that others, especially their friends, will like their future mates.

As for number of children, two continues to be the favored number, though fourteen percent of girls speak of four or more.

5. Interpersonal Relationships

If only Thirteens wouldn't snap back so, cut their parents short with a one-word answer, seem touchy, go off by themselves—then their parents might know better how to approach them, how to deal with them. Thirteens don't want to compromise their position in the family, but they know full well that they are not "as nice to my family as to my friends." Not quite sure themselves how things have changed for the worse and a bit bewildered, girl or boy says, "I don't know why we don't get on better."

Some Thirteens, however, get on "pretty well" or "okay" with their parents. They often recognize that their mother is understanding and sympathetic, but they are reticent about asking her questions, especially questions about growing up. They might tell her about things that have happened, especially away from home, or they might come to her to settle an argument, but they don't often confide in her. They might want to talk things over with their mother, ask her advice about social things or complain about school, but they don't want her to go to school and fight their battles for them, no matter how much she could help.

As one mother put it, "I'm needed now in a different way from when she was younger. I'm needed to provide productive and inventive outlets that will enrich and safeguard her potential. I'm needed to help in continuing the effort to instill in her a worthy code of ethics and to further establish a high standard of morality and values."

Thirteen is often embarrassed by his mother, especially when in the company of friends or someplace where somebody might recognize him (or her) as at the movies or the beach. But if in a strange place, a distant city where one is safe in his or her unknownness, the child of this age will get on better with her.

At home Thirteen is often critical of mother in little ways. This is truer of girls than of boys. If it isn't her hair, it's that she forgot to put on lipstick when she went out. (Or put on too much.) Or something is wrong with her clothes or even her handwriting.

Hopefully in perhaps the majority of instances, withdrawal from a close relationship with mother and criticism of her looks and behavior may constitute the extent of Thirteen's rebellion. However, especially with some girls who may be veering toward delinquency, things can be much worse than this. A thirteen-year-old girl whom we saw on our clinical service (not as one of our research group) told us quite explicitly that she was giving her mother just one month to "shape up." We asked if her mother knew about this time limit and the girl said, "No. She's just got to shape up on her own." Asked what would happen if she didn't, the girl replied, "I'll fix her. I'll just run away from home or maybe get pregnant."

On the other hand, some parents are almost too critical of their thirteen-year-olds. This expression of criticism can be so common and so persistent that parents are said to "din" or "nag" at Thirteen. The more usual criticisms concern keeping rooms picked up, helping more around the house, and improving table manners. Fathers may feel that Thirteen should try harder in school; that mother does too much for the child; that boy or girl should stick to things better; that there should be more work and less fooling; that the child should practice music lessons more; should have a better disposition, better judgment, more common sense. Fathers can be quite biting when they speak of their daughters as messy and selfish. These criticisms don't endear their parents to Thirteens. In fact, a few Thirteens feel persecuted, and some are so easily hurt that they burst into tears over any criticism. All of these criticisms leveled against Thirteen may be accurate, but girl or boy can't change too much or too fast. One thirteen-year-old daughter was heard to say, "I partly try to change but partly think that time will take care of it."

If only parents would recognize that time is indeed on their side. This is an age of inward absorption, of withdrawing, of thinking things over. This shift in attitude, this inner concentration, may actually produce a social deafness. Thirteen truly doesn't hear when parents call. The wise parent comes to realize that everything goes all right if he or she leaves Thirteens alone or stays on the surface. The parent further realizes that it is necessary to be tactful and reasonable with Thirteen in a grown-up sort of way, to be careful of criticism, and to know that Thirteen is very touchy. Failing to recognize this, he or she will feel the impact of Thirteen's snappish manners, antagonism, or even open resentment, and will produce a further withdrawing in boy or girl than would otherwise occur.

Generally Thirteen's relationship, such as it is, is closer with mother than with father. Most recognize that their relationship with father is "different" and "less close," though some girls have their first warm relationship with their fathers at this age. Thirteen often admires father and is less apt to criticize him than mother. Thirteens state that father is often too tired, too busy, or not around enough for them to do things together. But they do not usually say this in a complaining way. Father may go to sports events with them or to the movies or fishing or swimming.

But where father comes in most handy is in helping Thirteen with homework. From Thirteen's point of view, "Daddy is easier to work with now." But from the father's point of view the improvement may lodge in the child—"She's beginning to think. It's a pleasure to work with her." And probably there is an ounce of truth in both opinions.

When and if Thirteen withdraws from the family group, it is more often to get away from siblings than from parents. Perhaps it is because Thirteen is so touchy that he is so constantly annoyed by younger siblings, especially those in the six- to eleven-year range. A boy himself may be able to explain it by saying, "I'm going through a stage when everything bothers me." But all too often, "It's hard to explain," or he really doesn't know why he gets on so badly with siblings. Both boys and girls often speak of a younger sibling as a "spoiled brat," a "pest," a "nuisance," or a "pain in the neck." This horrible creature does undoubtedly "annoy" him, "get on his nerves," "interrupt" him, and get into his things, though this last is less of a complaint than formerly.

Thirteens on their part may not realize that they are too often assuming an adult role, trying to improve younger siblings, trying to make them do things a Thirteen knows how to do. They quarrel with younger brothers and sisters most often over "trivial things," "just little things." Usually fighting is in the form of "bickering"; often it is for fun, but sometimes it is in earnest and may need adult intervention.

Even with their sibling difficulties, Thirteens would not wish to be without siblings. They might wish to shift their age to younger or older, but they do feel that sibs help to prevent them from being spoiled. Boys, especially, would like a brother just their age, not realizing that this close relationship at home with a supposedly ideal brother would still produce many problems.

Thirteens' wider age separation from younger siblings under five allows them to assume a grown-up role more naturally. They often like to care for those much younger, get on fine with them, plan surprises for them.

Also, boy or girl is getting on well with older siblings, especially those fifteen or older. There may be some bickering, but squabbles can usually be settled without family interference. Thirteens may feel that an older sibling takes advantage. But on the whole they are beginning to enjoy each other's company. Thirteen may feel, at long last, that an older brother or sister is really acting as a brother or sister should: "She's a real sister." Sometimes these older siblings are quite convenient. You can talk things over with them. But when an older sibling criticizes until it hurts, Thirteen will retaliate in kind. As one Thirteen declared about his brother who had criticized his drawing, "Well, I don't like his attitude toward cops."

There is a considerable difference between boys and girls in their relationships with their own sex. Thirteen-year-old girls recognize a shift from being a part of a total group at twelve to having a number of separate friends at thirteen. As one girl put it, "Last year we had a sort of a gang. Then I think I learned my lesson. You make more friends if you don't go in a gang." Friendship is important to a thirteen-year-old girl. She wants and needs someone to confide in, someone to tell secrets to—even though what she tells may not be very confidential by adult standards.

Girls often go around in groups of three. The threesome often shifts into a twosome, as two gang up against the third girl. Often this is meant only as kidding, but Thirteen can also be quite pointedly critical, even of her friends. As one girl aptly remarked, "With the best of friends there are always arguments; the better they know you, the more they can criticize."

Boys of thirteen do not have the closely knit groups that girls have. They are more likely to cluster in gangs of four or five, with each member considering all the others to be his best friends. Boys don't seem to need the intimate atmosphere of imparted confidences that the girls demand. The boys are more concerned about *doing* things with their friends, and they more often group along activity lines. Friends are apt to be together mostly at school, though some do things together outside of school. There are always movies to attend, sports, hunting, and fishing to share. But boys less often stay overnight at each other's houses, especially since they may feel, "That's for girls."

Some thirteen-year-old boys get mad at their close friends in the gang, but on the whole they get on well, and if a controversy arises they can settle things peacefully. In fact, just the opposite of conflict often prevails in a group of thirteen-year-old boys. Each wants to be sure the other boy gets a chance, especially at sports.

Thirteen's general calming down is especially evident in relationship with the opposite sex. Some girls are, unfortunately, finding their male contemporaries too short of stature and too immature. They often refer to these same males as "drips" or "idiots" or "the awfulest dancer," though they must admit at times that some are "kind of cute." They also recognize that boys affect them so that they giggle and act silly, but they try to control this. Many Thirteens have one boy they are interested in and who may be interested in them, though they may shift to others from time to time. However, girls themselves recognize that some of their friends like boys and some don't. They also recognize that they don't talk about boys quite as much as they used to. Now they talk "about boys, but also about everything."

Only about one third of girls seem to do much dating, though nearly half claim to go steady or to have gone steady. "Making out" appears to be almost universal among those who do date, though only about one fourth of the Thirteens interviewed say that they even know any contemporaries who have "gone all the way."

Some boys make such remarks about girls as "My friends can have them, but I don't care." Or, "I don't give a snap about girls now." A few, in fact, have gone to the extent of being self-styled "woman haters." As one boy said, "Girls can be or cannot be just as they like. I don't find them repulsive. I just don't care."

As with girls, about one third of boys do date, and nearly half say they go steady or have gone steady.

General behavior at a party has improved over last year for most. As boys themselves report, "We don't have riots anymore." But still, without supervision and good planning, they are apt to end up throwing things. And there always seems to be at least one boy who has his eye on the light switch, ready to douse the lights at what he considers an appropriate moment.

Girls are usually the more eager to attend these parties and often come early. Boys straggle along. It is some time before all the invited have assembled. There is that hiatus when the boys go off in a room by themselves and the girls may start dancing with each other, and you wonder if this is really going to be a party. It is at this point, when the party needs to be swung into line, that organizational ability is needed.

The party, once it gets going, can rise to quite a pitch, and the master of ceremonies (if any) will need, besides finesse, a loud voice. Games with forfeits and prizes are what the less mature Thirteen wants. Any kind of prizes will do. It's the fun of the games that's important. From one third to one half of Thirteens may have moved on to at least occasional use of alcoholic beverages. Drug use has, it seems, not invaded most parties but is surely well on the way.

6. Activities and Interests

Mothers may report that their thirteen-year-old son or daughter has put away "all childish things," but this is more a trend than an accomplished fact. It is true that Thirteens realize that they are "outgrowing" certain types of books, that they use to send away for pictures but don't anymore, or that they are now "bored" with mysteries which they once thought so fascinating.

Both boys and girls recognize and chalk up the change. But that doesn't mean that they won't enjoy a younger sibling's comic books, even though they might not buy them for themselves. Some Thirteens are all too aware that they are holding on to childish things; a few even gloat about it.

Sometimes it's difficult just making a start. As one Thirteen says, "I think I should improve. One of those things that goes around and around. But I never get around to starting to improve myself." Another might report, "I like to do something silly and too young for me. I love to gallop around and pretend I'm riding a horse." And another, misjudging the interests of many adults, candidly reported, "This may be a shock to you, but I love detective stories."

Whether Thirteens are more childish or mature in their interests, they are always busy, and even passionate in the expression of their chosen activities. This passion may be expended over a dog or a horse, over sports, or over reading about rock or TV stars.

Many thirteen-year-olds are "sportsminded," "sports crazy," or "wrapped up in sports." Even the less athletic Thirteens may sometimes play so hard they almost knock themselves out. They give their all. Though Thirteen has a continuing interest in football (touch football for girls), now basketball and hockey are coming to the forefront. Baseball isn't quite as strong as it was, but it is even stronger as a spectator interest on television or as an actual game.

Whatever individual sports were started at an earlier age (sailing, skiing, skating, tennis, golf) are now receiving a good workout and even a little polishing. Horseback riding holds its place for some girls, but on the whole it's not the craze that it was. Hunting and fishing are enjoyed by a few boys.

The indoor interests of boys and girls are now showing a more defined separation because the pursuit of hobbies and the expression of greater interest in one specific line are growing more common. Boys' interests are more sharply defined than girls'. Photography has perhaps shown the biggest leap and now often includes developing and enlarging. Many thirteen-year-olds have earned enough money to equip their own darkrooms. Thirteens continue their interest in making models, especially midget racers, and enjoy designing cars, rockets, and planes. Some boys now participate less in constructing but observe more. This ability to observe the lines of cars accurately may even be classed as a hobby. The eagle eye of a thirteen-year-old boy espies every quality and shift of line in a design.

Girls are interested in knitting, weaving, or sewing for themselves. They may dabble in photography or with radio. They enjoy creative expression through drawing, painting, or writing. Or they will apply themselves to lessons in music, art, or dancing if they can give the time. But girls still need to spend a lot of time just "talking things over" with their friends, either in person or on the telephone.

Collections no longer have the fascination they once had. Stamps may be left lying around.

Telephoning, as at all teen ages, is a major and time-consuming interest.

Sedentary Looking and Listening Activities Parents are often pleasantly startled by how relatively little time Thirteen spends before the TV screen. The average girl of our group claims to watch no more than fifteen hours a week; the average boy, no more than twenty. Favorite programs for girls are comedies or soaps; for boys, comedies, action shows, or sports.

Radio may be preferred by some to TV, though both are strong. Rock, played very loud, is the favorite. Otherwise they listen to whatever is on the air. Thirteen is just apt to tune in and see what's on radio or television. Music is enjoyed as a background for whatever Thirteen is doing. A rising number may prefer their music on records or tapes.

Thirteens often wish they had more time to read. Often they are too busy with other things. It may be their homework that cuts into reading time. Or it may be a hobby like photography that "puts a dead stop" to reading. Some Thirteens, however, are ready to read anything. Dog more than horse stories, mysteries, and adventures lead the list. Some boys restrict themselves to sports. But the classics are being plumbed by a few, and historical novels are favored.

Newspaper reading is becoming more prevalent. A few read the paper thoroughly. But the majority concentrate on the front page, funnies, and sports. Magazines may be read more than newspapers: *Mad* magazine, science and sports magazines are preferred. The pictorial magazines are favored by both sexes. A few girls enjoy movie magazines.

As at twelve, Thirteens wish to select the movies they see and usually restrict themselves to what they consider "good" movies. If the movie is not extra special, many prefer to be out of doors participating in sports. Thirteen prefers to go with a friend of the same sex but may meet and sit with a friend of the opposite sex after getting into the theater.

7. School Life

Such adjectives as "sophisticated," "more inhibited," "calmer," "conscientious" all give some idea of a real inwardizing change that is occurring in Thirteen. The rapid, almost pell-mell enthusiasm of Twelve is now withheld and concentrated in more organized and sustained eagerness to learn. Thirteen stands off as he or she watches the antics of the twelve-year-olds, chasing each other up and down the halls, snatching any loose pieces of clothing they can grab from each other to produce further chase and interplay. Boys call it "kid stuff." They may not chase as they once did, but do jostle any nearby companion and are notorious for their inability to stand in line. They still snatch things from classmates, but selectively.

Thirteens are basically happier in school than formerly. They say themselves, "It's better this year—just nicer." They may qualify this statement by adding, "Better because I'm probably more willing to learn, but it seems to me as if they teach better."

The open, wholesome lack of inhibition of the usual seventh grader is refreshing. But the child's energy may not be sustained;

restlessness sets in. Whether there is a clock in the room or not, there comes the oft-repeated question, "What time is it?"

Now time is better organized, concentration more sustained, self-control more evident. Thirteen has an improving sense of responsibility, is more dependable. A teacher can enjoy shared intellectual experiences.

However, Thirteens don't show these more sterling qualities immediately. They seem almost to hide them until they can show them fully formed. They feel that they are now entering the adult world and that they wish to be treated as adults. They are galled when they meet the cloak of authority. They wish to feel independent as well as to be independent. They gripe when they feel restricted by authority. They want freedom of decision. But all too often they find that they need to come sheepishly back to the teacher for further help or advice.

Then it is up to the teacher to make this return possible by treating boy or girl with respect and not with an air of "I told you so." However, when Thirteens are resisting some task such as learning the complications of English grammar and strenuously feel that they "won't need to know this in life," the young person is almost begging for authority, an authority that says there are certain things you have to do whether you like it or not.

Thirteen wants to get to school early, likes to settle in slowly, wants to visit with friends. In fact, the appeal of school may be largely that it is a social spot where one can meet friends and socialize throughout the day.

If students come on a bus, they are usually calmer than at twelve. But Thirteen can become boisterous, with the piercing tones of a high, shrill voice as he chats mainly with friends of the same sex in the halls. There is so much to talk about—future parties, what they are going to do over the weekend, who likes whom. Close proximity produces some form of physical contact, either in pushing each other or draping an arm around another's shoulder.

Some now favor basketball over baseball. The constant action, team interplay, and need for precision of shots give Thirteen the kind of exercise he desires. Wrestling and gym are also favorites. Optional athletics at the end of the day allow the more athletically inclined to participate more fully.

Whether Thirteen needs to or should be asked to shower after strenuous physical activity is still debatable. If given a choice, most don't feel the need and would probably vote against it. They don't feel it is necessary and resent undressing and dressing again; and if physically immature, may be reluctant to expose themselves.

Thirteens' conduct in the classroom is closely related to their attitude toward their teacher. They are very critical of her. They may approve of her because "she treats us like we're people." Or may disapprove of her because she is "insulting," "always criticizing," "always interrupting," "too strict," "not strict enough," "boring," or "always cracking jokes at our expense." But they like things said in fun and even good-natured teasing.

Thirteens seem to have an intuitive sense about when a teacher is a good teacher. The good ones just seem to have something about them. They seem to know what they are talking about and can maintain discipline. It is not hard for Thirteen to respect a good teacher.

But if they don't respect her, they try to get away with things. Supported by the group, they may play practical jokes on the teacher. An undercurrent of belligerence flows beneath the surface at this age. In some schools, bad behavior goes far beyond the usual juvenile tricks.

School principals are often ill-thought of by Thirteen, for they not only represent authority but also exercise it. One may be referred to as "a big show-off, strutting around the halls like a peacock, always making stupid rules and always making speeches." Another may be said to "get in the way and mess up classes."

Previously, the teacher was often identified with the subject she taught. Thirteen, however, is beginning to separate the two. Girl or boy may like a teacher but not the subject she teaches. This shows greater discrimination and independence of thinking on the part of Thirteen.

On the whole, the group acts as a unit, and its members are more poised than earlier. Though Thirteen has difficulty in settling down, once started most can concentrate well. Sometimes they concentrate so hard that they are not disturbed by noises around them, but at other times they are distracted by a noisy classroom or by a teacher who keeps interrupting.

In their studies, Thirteens don't mind English but may not like grammar. Many don't understand it, and don't see why it is important for them to learn it. Some love to write stories and may show a lively imagination. Sometimes they write better than they speak. Some especially like to write about themselves and often enjoy hearing stories others have written about themselves. Thirteen's greater ease of expression makes letter writing less of a chore than it used to be. Boys and girls now can be more successful in keeping up with pen pals. This greater ease is evident not only in the words chosen but also in actual handwriting. Writing is now more uniform, but often very small, often to the discomfiture of the teacher.

In their reading, boys favor sports or adventure stories. Girls prefer teenage stories about people their own age with such suggestive titles as *See You Thursday*, or *The Golden Girl*. Some girls persist in their interest in animals, especially stories about horses, and are becoming more aware of style in what they read.

Thirteens are, above all, interested in trying new things. Those who like mathematics may like it even if they consider it their hardest subject. They feel a sense of accomplishment when they have successfully solved a problem. Boys especially like to check back over their work and use the practical applications of measurement. The newness of algebra, or even geometry if they have come to that, is devoured eagerly by some Thirteens.

They also enjoy the broadened outlook of world affairs in social studies. They enjoy reading newspapers or newsmagazines, and looking at cartoons and puzzling out their meaning. They enjoy discussion periods and can now recognize more shades of gray, going a step beyond the black versus white debates they waged the previous year. They like to delve into political history.

Thirteens persist in their interest in the solar system, the universe, and, closer to home, the weather. Atoms and atomic energy intrigue them, especially their peaceful uses, which offer so many more possibilities than just blowing things up. And they are becoming interested in natural and man-made substances, such as coal and plastics. It's the experimental part of science that intrigues them most. They want to get in and demonstrate a thing for themselves, and should have the facilities for doing so. And they are becoming aware of new branches of science, especially in the field of psychology. Computers also fascinate.

A future era of specialized course work and extracurricular activities is foreshadowed in Thirteen's increasing interest in hobbies. These should, as far as possible, be fostered on an individual basis, according to the individual's special interests. Music, especially the playing of an instrument, is strong with some, but with others (especially boys) a regular music class is anathema. Painting and drawing can produce similar extremes of response. Boys would often prefer to study radio or computers if the facilities were available.

In shop, Thirteens "feel their oats" and may talk back a bit, but on the whole they are good workers. They can, in metal work, even carry through the demands of making a hammer, with the demands of sawing, filing, and drilling.

Thirteens may assume a rather blasé attitude toward home economics, but they show their eagerness as soon as they are into a project. They still may use an eggbeater backward and cut with the wrong edge of the knife. But they can often handle a total meal quite well.

In spite of Thirteen's reputation as a griper, the child's protests need not interfere with his or her ability as a student. Some may appear restless as they are settling down, putting their feet out in the aisle, wiggling, talking, sharpening a pencil, but when once they settle down, they are good for a twenty- to thirty-minute period of intense concentration. Most want to finish their work and would prefer to finish at school rather than take it home.

If they do have homework regularly, they are usually conscientious and on their own, whereas they needed help at twelve. It is the long-term project that may suddenly catch them short of time. This may throw them into a sudden panic, for the task may seem interminable. But most do organize and come through eventually, perhaps with some help from parents.

At the end of a busy school day Thirteens like to hang around the lockers if they don't have to rush to catch a bus. They don't burst out of the building the way they did at eleven and sometimes at twelve.

8. Ethical Sense

Thirteen is moving in a more complex ethical realm than did Twelve. Children are thinking less of what would be to their advantage and more about ethics in general and how they help you to relate to others and to yourself. With the greater definition of Thirteen, extremes of ethical behavior are brought out. There are the puritanical, almost prudish girls who are scrupulously honest, have an exaggerated sense of right and wrong, and who may not tolerate those who veer from what they consider to be an established ethical code. Then there are the Thirteens (more often boys) whose consciences don't bother them and who are more apt to veer from an established ethical code. But the majority of Thirteens are finding it easier to make ethical decisions. They now enjoy a new freedom which their sharpened sense gives them.

The question of what is right and what is wrong is determined with a fair amount of ease. Most Thirteens can "tell pretty clearly" and can usually reach a conclusion "without any trouble." Some seem to know automatically, and some boys, oddly enough, speak in absolute terms of "I always know." They recognize that various forces guide them: their conscience, what their mother and father think, or "what people would think." There is a new force operating, however, and this they call their judgment. Though Thirteens know what is right and what is wrong, that does not mean that they will never do wrong. The fun of being bad still lurks around the corner, especially at school. And can one really criticize Thirteen for "going into an old empty house," if he does no harm to it?

Thirteen pretty much accepts his conscience as a part of self. He or she is aware that conscience is active, that it is often firm, in fact very firm, especially about big things! Thirteens know that the conscience doesn't bother them too much over little things and will even let them "get away with little teensy-weensy things." It is when another person is hurt, when Thirteen is mean to somebody, that conscience rises up in no uncertain terms.

Thirteen has come to fuller knowledge of what relative truth is; tries to be truthful and wants to tell the truth, but sometimes tells only part of it. Sometimes they tell "white lies," as much to protect a friend's feelings as to save their own skin. They especially dislike telling their parents about low grades, even though they know their parents won't "beat them down." Thirteen is apt to evade a question, give an excuse such as that a paper hasn't been returned or smooth things over by diverting parents' attention. But most tell the truth if they know that someone else will suffer from a lie.

Thirteen has made great strides in taking the blame when he is responsible and is beginning to admit his own shortcomings. There are still times when boys and girls are not ready to take the blame and find it easier to "push it off on others." Still, fairness is especially important to them at this age, particularly that parents and teachers be fair.

As at twelve, Thirteens rarely argue with parents just for the sake of argument. They may argue for fun but more often to get what they want. Most are now capable of discussion and have their own ideas on social issues. They feel that they are open to reason but are really not very easy to convince or to have their minds changed. Thirteens may accept their parents' demands just because they feel they should, and even against their own will, but usually remain unconvinced.

Some are even more critical of swearing than they were at twelve. They may feel that it is "horrible" or "ill bred" though perhaps "excusable" under certain circumstances. Most try not to swear, though some boys do to be "one of the gang."

The questions of smoking and drinking are now coming very close to Thirteen's own experience. Eighty-four percent of the girls, sixty-eight percent of the boys, say that they or their friends smoke; about two thirds of each sex (of those interviewed by us) say that they or their friends drink. Just under half admit that they or their friends use drugs, at least on occasion.

Thirteen is concerned about overdoing drinking to the point of getting drunk—unless perhaps there were "some good reason for getting drunk, like a celebration." Boys are more casual in their thinking about drinking than are girls.

Approximately two thirds of our subjects think that politicians are dishonest. Girls more than boys think that they personally, when older, might do something to improve conditions. More boys than girls favor ERA, though one male chauvinist says he does not favor it because "the male sex is definitely higher than the female sex." Half the girls and two thirds of the boys think we are doing enough for integration.

Thirteen-year-olds are reported to have positive attitudes but poor knowledge about social issues in general. Nearly all expressed concern for the physical and psychological welfare of people who have to live in poor housing conditions. However, only a third could suggest ways to fight poverty, and fewer than one fifth could state reasons why poverty exists.

chapter eight

THE FOURTEEN-YEAR-OLD

MATURITY PROFILE

The age of fourteen for many adolescents tends to be a time of verve, vigor, energy, and excitement. Boundless energy combines with optimistic enthusiasm and goodwill to encourage boy or girl to attempt almost anything.

Friends of both sexes delight, school is okay; and extracurricular activities fill the days with fun and pleasure. Nothing seems too much for boy or girl to undertake, though as one mother put it, "Fourteen's plans are sometimes so outsize that she just plain runs out of time. Unfortunately there are only twenty-four hours in every day."

Some parents blame the school for "piling on all these activities." If the school does so, it is largely in response to Fourteen's demand. Girl or boy likes to have life a little too full.

Fourteens enjoy friends, enjoy school, and are even interested in community affairs, at least to the extent that they themselves are involved. In fact, their interests tend to extend far beyond their own communities. If family and finances permit, they would gladly venture out far beyond the confines of their own hometown.

With life so sunny, is there no fly in the ointment? There is, indeed. It is the child's family. Especially his parents. Up till now it has been mostly mother who has been criticized and made to feel totally inadequate and antique. Beginning around the age of fourteen, both boys and girls—who may have admired father inordinately up till now at the expense of mother—now may include their father in their criticisms and consider him, too, hopelessly antiquated. Most, however, accept discipline from him better than they do from their mother, and may even comment that it is best for the family if father has a firm hand. (They just don't want to hear about when he was a boy!)

It is almost as if, during the time when your typical thirteen-year-old was brooding in his room, both father and mother have aged and deteriorated in a horrible way. A wicked witch has been at work on these formerly rather lively and acceptable people. Certainly children of any age may fight with and lash out at their parents. But earlier, for the most part, what the child objected to was the rules parents made and the thing they made them do.

Now what Fourteen objects to is the people themselves. Their peculiar looks! Their odd way of dressing! Those interminable stories about their younger days! Their peculiar notion that they are still young! "Oh Mother!" a girl will exclaim in despair at almost anything her mother says or does. Or, "Oh Father!" when father expresses some revolting trite and old-fashioned opinion. A boy may warn his father before some school gathering, "If they ask you what your name is, just say 'Ed.' " A girl, while shopping, may stay as far from her mother in a store as possible. This is the age when boy or girl walks at least five feet behind father if they are forced to go downtown together. Or, if possible, rides in a different car in the train for fear that somebody might know that they are related.

All of this is by no means true hostility, unfriendliness, or meanness. It is just that Fourteens, still in a painful search for self and identity, seem to feel that in the eyes of the world they and their parents are still closely identified. It will, they believe, count against them if their parents, as so often, do something just impossibly embarrassing.

Yet Fourteen is still very much a part of the family, for all that they embarrass him so. And, actually, deep down, many children of this age still love their parents. A typical mother gives this encouraging report:

> This is just a note to thank you for your most heartening and helpful letter regarding my combustible fourteen-year-old, Arthur. Arthur hurled himself off to school the other morning after a particularly explosive scene over a minor matter. I decided to try smoothing matters over by the old "heaping coals of fire" method, so I went out and bought him a very loud shirt he had been wanting.
>
> When he stomped in from school, not speaking to me as he

went through the kitchen, I heard him throw down his books on his bed and pick up the bag in which the shirt was folded.

Suddenly I could hear him running down the hall. He flung himself into the kitchen, was on me in an instant with a kiss that nearly broke my jaw, and he said in his cracked and splintery voice, "Gosh, Mom! I'm a terrible crumb sometimes, aren't I?"

Now I know that my lovable small boy is still there in the midst of all the adolescent noise and confusion; and waiting for him to emerge is a little easier.

A letter from another mother of a fourteen-year-old tells a somewhat similar story:

Before I get started on my housework this morning, I just have to sit down and write some suggestions of things which have helped me with my difficult fourteen-year-old. My boy seems to hate me much of the time and does exactly the things he knows bother me the most.

I think the reason may be largely that he needs more attention and affection than he can allow himself to accept. The only time he will ever accept it is just before he goes to bed. Then he wants to talk. I try very hard not to mention all the absolutely revolting things he has done all day; and I try to keep my good advice to a minimum, since anything I say he regards as *bugging* him. Then I cuddle him a bit, and he seems pretty content and goes right to sleep.

Another thing is that he needs to do things that really interest him. School, unfortunately, doesn't. He needs lots of physical activity and construction work. We've found that a chinning bar, basketball setup, punching bag, swimming at the Y and boxing lessons all help. He also likes the violin, model building and reading up on his interests—electronics, chess. Also he likes to be doing something useful—he helps run a nature program for little children and also works in the school library.

We are trying to do all we can for him—but he is still very *trying*. Period.

Yes, in spite of Fourteen's frequent lapses into niceness, many parents find themselves almost constantly on the defensive, trying to please a child who demands everything, appreciates little, and tends to be highly insulted if his family does not provide all the luxuries to which he considers himself entitled.

Most fourteen-year-olds, like the boy described, consider any efforts to improve them are *bugging*. As one girl expressed it, "I don't like to be preached at because usually I know what the person is going to say before they say it." Many Fourteens feel that they know how they should behave without anybody telling them—even if they do not always do what they know they should.

Fourteens, in general, probably get on better with father than with mother. They criticize him less. Also, they feel that he does not nag them as much as mother does; does not have to have everything just so.

A new aspect of father-child relationship, however, comes in at this age and in some families makes considerable trouble. Many girls have been very warm to their father up to now and the feeling has usually been reciprocated. Now girls are dating, and many fathers—though they would be loath to admit the fact—become extremely jealous. They scold their wives for what they claim are the excessive privileges allowed the daughter in the dating department. Much tact on a wife's part may be needed if a girl is to be allowed to date. (This, of course, applies more to middle-class than to inner-city families, where by this age dating may be taken for granted.)

Behavior with siblings still leaves a lot to be desired. The worst difficulties occur with those between six and thirteen, whom Fourteens describe as "a nuisance," "pain in the neck." They complain that these brothers and sisters argue all the time, "get into my things," "tag along." Parents feel that things should go better but are usually not too effective in bringing about much improvement.

Unrewarding as family living may seem to many Fourteens, it is perhaps encouraging that it does not deter them from planning for families of their own when the time comes. Nearly three quarters of both girls and boys say they plan to get married, and more than three quarters say they hope to have children. (Slightly more, apparently, plan to become parents than spouses!)

There is a vast difference between the way an ordinary fourteen-year-old behaves in relation to his or her family and to the rest of the world. Outside the home, one would not know that this person who is so totally unappreciative of family is the same individual. The fourteen-year-old the world sees is energetic, lively, dramatic, daring, sparkling, ready for anything. He or she bounces and bubbles and dashes about, enjoying life to the hilt.

Fourteen is at his very best with friends in every aspect of their lives together. Both girls and boys now tend to have a whole crowd of friends and move among them with practiced ease. No more "If you're speaking to Laurel, I'm not speaking to you."

Girls and boys both choose their friends partly on the basis of shared activity interests and partly (especially for girls) on the basis of their shared interest in the opposite sex.

Girls talk about boys (when they are not actually with them) in every spare moment when they are together, and by phone when they are not. For many, telling a girlfriend about a date may be almost as satisfactory as the experience of having the date.

Of Fourteens interviewed by us, sixty-eight percent of girls, fifty-four percent of boys tell us that they are going steady or have done so. And well over half say that they "believe in" going steady. "Going steady," of course, has many different interpretations and definitions. Some "go steady" half a dozen times in as many months. For others there can be a real and long-lasting commitment.

As for the intensity of the commitment, many such relationships are fairly bland (from the adult point of view). But more than three quarters of both boys and girls interviewed by us say that either they or their friends "make out." More than half claim that they or their friends have "gone all the way." And nearly half say that at least some of their classmates have "gotten into trouble." That this may indeed be true is vouched for by the increasing number of fourteen-year-old girls who do get pregnant.

At the opposite extreme is the occasional immature boy who will tell you, "I like people—every kind except girls."

Parties are popular and now go much more smoothly than a year ago when boys and girls tended to be rather gauche in their approach to each other. Now they are really interested in each other and enjoy being together. "Making out," real or reported, is now by far the leading activity. Eating, dancing, and "having fun" are other activities commonly mentioned, though a substantial amount of drug use is reported.

Party-time or otherwise, smoking, drinking, and drug use are now widespread, if the reports of our young informants are anywhere near to be trusted. Close to one hundred percent of both sexes claim that they or some of their friends smoke, drink, and/or use drugs, at least to some extent.

Dating, going to parties, and talking about the opposite sex does indeed use up a great deal of the young person's spare time. But interests go beyond this. A girl may plan a too-lengthy bicycle trip in the morning, lunch with friends, a movie in the afternoon, followed by a ball game, and a dance in the evening. This overcrowded schedule inevitably breaks down at some point or other, and then somebody (usually mother) is blamed because this plan for the day (about which she was not consulted in the first place) doesn't work out.

School is just one of the many usually well-accepted parts of Fourteen's crowded day. The majority (not all) now enjoy school. Those who are dissatisfied have moved on from criticism of the teacher to a broader criticism of the way the school is run, the "system," or the administration.

Fourteen thrives best on a varied program and most especially enjoys extracurricular activities and clubs—athletic, scientific, dramatic, musical. He likes to be busy. Many enjoy classwork, but it is the "other kids" and the activities which are now the true meaning of school. They are nearly everything to him, and he wants desperately to be just like everyone else in the crowd. This is not an age for being different.

The fourteen-year-old's easy ability to relate to adults—and yet the relative unimportance of these adults in his scheme of things—is nicely illustrated by his response to our interview procedures at our Institute. Fourteens in an interview are friendly and outgoing, quite unlike their closemouthed, thirteen-year-old former selves.

They are frank in what they have to say and even at times ask the interviewer's opinion as to what *she* thinks about things. But—and this seems to be the essence of Fourteen—cooperative as they are, they really do not have too much time for this procedure. They usually arrive late (with many breathless explanations of why they were late.) They often need to interrupt the interview to make an "important" telephone call to a friend. And they very often need to leave early—just have to rush off to their next appointment. Life is busy indeed for the average Fourteen. Fourteen in an interview is delightful but rather like quicksilver. He or she runs through your fingers.

Most Fourteens basically mean to do what is right. Many are no longer willing to rely entirely on their parents' teachings. They are trying to make up their own minds, trying to reconcile their parents' teachings about right and wrong with what their friends do, and with their own feelings about what is and is not appropriate.

Many are bothered by the discrepancy between what their

mother thinks they should do and the way they feel and what they want to do. Often mother and child are radically different. As one girl put it, "I do what would work out best with the kids, and then I sort of temper it down with my mother."

The social pattern at this age often changes with remarkably frequency. Sometimes there is a falling out with a same-sex friend, and very often a falling out with a friend of the opposite sex. Couples change constantly as they quarrel, make up, and quarrel again. As one Fourteen put it, "How can you invite a couple to a dance? How do you know they'll be a couple by the time you have the dance?" In fact, to the adult, Fourteen's description of who likes whom, who doesn't like whom, and who is expected to like whom can be very confusing indeed.

Fourteen has other problems. As mentioned, the days just aren't long enough. And school does not always go well. One's team does not always win. Allowances do not always stretch. And, of course, parents are embarrassing.

But for the most part, boy or girl of this age sees the world as a big, wide, wonderful place and means to take in as much of it as possible in the course of every livelong day.

With things so rosy, not much advice may be needed by the average parent, except in relation to Fourteen's less than appreciative treatment of said parent. Our suggestion would be to back off and tread lightly.

It is *not* pleasant to have somebody whom you are forced to see on a daily basis, and for whom you feel responsible, constantly criticizing. It is especially unpleasant, even destructive to your own sense of self as a worthwhile and valuable person, if you are a single parent. You need a great deal of support at a time like this—somebody to assure you that you really are all right.

If you do not have a sympathetic spouse, seek support from friends, preferably friends who are in the same position as you. Fourteen's harshest criticisms or most wildly denigrating statements take on a certain humor if shared with another parent. Support groups in all sorts of problem areas are springing up in this country. We strongly recommend a support group for normal parents of normal teenagers. If you can laugh with others at what you jointly are going through, it helps diffuse your own feelings of hurt and resentment. It helps you bounce back after criticism with that poise and security which are needed if you hope to remain the mature, secure, interested and interesting, but slightly detached person who makes the most successful parent for a fourteen-year-old girl or boy.

MATURITY TRAITS

1. Total Action System

The tight, withdrawn ways of Thirteen have loosened up at fourteen. A profound change has occurred, not only within the child but also in his or her impact on surroundings. Young people now seem to be more persons in their own right, more capable of easy give-and-take. They generate a friendly and relaxed atmosphere. There no longer seems to be the need to walk gingerly around them, to choose some special method of approach, as was often necessary at Thirteen. Fourteens, feeling more secure in themselves, are more outgoing, more straightforward. No longer so much on the defensive, so fearful that people will pry into their personal affairs, they can talk freely in a genuine, agreeable way with other people—even with their own parents on occasion.

In an interview, Fourteen's demeanor is quiet and relaxed. Posture is symmetrical, feet are often placed flat on the floor. They show few tensional outlets or shifts in interest from the task at hand. They listen and respond well, having both the desire and the ability to communicate. Even when they do not talk much, their smile shows interest. Fourteens throw in incidental comments, as does the examiner. They also add humorous asides, dramatize an answer, and laugh in a pleasant, mature manner. They can laugh at themselves or express mild, good-natured sarcasm: "Very simple, eh?" (This same expression might have had a biting quality if voiced by Thirteen.)

Fourteen shows a good, direct attack on a task, wants to "work things out." Though some may express self-depreciation, they do not get panicky and if they do have to give up, can do so gracefully. Even the excuse that they "didn't have enough sleep last night" is offered with good humor.

One of Fourteens' chief problems is that they often want to include too much in their thinking or plan too many activities. This is all a part of their new expansiveness: a loose inclusiveness that can sometimes swamp them. This is why it might be hard for some to formulate an answer and why they may, in the midst of trying to solve a problem, comment, "This is driving me crazy." The tangles in Fourteen's social life are likewise part of their overinclusiveness.

Fourteen is gathering a new sense of larger totals. Mobile eye movements give some idea of the multiple thought processes that are taking place. The child's very concept and use of the word *personality* suggests that he or she is judging others from a more comprehensive point of view.

Health Fourteen's health frequently is not just "good" but "really wonderful." Very little school is missed because of illness. Most can still attend even when they have a sniffle. Few Fourteens have the "habit" of being ill, as they might have had just earlier. They can actually go to the other extreme of putting up with illness when necessary. One boy was quite willing to suffer asthma if only he could keep his dog, to which he was allergic.

At this age nearly all young people (one hundred percent of our girls, eighty-eight percent of boys) say that some of their friends drink. Also, *this is the first age at which not only a majority but an overwhelming majority* (ninety percent of girls, eighty-two percent of boys) are reported by friends to use drugs. Fortunately, the majority do, or are thought to, use them only occasionally or to go along with the crowd. Marijuana is the drug kind most frequently reported. Others mentioned are LSD and amphetamines.

Tensional Outlets Fourteen may have a few remnants of past tensional outlets, but these are only incidental. Fingernail biting may occur with some, but only during tense situations such as viewing a scary movie. Headaches may occur when Fourteen can't adjust to the demands of the environment—or vice versa.

Vision Visually, Fourteen is usually in good shape. Eyes handle the usual visual skills tests (fusion, suppressions, stereopsis, usable vision, centering) quite adeptly. Eye movements in following moving objects are good. The trend at fourteen is toward a more stable amount of hyperopia (farsightedness). It is often the Fourteen with supposedly perfect ("20/20") vision and very little hyperopia who complains that his eyes bother him, especially when reading. A reduction in the reading program might alleviate the symptoms, but school demands will not always allow this. Fourteen then needs visual help—lenses or training—to build up the flexibility lacking. Most are well motivated and cooperate better in a training program than they would have at thirteen or will at fifteen.

Fourteen combines fixating and focusing mechanisms better than earlier. Responses are more like the usual adult patterns, and it is possible to predict more accurately than earlier what the eyes are going to do under certain test situations.

With the exception of those with very low hyperopia, Fourteens do not have as many visual complaints about reading as they did at thirteen. However, often they do not read as extensively as they did then. Reading, in addition to that required for school, often is confined to magazines.

Fourteens are more certain and dogmatic in their desire not to wear glasses, though they will "concede, if it is necessary." But if given the alternative, Fourteen is willing to do whatever is required to make glasses unnecessary. Even those who are nearsighted and really need their glasses will work hard in a visual training program in order to become less dependent upon them and to be able to take them off for special occasions. The motivation to work and to improve comes from within, and is not just imposed by others as it was in preceding years.

Physical Development and Sex Awareness—Girls Although there still are marked differences in rates of growth, the fourteen-year-old girl's body seems typically to be more that of a young woman than that of a child, and, for this reason perhaps, she is intensely concerned with her body build. Females in early adolescence are often less satisfied with their body than are males. In a nationwide survey, when early adolescent girls were asked what they would like to change in themselves, more than half expressed a desire for some change in looks.

Height growth is nearly completed during this year; after the fifteenth birthday, few girls will add more than an inch to their height. Increase in weight too has slowed down, though this may continue after height growth has ceased. Maturity features now approximate those of young adulthood. The breasts approach full adult size, and pubic hair is full and dense.

For all their feminine softness, however, the bodies of many fourteen-year-old girls give an impression of strength. Face and neck seem stronger. And the filling in of hollows gives a suggestion of greater compactness, even in the slimmer girls.

Very few girls have not menstruated by their fourteenth year. The majority are becoming well established in their menstrual patterns. Many report premenstrual symptoms which occur a day or two ahead of their periods. They may have cramps, a backache, or just a general state of emotional tension and nervousness. Their periods may be accompanied by slight cramps, and they may at times feel bad enough to lie down for an hour or so. A few may feel dizzy or sick and may actually miss a meal. At the other extreme are the girls who have no pain or other symptoms, and whose ordinary activities are in no way curtailed.

The menstrual cycle is now becoming more regular and is approximating a twenty-eight-day cycle, though in many it is longer. The menstrual flow may last as long as five days or even extend to six or seven days. Fourteens tend to use sanitary napkins or tampons lavishly. This is no time to economize. An ample supply should be on hand so that at least this aspect of Fourteen's adjustment to her new function of sexual maturing is made easier.

Girls are now interested in the complex aspects of reproduction—contraceptives, miscarriage. They not only understand more themselves, but may ask how you go about explaining sex to children.

Physical Development and Sex Awareness—Boys Fourteen seems to be a transition zone for most boys. At thirteen, despite newly acquired features of maturity, the majority seemed to look like young boys—more akin to their ten-year-old selves. By fifteen most will look like men. Though at fourteen they are still far from mature in total development, they seem to have crossed a line. Actually, of course, this line may be crossed at thirteen or earlier, or at fifteen or later. But most often it seems to lie between the fourteenth and fifteenth birthdays.

At fourteen the size increase in most boys is quite marked. This is the period of most rapid height growth for the greatest number of boys. The body form appears more heavily muscled. The adolescent fat period is a thing of the past for most of the boys who had showed this at all. The larger physique, together with its newly developed maturity features, gives a strong impression of adolescent masculinity.

Pubic hair is now fairly dense and is darker in most boys. Hair on forearms and legs has become denser, and sideburns have started to elongate. Deepening of the voice has become more noticeable. The voice change may occur slowly and steadily, or through a cracking process, or all of a sudden. The sudden change can be mistaken for a cold. It is as though Fourteen develops a hoarseness which never leaves him. With this sudden change of voice (which occurs in a minority), there are often accompanying sharp changes. Lack of self-consciousness may suddenly switch over into extreme modesty —almost as if the voice change shocked Fourteen into an awareness of his own sexual maturing.

The genital developments already visible at thirteen are quite advanced in many Fourteens. By the end of the fourteenth year, a large majority of boys will have experienced ejaculation in one situation or another. By far the most common source of this first ejaculation is masturbation, a phenomenon that most boys have known about and a majority have experimented with since age eleven or before. So far as we can determine, few young people today believe the old wives' tales that masturbation is evil and produces idiocy or worse.

Very soon after the first experience of emission, nearly all boys develop an individual, more or less regular pattern of sexual activity. Masturbation is common, and nocturnal emissions may begin to occur in the period just before fourteen, though many boys do not experience these until later adolescence. Boys respond quite individually to the experience. Fortunately, nowadays more boys are informed about this possible occurrence and are less likely to be disturbed by it, but, even so, some feel ashamed and hide their pajamas, while others take it naturally as a part of life.

Fourteen is an age when further sex education is both needed and eagerly received. Besides information requested about individual sex development, including the physiology and functioning of sex parts, many questions concern intercourse, both premarital and marital. Such topics as birth control, unwanted pregnancy, venereal disease, herpes, AIDS, prostitution, abortion, and homosexuality are also raised. Fourteen not only wants information about those topics, he or she wants to discuss them, to work out some kind of evaluation of them.

Fourteens are trying to find their own way, to clarify for themselves how they feel, and to decide what paths are best for them. They can do this best on the basis of accurate information, presented in the context of a philosophy compatible with their own values. Unfortunately, they are too often left to make their own decisions when they are not adequately prepared to do so. It is the uninformed adolescent who is most likely to get into trouble. Thus a fourteen-year-old girl, with her expansiveness and her preference for older boys, may in some cases be extremely vulnerable. All too often a pregnancy may occur, either because she was inadequately informed or because too great license was allowed. Parents need both to inform and to protect their daughters—not by prohibiting dates or setting unreasonable curfews but by helping them to develop reasonable inhibitions and an understanding of the need for control when they are not ready to assume the consequences of their actions.

Many mothers and fathers today are faced with the problem not so much of how much information to give their growing daughters, but as to whether or not—if it seems clear to them that their daughters are sexually active—to provide them with contraceptive materials. This is a hard problem for parents to face.

2. Self-Care and Routines

Eating Fourteens are becoming more discriminative in their eating. They still have a very fine appetite, especially if athletically inclined, but this appetite is on the whole under reasonably good control. They are now especially aware of the smell of food, either the smell that repels or the smell that beckons. The aroma from a Hungarian goulash may repel, whereas the aromas from food cooked over a campfire may have special appeal. They are also aware of the consistency of foods. It may be the sticky consistency of peanut butter which causes some Fourteens to dislike it, while the crispness of an apple delights them.

Fourteen is still a snacker, especially after school. However, there isn't that urge to eat that there was at twelve. Most are satisfied with whatever mother happens to have on hand, especially fruit. They are less apt to eat before bedtime than they were; may say they are too lazy to prepare a bedtime snack, but this may really be because appetite is less. If they do have a bedtime snack, they don't "sit down and make a feast" as earlier.

Fourteen frequents the snack shop but it may be as much in search of sociability as of food. There are, however, the two extremes—the sweets eaters and the nonsweets eaters. The former have to tussle with themselves to restrict the elaborateness of the sweets they order. The depletion of their funds may solve the problem.

Mealtime can be reasonably pleasant for Fourteen and the family. Girl or boy has likes and dislikes, but the latter may be minor. Apple pie is much preferred. One fourteen-year-old boy was heard to say, "I'd like to sit down and eat myself a whole apple pie, but I'd probably get sick." Fourteen does seem to know his digestive limitations.

There is some complaint about Fourteen's table manners but mostly in reference to an elbow on the table. They may use their fingers as pushers, but this can be easily curtailed. In general, the parental attitude toward Fourteen's table manners is noncomplaining and can be summed up in one mother's remark, "It's all that can be expected."

With Fourteen's increase in height there comes in general a slimming down. The need for dieting is less in evidence. There are always the few who may nibble at food, especially when they are bored, but on the whole Fourteen doesn't have that consuming interest in food that was present earlier, especially at twelve. Most feel confident in their ability to cook and still enjoy watching food being prepared. Fourteen may tell you that he or she "likes to cook not so much for cooking's sake as for the enjoyment of seeing other people enjoy it."

Sleep

BEDTIME: Fourteen is pretty much at the helm as far as sleeping goes. As one Fourteen puts it, "I usually go to bed myself. I know enough to go to bed." The hour of bedtime ranges from nine to eleven, with the commonest time at nine-thirty or ten. Each Fourteen seemed to have his or her own variation of bedtime within the range of an hour. If they are tired, they are apt to go to bed early. Many are busy with homework right up to bedtime. They may listen to the radio or read a bit after they are in bed, or they may daydream a bit about the near future or present. But on the whole Fourteen is most likely to fall right off to sleep.

SLEEP: Most Fourteens report that they dream but also that they are apt to forget their dreams when they wake up. If they do remember them, they often report them as "rather uninteresting," "perfectly logical," or "just incidents." They often tell their dreams at breakfast and find that "people are usually reasonably interested" to hear them recounted.

MORNING: There is a great variety of waking times at Fourteen, ranging from six to eight A.M. There are those who seem to need little sleep—who go to bed late and get up early. Then there are those who are establishing a routine. They may awake on the dot of eight. They like the feeling of getting into a habit. Others have to establish the habit through use of an alarm clock. And, lastly, there are those slugabeds who always want to sneak in that extra ten or fifteen minutes. They are the ones who have to be called not once but twice or three times over. They happily sleep until noon on Saturday and Sunday or during vacation. They may be even harder to rouse than earlier.

Bathing and Care of Hair
When parents can report, "She's reached the clean stage now," it is evident enough that girls, if not boys, at fourteen are more surely responsible for their own cleanliness. Though most girls bathe every other night, an increasing number

like to bathe nightly. They even miss their bath when they don't have time or are too tired to take one.

Boys don't come up to the level of girls. In fact, many still have to be reminded and are even said to be "allergic to soap." They quite often need to be reminded to wash their hands before mealtime, and they have a way of slipping up on their bath. Fortunately, showers after athletics make home bathing less imperative.

Shampooing and care of hair is not the task it used to be. Some need not shampoo their hair more often than once a week. Others with a tendency to oily hair want to shampoo it a good deal more often. Fourteen-year-old girls are quite adept at blow-drying their hair.

Boys groom their hair well, including washing. Some feel that hair is "the only thing that counts." Most are now responsible for seeing that it is cut, at least as often as they wish. A few boys are beginning to shave. This is accomplished very privately and when necessary.

Fingernails are now becoming a part of Fourteen's total care of self. Some may need a little reminding about both care of fingernails and brushing of teeth, but on the whole most are doing a quite passable job.

Clothing and Care of Room Fourteens earn a few gentle compliments from mothers: "She is pretty good about her clothes"; "She hangs them up most of the time"; "He is essentially neat"; "He makes a nice appearance."

Most are interested in clothes. They like variety. Boys will splurge on shirts and sports jackets. Some are on the more conservative side, others are a little off-beat. Girls' tastes in clothes may differ from their mothers'.

Styles of dress vary with the season, the region, the latest fad—but within the limits of "what everyone else is wearing" both boys and girls usually manage to show reasonably good taste and control in their dress. Now they are slightly less swayed by fads and less dependent on the protective coloration of group uniformity. So though they stay in style, they may not swing too violently to extremes. Most seem to gravitate back to the old standbys—skirts or jeans and sweaters or blouses for girls; plain shirts, sweaters and slacks, jeans, or khakis for the boys.

Few girls overdress or accentuate their sex through their dress—though some do. Most are using lipstick more skillfully than previously.

Both sexes are pretty well aware of what they need in the line of clothes. They seem to understand the makeup of a total wardrobe. This is the age when boys or girls are aware of the need for a top-coat. Some girls would go out of bounds in their purchase of clothes if permitted. Oddly enough, it is the girl whose closet is most stocked who is most apt to moan, "I have nothing to wear."

The purchase and choice of clothes is not too difficult for Fourteens. They take care of the small purchases—underwear, socks, or shoes—by themselves, but do like to have a parent help with the bigger purchases. There is a fair amount of agreement between the parent and child, unless their basic tastes differ drastically. Then there may be a "big disagreement." By this age, the mother has or should have learned that her daughter won't wear something she doesn't like and that any clothes brought home by mother on her own are likely to hang in her daughter's closet unworn.

A few Fourteens may demand or be given a clothes allowance. It is, however, the unusual Fourteen who can budget wisely. Also, it can be a great strain on Fourteen to keep track of expenditures and not go broke.

Fourteen's care of clothes is showing increasing responsibility. A boy tells us matter-of-factly that "we have a closet where I hang up outdoor clothes when I come in," as if the hall closet had not been there for some years past. Many are more careful about hanging up their better clothes but still may have trouble in the proper use of hangers. A boy may even avoid the use of hangers and pile one piece of clothing on top of another on a single hook until the effect, according to the parent, is that of a "hunchbacked person."

Fourteens are more apt now than formerly to report rips and miss-ing buttons, and boys as well as girls may even remedy matters themselves.

Disposal of dirty clothes in a pile or hamper is becoming a habit, and this pile can become pretty large if there is a daily change of shirts. Some Fourteens wash and iron their own shirts. They also may be quite expert at pressing trousers or skirts. But it is not sur-prising to see a fourteen-year-old boy all resplendent in a freshly ironed shirt yet unaware of obvious spots on his trousers.

The majority of Fourteens keep their rooms passably neat. Some even enjoy a tidy room. Fourteens still tend to leave clothes around the room but do pick them up sporadically. They are less interested in decorating their room with pennants and pictures and may re-move many of the trappings they enjoyed so at twelve and thirteen. Girls who have a crush on a rock or television star may focus the theme of their decorations and interest on that one person. Some Fourteens, like Thirteens, are apt to spend considerable time in their rooms. But on the whole Fourteen uses his or her room for sleeping and studying, and would prefer to read in the midst of the family group.

Those Fourteens who are not too good about keeping their rooms neat may nevertheless maintain order in parts, especially their desks. But Fourteen is apt to leave books strewn around. The best stimulus to urge them to clean up their room is the thought of guests coming. They are apt to slip up on bedmaking, especially toward the end of the week, but a new week may bring a fresh start.

Money Parents are now feeling the fuller impact of how much it costs to rear a child, especially at this expanding, demanding age of fourteen. The weekly allowance of four to six dollars, plus extras, with simple budgeting, may or may not be sufficient. But with an increased demand for extras, and especially clothes with girls, it is very difficult to work out even a monthly allowance.

A few families find it easier to give up an allowance and give out money as needed. This method is easier with those Fourteens who are more conscious of money and are guided by what the family can afford.

With those who have expensive tastes but little desire to earn money to pay for these tastes, the planning is more difficult. Their idea of money may be very inflated, and it may be the one topic of discussion that produces the most quarrels with their parents, especially with their fathers. With these Fourteens, it is necessary to set boundaries and stick to them. Clothes-hungry girls need to have a clothes allowance, not just for them to enjoy but rather to keep them within bounds.

Fourteen is more of a spendthrift than earlier. A number spend money foolishly and are usually "broke" at the end of the week if they are on an allowance. They may buy good books and records, but they have little money on hand.

Earned funds, however, are increasing. Summer jobs often net substantial sums which can be banked and left to gather interest.

Work Fourteens recognize their own change in attitude toward work. They remember how terrible they were two years ago and feel that they are "now quite good at it." They may not only do chores willingly but also automatically. Those who are less cheerful about work and more resistant may realize they are not "acting their age."

Girls are now extending their activities in the home. They dust and clean, scrub bathrooms, and may be capable of cleaning an entire house.

Boys not only wash the family car but may be able to change a tire and even keep the car in good mechanical condition. Some are beginning to do real man-size jobs.

Regular jobs are usually summer ones, such as working at a garage or helping in a store. Baby-sitting may also take on a steady pattern over a period of months. But often Fourteen does not have the time to give to demanding steady work, nor is he or she quite ready to take on fixed demands.

3. Emotions

The first acute throes of what is often thought of as adolescent behavior—which appeared so strongly in the withdrawal and touchiness of Thirteen—have now been gone through. A new, joyous, happy note is struck in Fourteen. No longer is it necessary for parents to skirt gingerly around their "pathetically edgy" sons and daughters. The atmosphere has cleared—laughter rings out in the house, singing, so long neglected, may be heard even in the morning. Fourteen has indeed taken a turn for the better. Fourteen loves living. As parents remark, "He's just full of life"; "She has burst out all over." If less exuberant, boy or girl is at least "in general easygoing" or "happy in an adult way." It is the agreeable note in the child's voice, the humorous twist of a phrase that now makes girl or boy so much more pleasant to live with.

Not that Fourteen stays within the positive realm all the time. Actually, many seem to have two sides to their nature. A mother will say of her son, "Though he is easygoing, he gets moody." "Though he usually takes things in stride, he is sometimes irritable and makes issues of little things." Or, of a girl, "Though she is awfully happy at times, she can also be thrown into the depths of depression."

On the whole, Fourteens enjoy life. They recognize that as they get older "life gets more complicated, but it's lots more fun." They are moving with life, and many say, "It gets better as I go along." Fourteen is becoming ready to accept added responsibilities and also recognizes that you come to "nasty places" every once in a while.

These "nasty places" don't come often, but when they do they are something to cope with. They are inner tangles that produce outbursts such as violent anger or distressed crying, which are out of keeping with Fourteen's usual responses. When these moments come, it is important for the parent or teacher to try to find out what lies behind the sudden flare-up of violence that seems all out of proportion to the occasion.

Fourteens tend to have moments of being "awfully happy." These are most likely to come when they are not in school, though they can be extremely pleased about being on the honor roll or having their team win. But it is their social life—going out on a date, getting something new to wear—which gives Fourteen the greatest happiness.

Happy moods far outstrip Fourteen's sad ones. Rather than being sad, they are apt to be annoyed or moody. This moodiness can move into more active brooding or depression. But Fourteen is not likely to stay in these somber states for very long. Girl or boy may drop into the depths occasionally, but is able to bounce back rather quickly.

Fourteen is less inhibited than earlier about his or her temper and is apt to get angry quickly, though not often. Both sexes show short, explosive outbursts, especially against a sibling. They will suddenly "let off steam" before others, whereas at thirteen they more often controlled themselves and withdrew to their room. If they now do retreat to their room, they may stomp off noisily. Fourteen is not one to keep things bottled up, but lets you know when he or she is "mad" or "annoyed." A boy, especially, likes to "throw his voice around" and is especially likely to yell or shout at his siblings or swear to himself in his room. But he less often strikes out physically, except at his siblings. If mad at his teacher, he can contain himself and remain silent. This is also usually true when he is mad at his parents.

Fourteen is not really a fearful age, though quite a variety of fears are reported. It is almost as though each child has his or her pet fear that has come to the surface. There are those who are afraid of bugs, spiders, bees, and other insects. A fairly large number of boys and girls are afraid of snakes. Some are afraid of high places, of deep water, of being out in the dark, of walking on a soft, mushy bottom in the water. They are afraid of being embarrassed, afraid of people, of being "left out," of social gossip, of "just what's going to happen," or "how things will turn out." This is an age when experience may resolve the fear.

Worrying now has the same quality as fearfulness, although Fourteen really isn't the worrier that he or she was at thirteen. A few declare that they are too busy to worry. A large number worry about schoolwork—getting homework done, getting good grades, passing examinations. Others worry about being late for school. They worry about friends if they haven't got them. They worry about what kind of impression they make on people, about their boyfriend staying or leaving them, about family relations, about popularity. They worry about their reputation or lack of ambition or diseases they might get. But though the list is long, Fourteen's worries don't overwhelm him any more than do his fears.

A discussion of Fourteen's main problems shows that things don't disturb the boy or girl too deeply. Their main problem may be body build—that they are too fat, too short, or too tall. It may be something about schoolwork (especially exams), or it may be in the social sphere. But even when they complain, as one boy did about his eleven-year-old sister who got on his nerves and made it difficult for him to concentrate, they may add, "But I don't mind it too much." And though Fourteens complain about not getting on with friends, they are apt to end up with, "But it's much better than it used to be."

Fourteens are not ashamed to show how they feel. Some may still cover up feelings, but on the whole they are open about emotions and like to have people know how they feel. Fourteen is made of tougher stuff than was Thirteen; is not as vulnerable as earlier. They feel the impact of the other person, and though feelings can be hurt, most are able to take it. The child may strike back immediately with a few words or may postpone this thrust to a later date. But girl or boy tends more to be nonchalant—"so what?"—or to take things as a joke and laugh them off.

When Fourteens are asked if they are ever jealous or envious, they reply with ease that they are "not really jealous" or "only in a way." They may wish they had the privileges of someone else—"going to dances," "having more freedom"; may wish they were as popular as some of their friends. They may wish they had the choice, like some of their friends, to work on a farm and drive a tractor. But as a boy thinks it over, he begins to realize his lot isn't so bad, that he's "pretty lucky," that he "gets as many breaks as anyone," that he really doesn't want to change places with another person. ("Oh, no!") You can almost hear him and feel him hurrying back to himself as he says, "When I get right down to it, I'm just *darn glad* I'm myself."

With this good feeling of being himself or herself Fourteen can enter into competition with a different feeling from the one he or she had at eleven. Then children were almost viciously competitive, demanding to win at any price. At fourteen they love competition, but in a different way. Fourteens like to compete in what they are good at, more often in sports than in lessons. They want, above all, to do well. If they win, so much the better. They are especially happy if their team wins.

It is their witty, light touch that makes Fourteens more fun to have around, at least in those moments when they are exercising this talent. Fourteens are reaching for the intangible, a new kind of sharing of experience. When they form imaginary clubs and name them meaningfully "The Tennyson Brook Club" or "The Black Mark," it is the common experience of the members of the group which allows them to enjoy the humorous meaning of the names. Without explanation, they will know that the babblers belong to the former, and the heavy receivers of demerits belong to the latter.

4. The Growing Self

By now, the most intensely inwardizing work of Thirteen has pretty much been accomplished. The reflective process, the living with oneself, the thinking about oneself which characterize Thirteen are all a bit like an active hibernation process. Then comes the time when the inner biological clock is turning, and the time for emergence into the sun arrives. And that time in many is fourteen.

The boy or girl of this age seems "so like himself." He feels like himself even though he might desire a few changes—a little less fat, a little taller, a little shorter. Young people are now aware of their difference from other people and of their own uniqueness, even though they are not quite ready to accept it fully. They are still influenced a bit by the idealized perfect form.

As one father remarked of his son, "He is finally absorbed in something outside himself." And that can be true. That is one reason why Fourteen is so ready to take the world as it is. Fourteens are learning the art of how to master life. And in this mastery they come to know that as one becomes capable of adapting within limits to the demands of the outside world, one also learns how to choose. Fourteen is beginning to know more clearly what he or she wants and how to discriminate; thus is capable of saying no because of making a choice and not just being resistant. Fourteens can choose their friends and their literature, though they still tend to choose too much and then to be swamped by their own exuberance.

Fourteens feel good about themselves. You may hear them say, "I like myself the way I am." If they have not quite reached this state, they may overstep in their desire to take responsibility and to plan their time on their own. They may still need more adult guidance than they think they do in talking over their plans before putting them into action. Many are able to look back on their former selves with more perspective, more tolerance. Did they not once do the very things they now see these younger children doing?

Those Fourteens who are immature or just resistant to growing up are often quite aware of how they are expected to act, but prefer acting like a younger child. Others who were slow in their social growth at twelve and thirteen are now eager to make up for lost time, and become gluttons for social experience. The days, weeks, and months don't have enough time to contain their plans. They tend even to overdo the customary characteristic tendency of Fourteens to go out of bounds. They spill out all over and, in their attempt to organize their excess, often produce considerable confusion.

Fourteens are very aware of their outward appearance. Their complexion often distresses them. They may desire some changes physically, but on the whole get on with themselves and groom themselves according to inner dictates as well as outer appearances.

Fourteens don't like to brag and may be very critical of classmates who do. They can recognize in themselves such good qualities as getting on with people, having a good sense of humor, and the "ability to appreciate things." A few still consider getting good marks their greatest asset, but more, especially among the boys, are concerned with their good athletic ability.

Fourteens are willing to face their faults rather squarely, even though they are not too good at overcoming them. Typical faults mentioned by Fourteens include being sarcastic, critical, unable to keep a secret, having a weak personality. One fault many Fourteens have in common is their loud voice. This can be used in fun and sociability with their friends, or it can, all too often, be used to express anger. For Fourteens do not hide or control their feelings as some did at thirteen. And anger, especially toward siblings, seems to rise all too easily to the surface.

Fourteens are well aware of their parents' displeasure about this kind of behavior. But it will take another year for most to have the perspective needed to view their own emotional episodes from a more adult point of view. Eventually they will find themselves becoming far less upset by things their siblings do.

In telling what they would wish for, Fourteens are not thinking of themselves alone. Rather, they are thinking of the kind of world they would like to live in. First and foremost, they wish for a world at peace or for an end of wars. Then they wish for a better world in general, in which there is a "unity of nations," "a union of all religion," a "high standard of living," and "a better chance for people to grow up." More specifically, they wish that there were a more properly run government ("one that wouldn't allow taxes to go up!") and a better educational system.

They are especially desirous of happiness for both their own family and people in general, and in their own future marriage. They want to be successful both in getting into and through high school and college, and also want to achieve well in their career. A few are more concerned about personal attributes of intelligence, good health, popularity, but on the whole Fourteens accept themselves as they are, though they are becoming interested in finding out more about what they are like as persons. Money and what money can buy are more often wished for by boys than by girls. But those who desire material possessions are in the minority. This is, however, the age when the desire to have a car rears its disquieting head. Many conflicts will be fought over this consuming passion before the prize itself is within the individual's possession and control.

Fourteen is in a delightfully fluid state in relation to the future. Though they wish they were old enough to drive a car or to have the privileges of college age, they are really having a fine time where they are. They play around with the thought of the future but say they haven't made up their minds. Fourteens may say they have "no idea" what they want to be or will be. The future is ahead of them. Medicine still entices a certain number. Fourteen is especially interested in any job that has to do with people. This may be expressed in social work, politics, psychiatry, psychology, diplomatic work, history, and on and on into any other ramifications that include people. However, with girls, veterinarian, teacher, musician, doctor, or dentist are the leading choices. Boys choose most often to be a doctor, sports figure, carpenter, or businessman.

There is no hurry for Fourteen to decide about his or her future career. They may be more interested in immediate high school or prep school training than in college. Most (seventy-eight percent of the girls, eighty-four percent of the boys) do want to go to college, though they often do not know where. Even these have definite moments when they're not quite sure if they want to go to college and "spend all that money" or not. Some are wondering if a vocational school might not be better.

Fourteen is less intense in thinking about marriage than a year earlier. Only seventy percent of the girls, seventy-two percent of the boys, plan to marry. Fourteen says things like, "I probably will," "Most people do," "Haven't decided," or "Want to grow up a little more first." These figures contrast interestingly with those for our 1950 subjects. At that time, more girls (one hundred percent) but fewer boys (only forty-three percent) planned to marry.

Fourteens, on the whole, are not in a hurry to marry, recognizing that they have much to do before that time will come. Many even like the thought of working for a while after college before marrying. But this does not prevent them from planning. Girls are so realistic in this realm that they are already rearing their imaginary children and desire husbands who will be handy around the house and capable of "fixing drains and putting up shelves." But girls want more than the practical side from their future spouses. They are now thinking more of love as a basis for marriage. Both girls and the few boys who have thought about it are most interested in their future mates having a good disposition. Looks are something, intelligence is something, but in the end Fourteen is beginning to know that it's how well two people relate to each other and to their children that is of prime importance.

Fourteen is thinking quite realistically about future children. Both boys and girls hope to have them but recognize the uncertainties of life. Eighty percent of our girls, seventy-eight percent of boys, say they do want to have children. Two children remain the favored number, though quite a few now say "two or three."

5. Interpersonal Relationships

The change in the atmosphere of the home when a thirteen-year-old becomes fourteen can often bring a wonderful relief. At least these young people have come out of their rooms and do communicate. But there are many Fourteens who have difficulties with their parents—especially girls with their mothers. Though many feel they are given as much freedom as they should have, others are champing at the bit and feel as though they are held in check. They storm around and shout about their "big problem," meaning their mother, though they often group their parents together as "they." "They" are often dubbed "old-fashioned," "antiquated," "living in the 1960's." Girls get into arguments with their parents especially over dating and curfew. Boys have troubles about going out at night. And there are the everlasting problems about homework, clothes, and helping around the house. There come intense moments when mother and daughter "fight like cats and dogs," and fathers are tempted to administer physical punishment to their sons. But after considerable energy has been expended on both sides, parent and child can usually work out a solution.

These intense moments seem to be a part of Fourteens' tendency to get so tangled every now and then that something must be done to help them untangle. There is a trend toward an increased feeling of confidence in parents, even though they may keep any approval they feel to themselves. Fourteens begin to feel a new understanding on the part of parents, a desire to help them, and a sympathetic attitude which seems new. This attitude on the part of the parents allows the child to confide in them and to discuss problems, especially social problems (more with mother than with father.)

Fathers are often not as critical as they have been in the past, which may indicate that there is less to criticize. Fourteen recognizes when father puts on the pressure and when he lets up. Girls, especially, approve of their father's method of handling and, as one girl frankly stated, "It's most important for a father to have a firm hand and keep things in order." Fathers are, on the whole, said to be more strict and less understanding and sympathetic than mothers, but many daughters get on better with their fathers. However, they may not wish to accept affection from him. Some girls, sensing their father's warm response to them at this time, may turn a cold shoulder toward him and act very casually. This puts father in a bad spot. He may even show some jealousy of his daughter's dates.

Considering the extent and sharpness of a father's criticism of his thirteen-year-old, his criticisms seem mild at fourteen. He wants his son or daughter to be more lively, more outgoing, more friendly, more desirous of his company. He is shifting from his more specific demands, such as the intellectual achievement he required at thirteen, to the looser demands of the social poise he feels would become Fourteen.

At long last, there is some definite improvement in Fourteens' relationship with younger siblings. They recognize that their family's criticisms are still valid, but they really get on better with sibs than the family may realize. Of course there are disagreements, quarrels, and occasional moments when Fourteen is really mad at younger siblings. But there are more times when the teenager can have fun with them, impart the benefits of his or her experience, and teach them things for the fun of it, such as dancing. However, younger siblings can be annoying, often do things on purpose just to irritate, and, what is most distressing to Fourteen, they take things without asking.

Though most older sibs get on well with Fourteen, discuss his problems with him, and give advice, the danger of a competitive urge is all too soon apparent. Older siblings will purposely not give Fourteen a break; may make him or her walk when they could have given a ride. Or when Fourteen is with friends, the very presence of an older sibling may make girl or boy feel self-conscious.

It is the fourteen-year-old girl who is more perceptive in all of these interpersonal relationships, especially with contemporaries. As one so aptly remarked, "It's like jumping into a different world— things are so different last year and this year." The quality of this different world is elusive, hard to pin down. But Fourteen's use of the words "clique," "circle," "fitting into a group," wanting to "get in," even though she has to "push" her way in, "feeling like a para- site"—all these expressions, and many more, tell of a new social order, of the magic strands that hold a group together. The group, which may be as small as two or as big as seven, may prove to be an exclusive one.

A fourteen-year-old girl's selection of friends is far less deter- mined by activity interests than it was earlier. In fact, she is at times shocked that she may have very little in common with a best friend except that she just feels "sort of pally." Reasons for choosing friends are different from earlier. Fourteen likes a friend because she's so "full of life," "free and aboveboard," or "ladylike and yet a tomboy." Fourteen is apt to have "more friends and not just special ones," "a whole bunch of best friends."

A group of girls have much to talk about: "We talk about clothes, boys, teachers, what we think about school or lessons, just a combi- nation of everything." Discussions of the personalities of their vari- ous friends are beginning. (These will become a more precise art in another year.) Discussions also may touch on social problems, but these, again, will come to fuller flower in another year. Fourteen is ready to accept a certain amount of trouble with a group because she says, "It's bound to be"; but she is ready to do more than this. There are times when she knows she has to talk things out with a friend "in order to get along" and to restore a certain amount of understanding between them.

The closeness and faddishness of individual cliques is important but can be uncomfortable for those not included. Those Fourteens who are on the outside of these groups are rather sorry sights. They try to "get in" by joining up with all sorts of activities. But all too often, they "meet the people and that's all there is to it." They walk down the corridors with another girl, hoping something might happen. At times, this social predicament is recognized by a more popular (and sympathetic) fourteen-year-old, and the unpopular girl may be included as an underdog.

Boys, as always, are more apt to "gang up" with each other and to have plenty of friends without necessarily having a close circle of friends. They maneuver socially and know that they choose friends just because they happen to like them rather than because of shared activities. They are not too aware of how they select their friends—"can't say how I pick them"—but they know which ones they want to be with. They feel a nice satisfaction in their friends and often continue with neighborhood friends, whereas girls are more often interested in newfound school friends. Boys are freer in their feelings toward their friends and show a lot of good-natured, back-and-forth kidding. Situations that would have been too much for them at a younger age, such as being pushed down in the snow, no longer upset them, and they may report, "I think I can handle that now."

Boys have a really good time together. They enjoy each other's sense of humor. There is often a comedian among them whose every word is considered funny both by his friends and himself, even though an adult may fail to see the humor. The forthright laughter from a group of boys is the evidence of good fun that is often the by-product of a stag party. Even poker games may be part of the group's activities, with relatively high stakes involved. It is like expanding, exuberant, exaggerating Fourteen to choose high stakes of a thousand points to a dime. As the game gets under way, there is much ado and you would think that Fourteen were dealing in millions of dollars instead of just dimes.

As do the girls, some fourteen-year-old boys sense the difficulties another boy may be having and are willing to protect him. A boy who is being blackballed by the others may be unobtrusively chosen as the tent mate of a boy who wishes to protect him on a scouting trip. And boys can help the "lame duck" with more sureness and trustworthiness than girls can. They stay with their problem and are more apt to see it through. Some Fourteens are still lone wolves, but even they are expanding a little more and may stop by at a friend's house on their way home from school—a thing that would hardly have entered their minds a year ago.

The expanding and social interests of Fourteen include a real drive toward the opposite sex, boys being as interested in girls (though in a different way) as girls are in boys. There are still the casual meetings on the bus, in the halls at school, at the drugstore, but these are often takeoffs for further activity together. Most boys now consider girls "more fun than a nuisance." They report that most of their friends are interested in girls. Suspecting they might be turned down by girls of their own age, some may protect themselves by cautiously asking such a question as, "If I asked you to go to the dance with me, would you go?" Girls are fairly sure which boy they want to go with and will blithely tell others they are busy even when this is not the case.

Arranged parties are more fun than they used to be. The boys don't stand on the sidelines so much. They mix better and carry on more of a conversation, even though the girl may have to talk about sports. Girls prefer parties with older boys because they are less rowdy. Dancing may now be the preferred activity, though ninety-five percent of the boys (only sixteen percent of the girls) say they "make out." The majority of the boys claim that they drink at parties, and drug use is reported by twenty-eight percent of the girls, fifty percent of boys.

The kind of parties fourteen-year-old girls especially enjoy are the spontaneous ones that just come into being with very little planning. They can be the most successful parties, especially when a room in the house is available and parents are on hand for the first half hour to make the group feel at home, then withdraw to another part of the house as the party develops on its own. There might be piano or guitar playing, singing, dancing, or just talking. Parents notice the difference between these parties and the ones in previous years. There is a greater ease of mixing of boys and girls.

Eating is incidental and just a part of the sociability, except with the party-crashing boys who might wish to raid the refrigerator. Firm parental control and understanding can usually bring these infractors into line.

About one third of the girls, one half of the boys, say they do a lot of dating. Well over half of both sexes say they are going steady or have gone steady. By far the majority say that they or their friends do "make out," and over half say that they or their friends "go all the way."

Girls know that boys date a number of girls and vice versa. Each has an idea of what kind of person he or she would like to date. First and foremost, the date should have a good sense of humor, and then such other qualities as intellect and ability to talk are helpful. Girls especially like boys who know their way around and who might be "a little forward," and they prefer a boy to be liked by other boys. Both sexes dislike the conceited date or the windbag. Girls are beginning to recognize that looks are not everything. And boys are coming to the same realization. The girl who might initially be thought to be the most popular because of her looks and easy ways can turn out to be the least popular. Reputations and rumors get around.

Activities in dating vary from the more usual parties at home to a movie, sports event, picnics, or skating parties. Fourteens like to go on double dates as well as in larger groups, but there are also the twosomes, especially of the fourteen-year-old girls and older boys.

Some girls give their dates rough treatment or just drop them, "break it off," "throw them over." Reasons for these shifts might not be too clear, but things can shift rapidly when the heart is involved. However, Fourteen may even be relieved to get rid of a too demanding relationship.

6. Activities and Interests

The life of a fourteen-year-old is all of a piece—an exciting, full, active, and usually happy existence. What Fourteens do specifically is less important than how they relate their activities to the whole of their lives. They have a capacity to think in terms of the whole year, relating their interests to the season. Thus, when asked about their interest in sports, they will often separate them into summer and winter types. The season that suits Fourteen best is usually summertime. Children of this age often don't want to go to camp. They may prefer the casual, active, and heterosexual social life of summer at home.

It is school that occupies Fourteens' time in the winter. They are at school for most of the day, have club activities after school, and homework at night; but they accept all this and fit in other activities around these more basic responsibilities.

Boys' and girls' interests in sports contrast considerably. Basketball is the favored sport of boys, but baseball and football are not far behind. The increasing muscular ability in boys needs to be put to the test. This is an age when the athlete begins to stand out more sharply and may be favored by his peers because of his prowess. But even when a boy knows he is "not top athletic material" or is "too light," he still often wants to be on a team of some kind. Intramural sports provide the kind of competition Fourteen enjoys.

Girls may not have the drive toward sports that boys have. What they do with sports is, in large part, determined by what the school provides and the kind of group spirit that surrounds a sport. Volleyball and field hockey are the more favored group sports. Tennis and Ping-Pong are also favored, and there may be a return to an interest in bicycling. Both sexes enjoy roller-skating.

Indoor activities have shifted considerably from the intense hobby interests of Thirteen to the looser social interests of Fourteen. Boys continue to like video games. Girls continue with their earlier interest in sewing, possibly designing and making their own clothes. Some of both sexes enjoy drawing.

But the greatest amount of time is spent in social gatherings, either of separate sexes or in mixed company. Group card games are on the rise, with the semblance of an adult pattern. The structure of a gathering is loose, flowing, and shifting, with the power of restabilizing itself. When both sexes are present, everything becomes a little more precarious. The social structure gets looser and shifts more rapidly. (It is not uncommon for a boy to shift his attentions from one girl to another in the course of the evening.)

Verbal communication of some form seems essential to girls at almost any age. Fourteen expresses this need in her talk fests, telephoning, and letter writing. Sometimes the telephoning demands are so great that an additional extension seems essential. Rules for the use of the phone should be laid down, though with a certain amount of flexibility.

Sedentary Looking and Listening Activities Television and radio are usually not a problem with Fourteen. Some watch or listen only occasionally, either because they have so much else to do or because they don't enjoy the programs.

More than fifty percent of the girls claim that they watch no more than ten hours a week; boys watch a little more—fifteen hours a week or perhaps less. Radio or stereo may be played for their own sake or as a background to doing homework.

The TV programs Fourteens select vary considerably, reflecting their personal tastes. With boys, comedies, crime, and sports programs are preferred, whereas girls are most apt to choose comedies, movies, soaps, or family shows. Rock is of interest to both sexes, and the disc jockeys know full well that their audience includes a good number of fourteen-year-olds.

Interest in rock and roll records, strong at thirteen, is increasing at fourteen. Fourteens enjoy having their own records but may feel that the expense of such a hobby is excessive. The radio, which they play loud and long, is less expensive.

The amount of reading Fourteen does is largely determined by the young person's own taste. Some do not have time for more than their school assignments. Others read a good deal and their interests are varied, especially since they are entering the adult sphere. They may track down a number of books by the same author. Or they will read, or avoid reading, certain subjects—"anything in ancient history" or "nothing in politics." Their reading may be influenced by their moods, and the books themselves may create a mood in them. Trashy magazines make them feel bad. But much of their reading makes them feel good.

Newspaper reading is spotty with most Fourteens, though a few read the paper thoroughly. The funnies and the news are read most. Some now like human interest stories, certain columns, and the society page. Sports, movies, and television news have their continuing place. Magazine reading is steadily increasing. Fourteen likes to be informed of any special articles that might be of interest.

Moviegoing varies greatly with the community. There may be certain movies that are a "must." But regular weekly or biweekly movie attendance is, for many, no longer as popular as it may have been in years just past.

7. School Life*

Fourteens are ready for a change, in school as in other things—a sizable change that will satisfy their expansiveness. Their decrease in suspicious belligerence readies them for new territory. They are quieter with themselves, even though, compared with Thirteen,

---

* The schools in which we made most of our observations were decidedly homogeneous so far as the student body was concerned. In many public high schools today the diversity of background of the students, and the size and complexity of the school itself, makes our descriptions of age differences of perhaps relatively minor importance. We recommend Sara Lawrence Lightfoot's *The Good High School: Portraits of Character and Culture* for any reader desiring a comprehensive picture of high school life in this country.

they are less inwardized and noisier with the group. Their greater inner quietness is linked with a paradoxical development—an increase in interest in themselves, yet a decrease in self-consciousness. They are becoming less dissatisfied and defensive about their personality, more calm and judicious.

Fourteens often seem to bloom forth with new qualities that can make them an asset to any school setup. They intermingle well, are more respectful, have ideals. This is Fourteen at his or her best. However, they can also be disappointing to a teacher, for they may spread themselves too thin, emphasize the froth of life, and fail to spend time and energy on their schoolwork.

Schoolwork, for Fourteen, is only a part of a full school life— sometimes seemingly a rather minor part. Both sexes can be so busy with friends before, between, and after classes (and sometimes during them too) that schoolwork appears embedded in a much larger sphere of sociality. School provides the takeoff point for much of Fourteen's social activity. They even make plans to meet friends on the way to school. Those who come to school on a bus still show a tendency to separate along same-sex lines.

The homeroom, if available, is an excellent place to exercise student organization and to plan for certain activities, both social and business. Fourteens love to elect officers, though this still needs a certain amount of adult supervision. The athlete is most often chosen. At times other qualifications are needed for the job. It is here that a teacher might help by presenting the issues more clearly, to facilitate a better choice.

In homeroom too, girl or boy may be able to form group identity (unless the school is so impersonal, the classes so jumbled, that common ties do not exist.) Fourteens like their group to be close-knit, and like to identify it by a name. Whatever any member of the group does may reflect on the whole group, favorably or otherwise. They like to sit together as a group in assembly.

Fourteen often gets on better with his or her teacher than formerly and may even consider the teacher to be fun. Students know that they are nicer to the teachers than they have been, and teachers apparently respond in kind. Criticisms of teachers are now more valid, more closely related to fact than they have been. If a teacher is unsympathetic, indifferent, or clear thinking and full of originality, Fourteen says so.

A teacher of Fourteens needs to be especially aware of the group structure. But variety such as an announcement over the loudspeaker acts as a disturbing interruption. The teacher must then bring the group back to where they started from to keep the thread of their attention. The building of atmosphere is essential to a good learning process. Unfortunately the atmosphere may sometimes be so fragile that it breaks to bits. (And of course there are some schools in which not only confusion but actually violence often occurs.)

In periods between classes or in time off for socializing, Fourteens waste no time before getting together to talk. Girls often act as though they are suddenly released like a jack-in-the-box. They scoot over to a friend to chitchat. They may have interesting information to report. They look at the pictures in each other's billfolds. Boys are more apt to act like big dogs, cuffing each other. They may start quietly but soon become very loud. One teacher remarked that noise was so much a part of them at this age that they actually don't hear it.

The immature students stand out in a group of Fourteens. They are the ones who push, throw, talk too much. Their laughter is the loudest, and their jokes are made to draw attention to themselves. They play hooky. They are antagonistic. They do not get on well with the other members of the group. They might trip or pinch or hide another's book. It is this kind of child who especially needs a careful individual evaluation to determine where he or she can fit in, and whether or not some very special kind of help may be needed.

Boy-girl relationships come and go. Some boys are still so self-conscious about girls that they refuse to sit next to them in assembly. Others seek girls out in the halls, in assembly, in club activities. Girls are more eager to have boyfriends than vice versa. As one girl said, "You have no idea how secure you feel when you have a boyfriend." The relationship between the sexes at this age, as at most ages, would improve if the boys were a year older than the girls. It is the boys' immaturity that so often makes the girls look toward older boys. About a third of the girls and half the boys are now dating, but "going steady" often lasts for only a few weeks. There is a definite attraction to those of the opposite sex, and boys and girls both like activities in mixed groups: sitting together at lunch, serving on committees, planning for dances. All of these are welcomed by Fourteen, for they provide situations with some structure in which children know how they are expected to act, and through which they can communicate easily with the opposite sex.

Significantly, it is no longer possible within the compass of our presentation to give an overview of curriculum—for this has suddenly burgeoned out with new variety and intricacy. We can merely mention a few items. The more gifted students are usually good in mathematics (including algebra), creative writing, English, and Latin. Though a fourteen-year-old may be warned against taking Latin, he or she may like the challenge. Fourteen is a person of action who learns through trial and error. When it is practical, girl or boy should be allowed a trial run even though it may end in failure. So long as such a failure is not viewed as a disgrace, it can produce far healthier growth in the fourteen-year-old who is not ready just to accept advice. Learning through error has its important place.

The whole field of social studies—politics, current events, reading the newspaper—may not be especially interesting to Fourteens. But they often like to express themselves in public speaking, giving oral reports, participating in dramatics. And there is a growing interest in the study of man—his biology, physiology, psychology. Fourteens are eager and ready to know more about themselves. Homework is accepted as a part of Fourteen's life, even though most complain that it is piled on.

After-school clubs are popular. Each student should be able to find his or her niche. There are athletic, scientific, dramatic, music, and photography clubs. There is the bowling club for the only moderately athletically inclined. A roller-skating club can perform a real service, for it is often sought by those who do not have a place socially but who can belong to a group through a shared activity. Each school will have its own variety of clubs—which, to a large extent, take the place of sororities and fraternities.

The lives of fourteen-year-olds are indeed active and full, and the more active the better they like it. The school needs to be ready to supply an active program and to help the boys and girls fit in, for Fourteens often need more help than they think they do. There may even be times when it is necessary to bring the parent into the school to unsnarl some special problem or difficulty. Fortunately, most Fourteens will accept their parents' authority when they feel that home and school are working together.

The idea of a separate school for Fourteen is still virtually untested. Where it has been tried it has worked most satisfactorily, and it certainly seems in theory to solve many problems posed by Fourteen's transitional status. It is no universal solution, and many telling criticisms can be levelled against it. But we believe that if Fourteens might be allowed to experience such a contained unit and then could speak for themselves, the odds are that they would thrive under the experience.

8. Ethical Sense

Fourteens are, in a way, less aware than earlier of their own ethical behavior because it is now more a part of them. They have lost the intensity, the scrupulousness, the sense of feeling "terrible" that they often experienced at thirteen. Now just as their clothes sit well on them, so do their ethics.

Though still conformists, aware that they must obey the rules, they are now developing their own concept of "morals." They recognize the multiple influences that produce their own ethical codes. As one girl explained, "You aren't exactly taught morals. But they are partly what you're taught, your own ideas, what you learn from experience, from reading, and what other people do." The diversified and easy movement of fourteen-year-olds makes it possible for them to mesh these various influences into their own sense of moral values.

And moral interests go beyond self, for they are now thinking of larger issues and of the relationship of one group to another. They are becoming aware of such issues as the treatment of minority groups, discrimination, and exclusion. They are basically tolerant, having both respect for and interest in other people.

Fourteens are ready and eager to share experiences with those who are different from them in race or social class. Fourteen, perhaps more than boys and girls of other ages, seems willing to give the other person a chance.

Fourteens, for the most part, do not have too much difficulty deciding what is right and what is wrong. Though they usually know what is best to do, they may quickly add, "But that doesn't mean I always do the right thing." They make their decisions about behavior from multiple influences. Some Fourteens "just seem to know," "have a clear notion," "go by common sense," or "just feel" what is right. Others are more influenced by the opinion of their family, other people or friends, or religious teaching. Still others are more calculating in their decisions. They weigh problems in their minds as to advantages and disadvantages or who would be benefited or harmed. Some feel the tug and pull of two different forces: what would work out with their peers in the one direction and with their parents in the other. Their parents' opinion is important to them even if only to avoid trouble, but they might "temper it down a bit."

Fourteen's conscience doesn't always figure too strongly in making decisions. It is there to direct them if they need it about big things, but it doesn't plague them. Fourteen doesn't see much point in worrying about what has already been done; is more interested in trying to fix it. The nonchalance of Fourteens makes them easier to live with, but may also get them into trouble in realms they are not yet capable of handling.

Just as conscience doesn't bother them too much now, telling the truth is not hard either. Girl or boy might "stretch" the truth now and then and might question whether *anyone* is "strictly truthful." But most don't tell out-and-out falsehoods. If things are important, they will tell the truth. They are ready to stand up for something they think is important, whether it is for their own good or somebody else's.

Where Thirteen preferred to avoid argument, Fourteen appears to enjoy it and treats it almost as a game. Most have had enough practice to know which way an argument usually ends or with whom arguing is the most fun. Fathers usually win, either through the advantage of their years ("I start to drop my reasoning when I argue with Daddy") or their ability to terminate a dispute ("No argument"). But mothers seem to be good bait for both sons and daughters and may well come out the losers. On the whole, Fourteen will listen to reason about important things.

Smoking and drinking are now strongly within the realm of Fourteen's own experience, for if they don't indulge themselves, some of their friends do. In fact, nearly all Fourteens say that their friends—if not they themselves—smoke; and about three quarters say that they or their friends drink. More than three quarters of both sexes claim that at least some of their friends use drugs.

Fourteen's attitude about these matters is quite casual and matter-of-fact. He or she is now rarely disturbed by adults' drinking as long as it is "in proportion." Most are concerned about friends being able to hold their liquor but don't condemn them for drinking. For most, neither drinking nor smoking has come into the problem realm at fourteen, but there are indications as to which way the wind is blowing, since half the girls and one third of the boys admit that they have friends or acquaintances who have gotten into trouble with drugs or drink.

Fourteen is much less concerned about swearing than formerly and also is less apt to swear. Thirteens swore both to release their own inner tensions and to feel a part of the gang. But now they don't have the same needs; don't have the same bottled-up tensions they had at thirteen and usually have better ways to feel a part of their group. Nevertheless, Fourteens seems to take it for granted that "everybody swears."

Cheating is not usually a problem with the well-adjusted Fourteens. Those who do cheat are apt to cheat or check with others only on subjects they are less good in. If there is a great amount of cheating in a school, the teachers and teaching methods should be considered. There are some teachers in whose class a student would never cheat. Fairness of a teacher is very vital to Fourteen, but also the fairness of students to the teacher.

Most Fourteens are not moved to steal, though they may reminisce about the time when they did a few years earlier.* They recognize that many such boys and girls are often not poor and do not need to steal. And so, in their accepting way, they might comment, "I think they just can't help it."

Two thirds of the girls but only about one third of the boys think most politicians are dishonest. About two thirds of all think we are doing enough about integration. Sixty-eight percent of all our Fourteens favor ERA. One of the girls who do not favor it comments, "No, I do not favor it. If it were passed, women would have to go to war against men. And it is true, we *are* the weaker sex."

---

* We refer here to shoplifting and not to mugging and purse-snatching, which as far as we know did not occur among our subjects.

PART THREE
Maturity Trends
and
Selected Growth Gradients

chapter nine
TOTAL ACTION SYSTEM

Body and mind are not two separate things, though for practical purposes people often speak of them separately. We devote an entire chapter to the child's body, or what we call the "total action system," because the young person's body, perhaps even more than his environment, determines his or her behavior. Few things have more influence on any adolescent boy or girl than body size and shape and level of sexual maturity.

Thus the eleven-year-old girl who has already come of age sexually is inevitably going to have very different interests in life from the girl who does not mature till she is fourteen. The boy who at fourteen still lags behind his classmates in size will, in most instances, approach life, and especially the opposite sex, with far less confidence than the boy who is big for his age.

Many of the physical changes of adolescence are so conspicuous that boys and girls alike become acutely aware of them. Although in earlier years a young person may have been quite careless about personal appearance, he or she now begins to visualize self with and without the aid of a mirror. He or she projects into the future: "Will I always be too tall?" "too short?" "too fat?" or "so skinny and gawky?" "And what about my nose?" These are very real worries and call for sympathetic understanding. Fortunately, in some matters of body size and disproportions, growth trends are predictably favorable and often grounds for reassurance.

Tremendous changes in size and shape of the body do take place in the years from ten to fourteen. Some of these changes are gradual. Others occur all of a sudden, as it were. Midway in this age range comes a marked spurt in height growth—in girls often between ten and eleven, in boys a little later, usually between twelve and thirteen. This spurt usually comes just before the onset of menstruation in girls, before the first ejaculation in boys.

Not only the body in general but especially the face may change. In some, the nose becomes temporarily prominent. Many, especially boys, develop a sort of half-finished look for a while before blossoming out into what is often the real beauty of sixteen.

Some of these changes, especially the gain in height, are well accepted and welcome. Others such as voice changes, excessive perspiration, and most of all, facial blemishes can be a source of real agony for many a teen. No wonder many feel so insecure when even their bodies cannot be relied upon.

One girl explained to us that the reason she was so upset when her family moved out of state when she was thirteen was that "I was just getting used to the changes in myself. That was hard enough without having to get used to a new place to live."

RELATING TO THE OPPOSITE SEX is for many teenagers the most fascinating and time-consuming of all activities, and the timing and extent of this interest depends more on physical drive than on wish for social acceptance. At few ages is the individual so strongly under the influence of his or her hormones.

Sex-related pleasures and problems in these years are so primary that it would be wise of the culture to pay more attention than it does to providing adequate sex education. Information about sex, whether accurate or inaccurate, has always come, at least to some extent, from outside the home. In fact, the home seems decreasingly to be the source of such information. A study reports that "Though the percentage of males who received their primary sex education from their parents declined from a third of those sampled in 1924 to eighteen percent in 1977, the corresponding shift among girls was more dramatic: from two thirds to one third"[10] At the same time, the percentage of girls citing friends as their most important source rose from one fifth to one third, making this source as important for girls as for boys.

Though there is still opposition from some parents, many people feel that schools must do their part in providing adequate instruction about sexual matters. This education should, of course, include not only information about the physiology of puberty and reproduction but go beyond that. It should provide practical information about birth control, wanted and needed in these days of rather free sexual activity in the young.

Some feel that information about birth control will encourage sexual activity in young people. Experience shows that this does not seem to be the case. The danger is far greater that teenagers will be sexually active without the needed information about contraception than that information about contraception will lead to sexual activity.

Concrete sex problems of individuals must be addressed realistically in terms of authentic information. But young people also need orientation as well as factual knowledge. They need to develop increasingly mature and respectful attitudes toward the opposite sex. They need to be helped to develop a workable code of morality in all of their personal relationships.

A broadly conceived program of pre-parental education, including sex education as well as formal courses in parenting and child-care, would assist the individual to realize what becoming an adult actually means.

THE HEALTH OF THE GROWING GIRL OR BOY is of course a vital aspect of the total action system. Few things, presumably, other than inadequate nutrition, lack of necessary vitamins, or unrecognized and untreated allergies have an even more negative effect on health than the all too prevalent habits of smoking, drinking, and use of drugs.

With inevitable exceptions, boys and girls in middle-class America tend to be reasonably healthy. However, such health-related activities as smoking, drinking, and drug use are of major concern to their parents and teachers. Adult reaction to these activities varies tremendously, ranging from great concern to a bland and unrealistic attitude that "it can't happen here." Parents in some of the schools which refused us permission to question their young on these topics told us flatly that drinking and drug use did not go on in their community, and if they did they—the parents—did not want to know about it.

Since it might be assumed that many young people, for fear of reprisal, might not be entirely frank when questioned about their own smoking, drinking, and use of drugs, we approached the problem somewhat obliquely by asking teenagers if any of the girls and boys they knew indulged in any of these activities.

Thus we assume that the responses were for the most part truthful. But the percentages obtained report how many, at each age, *knew people* who indulged rather than how many actually say that they themselves engaged in such activities.

Figures, as Table 5 in the Appendix shows, were high. Even at ten years of age, more than fifty percent of both sexes report that "some of the kids" smoke. By twelve, more than fifty percent report that "some of the kids" smoke and drink. And by fourteen, more than fifty percent (in fact from seventy-four to one hundred percent) report that "some of the kids" smoke, drink, and use drugs. However, in some parts of the country, teachers report that among thirteen-, fourteen-, and fifteen-year-olds there is somewhat less pot smoking and pill popping than a few years ago.

(Recent figures released by the Director of the National Institute on Drug Abuse show that one out of nine at the senior high level use marijuana daily and that "over the past five years, daily use of alcohol—beer and wine—has essentially remained at about the five percent level.")

All these behaviors represent perhaps, in teenager as in adult, extreme expressions of tensional behavior. *The more customary kinds of tensional outlet* seen in adolescence are certainly less worrisome, though in all likelihood still annoying to the adult. Parents in general are becoming more permissive about the very young child's tensional outlets—his or her thumb sucking, pacifier sucking, security blanket fondling. Most are less permissive about and more bothered by teenage tensional outlets such as ticlike facial movements, nail biting, fidgeting, and leg jiggling.

But even tensional outlets show a somewhat patterned progression and change with age. The more basic physiological outlets such as stomachaches and headaches, and the more overt behavioral outlets such as grimacing and excessive movement of arms and legs if not of the whole body, characteristic of ten, eleven, and twelve have as a rule by fourteen become much less gross and much less constant.

RESPONSE TO INTERVIEW PROCEDURES. One of the many areas in which the response of the young person seems largely based on changes in body and mind is the situation in which we personally interviewed a boy or girl, asking questions which ranged over the entire experience of living.

During this interview, the typical ten-year-old seemed almost totally active, moving about the room and touching or asking about almost everything in it. Though expressing few deep insights, girl or boy was pleasant, relaxed, extremely friendly and sociable with the interviewer.

Elevens might or might not sit in one spot. Even when sitting, though, they were still almost totally active as they sat in their chair. They showed themselves even more cooperative, if possible, than Ten and gave information, "telling all" with tremendous enthusiasm.

Twelve still wriggles in his or her chair and continues to be friendly, outgoing, cooperative. But a slight note of caution appears. Twelve is somewhat less confiding than a year earlier. And Thirteens, in contrast to the Tens and Elevens, are extremely withdrawn. Though friendly, they show themselves to be quiet, withdrawn, even a little sad. And even when cooperation is good, responses are not particularly revealing. No secrets are told. Answers tend to be brief and guarded.

Fourteen, with his usual exuberance, is once again very cheerful and friendly, sharing ideas as well as facts. But in spite of his friendliness, Fourteen tends to arrive at the interview a little late, to leave a little early, and perhaps to make a phone call during the visit with us. The child's own personal life now takes precedence over adult demands.

We have always maintained that behavior is a function of structure; that is, we behave as we do because of the kind of bodies we possess. Behavior changes with age as the body changes, and the behavior of any growing girl or boy, regardless of the environment, cannot transcend the body's development.

chapter ten
SELF-CARE AND ROUTINES

Among the more aggravating aspects of the growing child's behavior—of daily concern to parents—are the routines of eating, sleeping, bathing, care of room and clothes, and money earned and spent.

Boy or girl eats too little or too much, is picky and fussy about what is served and, above all, prefers junk food to things parents think are wholesome and nourishing. Increasingly as the years go by, preteen and teenager may find it difficult to go to bed at what parents consider a proper bedtime. They also find it even more difficult to get up in the morning, again at what adults consider a "proper" time.

Bathing and care of face and hands is stubbornly resisted until, all of a sudden, the young person monopolizes the bathroom, spending an inordinate amount of time especially in washing and grooming his or her hair.

Clothes, once the docile age of ten is past, can be a matter of constant disagreement, and hardly a teenager alive keeps his or her room up to what mother considers to be safe health standards, let alone neat and orderly.

As for money—adult and child seldom come to anywhere near agreement as to how much it costs any boy or girl for bare social existence, let alone to keep up with what "everybody else's" parents provide. And if parents are relatively older than other parents of teenagers and thus remember a preinflation era, something that "only costs twenty-five dollars" is going to seem very different to parent and child.

Routines may not seem a dramatic part of growing up, but they contribute a very great deal to family harmony or disharmony.

EATING BEHAVIOR: The typical ten-year-old loves to eat. He or she is willing to try new foods and with Ten's typical niceness is not as rejecting of disliked foods as in the past. Even table manners are not too bad.

Elevens are real eaters. On an automobile trip, even if you take provisions with you in the car, you will be barely out of the yard before they are asking for food. They will eat almost anything and state frankly, "I love to eat." At home they especially love to eat between meals, admitting, "I come home from school and I'm *starved!*"

Twelve's appetite seems equally large: "Enormous eater—always hungry—no end to his appetite." But possibly because girl or boy is, in general, a more agreeable person than Eleven this constant eating is not as irritating to the adult as it was a year earlier.

Thirteen is no slouch when it comes to eating, but food, even for the big eater, is not the absorbing interest it was earlier. In fact, some Thirteens are not particularly enthusiastic about much of anything, food included. And perhaps predictably, Fourteen, with his or her marvelous zest for life once again shows a tremendous enthusiasm for food—"the best part of the party." Some like everything—"anything, so long as it's food." In spite of their warmth toward food, many at this age contribute little to the pleasure or harmony of family mealtimes. They criticize the food (even while they are gobbling it up), monopolize conversation, or argue with family members.

These changes in eating behavior have far-reaching implications. In adolescence, as in infancy, nutrition is a most basic problem. Gone are the days when the mother worried that her young child did not eat enough. In reverse, she may now be concerned about the "terrible" intensity of appetite and the deepening of the seemingly bottomless pit. Now parents worry about the amount and kind of food ("junk food") which their children eat rather than whether they eat enough.

Studies by Feingold,[11] Smith,[12] Wunderlich,[13] and others suggest that the junk foods which many teenagers consume, with their poor nutritional value and their artificial colorings and flavorings, may actually be at the root of overactivity and of some learning disabilities. Feingold has proposed a synthetics-free diet which, in many instances, appears to cause young people to calm down, quiet down, and respond well to learning situations.

Other nutritionists, for instance William Crook, suggest that much unsatisfactory and uncomfortable behavior may result from often hidden food allergies.[14] He proposes a so-called elimination diet in which first one eliminates all the child's favorite foods, since the more of a food a person eats, the greater are his chances of becoming allergic to that food. The main foods to be removed from the diet are milk and all dairy products, eggs, wheat, corn, cane and beet sugar, oranges and other citrus fruits, chocolate, food colorings, and additives.

You remove all these foods from the diet for a week or so till any allergic reactions may have disappeared, then reintroduce these suspect foods, one at a time, and only one on any given day. By this method it should be reasonably easy to discover which food, if any, is the culprit.

SLEEPING: The changes which take place in the young person's response to sleep in the years between ten and fourteen are clear and definite. Number of hours of sleep shortens, as a rule, from an average of ten hours a night at ten years to nine at thirteen and fourteen.

But this shortening of the night does not begin to tell the whole story. At ten, it is the parents who not only set the bedtime hour but who have to insist upon it. "Just one more bike ride," "Just half an hour more TV." One gets the impression that without the parents' insistence, Ten might never go to bed. Eleven, too, not only has to be reminded but practically forced to go to bed.

Even at twelve, though things are improving, many admit that they are not "good" about bedtime. Many Thirteens, of course, are already in their own room. They may prefer to spend the evening there. If not, most know the time that has been set and accept it without much argument.

By fourteen, a big change has taken place. Though a few still need to be nagged or at least reminded, many just decide on bedtime themselves and are reasonable enough about it that even though parents may feel they are not getting enough sleep, they do not intervene.

BATH: Almost the same story repeats itself with the bath—from resistance and almost total management by parents to acceptance not only of the fact that one must bathe but of responsibility for the whole procedure.

Most Tens protest with comments such as, "I hadn't counted on taking a bath tonight." Most would seemingly rather be dirty than go through the torture of bathing. Though Elevens resist less than Tens do, bathing does not come easily. By twelve, bathing is less of an issue, and some have also begun to conceive of the possible need of a bath.

At thirteen, reminders are still needed. By fourteen, most bathe every day or at least every other day, though some, especially the less mature, are still averse to bathing.

CLOTHES: With clothes, as with other aspects of daily living, ten-year-olds are still very much mommy's girl (or boy). Mother as a rule decides which clothes to buy: "If I like it and she likes it, we get it. If she likes it and I don't like it, we get it. If I like it and she doesn't like it, we don't get it," says Ten. Though Ten may select his or her clothes for daily wear, Mother still checks on the selection and may do the selecting herself.

At eleven, as with so much else, clothes shopping is apt to involve an argument. And even daily choice of what to wear may involve disagreement. Eleven likes a good fight. Also the child of this age is apt to choose what mothers consider "outlandish" combinations of garments.

By twelve, a girl may say of shopping, "We pick things out together." Thirteen is usually the last age when mother makes the firm and final decision about buying. Most at this age do select their clothes for daily wearing and by now have rather definite notions of what they will and will not wear.

Fourteen-year-olds are pretty independent, and some even have a clothes allowance that theoretically covers all their purchases. Most are not ready for this much responsibility, though most now definitely decide what they will wear on a day-to-day basis and are, for the most part, the ones who decide what they will buy.

CARE OF ROOM: This is not a particularly cheerful subject. Most young people's rooms even through fourteen, or later, especially with boys, are nowhere near up to parental standards. Though the cans of worms, half-eaten apples, Coke bottles, comic books, and dirty socks of the twelve- and thirteen-year-old may be slightly less conspicuous by fourteen and after, there are many fifteens and sixteens whose rooms are still a mess.

WORK AND MONEY: Ten-year-olds, for all their basic good nature and friendliness, are not really good about helping around the house. "I hate it," they admit frankly. "Never does a thing unless you make a real issue of it," parents report. Still, they are not ugly about their noncooperativeness. They would just rather not do any work.

Elevens are something else again. "Tasks he has done willingly for years are now easier for me to do myself," a mother will tell you.

Any Eleven will not only do as little work as possible but will make maximum fuss about anything he is forced to do.

Twelves have reached the level of maturity at which some can say of work to be done, "Might as well do it the first time she asks. Have to, anyway." Of Thirteen a mother may say, "She can do her share without too much resistance. At least much of the time." Some Fourteens can go so far as to say, in talking about household chores or yard work, "My responsibilities are . . ."

Allowance: Allowance increases with age as, if one is fortunate, does responsibility about the use of money. Now and then one runs into a young person who is extremely "good" about money, not only saving but earning. There are some boys, especially, who can always be counted on for ready cash when everyone else in the family has run out. At the opposite extreme are those spendthrifts who never have enough money, no matter how big their allowance.

Most, today as in the past, feel that their allowance is pitifully small and their family tightwads. The situation is made worse in those cases where parents simply cannot believe the amount of money it takes a teenager to get through the week. Inflation proceeds so rapidly these days that we hesitate to give a presumed average amount of allowance for the different ages.

GROWTH GRADIENTS

1. Eating

10 Years

APPETITE: The majority "love food—eat tons—eat constantly," though many express this quite casually: "Sometimes I like to eat, sometimes I don't."

Even poor eaters have usually improved. They eat more, will try some new foods, will eat cooking other than mother's.

Many, however, do not eat a big breakfast.

PREFERENCES AND REFUSALS: Related with enthusiasm—eyes sparkle as they tell of likes, gesture of vomiting as they describe disliked foods. Variety of likes greater than dislikes.

Favorites: "Any kind of meat" (especially steak, roast beef, hamburgers and hot dogs, chicken, lamb chops). "Any kind of potatoes" (baked, mashed, French fried). Raw vegetables, especially carrots, tomatoes, celery. Cooked peas. Cake and ice cream.

Refusals: Liver (almost universally), fish, eggs. Cooked vegetables—

carrots, onions, celery, tomatoes, cauliflower, cabbage, asparagus. "Mixed things like stew." Some dislike desserts, and some turn against that old favorite, peanut butter.

SNACKS AND SWEETS: The majority eat between meals, and even the self-styled abstainers may eat a little. Quote mother in relation to this: "I can have all the cider I want between meals—it's good for me, my mother says."

Favorite between-meal snacks are soft drinks, cookies, especially fruit cookies, and fruit.

Marked individual differences in liking sweets. Some crave them, have a "terrific sweet tooth." Some are not interested. Others like them but try to cut down because of teeth or weight or parents' restrictions. Ice cream is among the favorites; candy and pie are not.

TABLE MANNERS: About half of our group are described as having adequate manners, and they themselves say their manners are "not mentioned" by parents. Of the rest, some are described as "bad" or even "terrible."

Poor posture is the greatest complaint. Also criticizing food, holding fork incorrectly, talking too much. Some children criticize table manners of parents.

Mother may let up on them when father is not present. Children try to do better when father is there.

COOKING: Considerable enthusiasm about cooking in boys as well as girls. About a quarter of our subjects do some cooking. Bacon, eggs, hamburgers, or hot dogs are the chief foods cooked. Some even try cakes or pancakes.

11 Years

APPETITE: Eating is a real pleasure to most. They spontaneously state, "I love to eat," and their parents say, "He will eat most anything." But in a few, appetite has fallen off and they are "finicky" or "picky."

Children themselves are aware that they are eating more (or less) than last year, and comment on the relation between amount eaten and their own size.

Daily variation in appetite: hungry some days and not others; will eat certain foods one day, then not on another. Many comment that they don't like to eat or even look at food when they are full, or that some foods take away their appetite.

PREFERENCES AND REFUSALS: Very definite tastes: "I love . . ." The widest variety of preferences of any age, yet much uniformity in preferences from child to child. With interest in cost of food, may say they like to eat "expensive things." Most mention only one or two dislikes, which may be determined by texture.

Favorites: Meat—especially rare or raw (steak, roast beef, hamburgers, hot dogs, chops). Potatoes—any kind, but especially French fried or mashed. Spaghetti. Fried foods. Corn and peas. Desserts—candy, ice cream, cake, pie.

Refusals: Liver. Vegetables: squash, turnips, broccoli, asparagus, cabbage, onions—raw or cooked. (Dislike of cooked celery, carrots, tomatoes less marked than earlier.) "All kinds of fish." Casseroles, creamed foods, mayonnaise.

SNACKS AND SWEETS: Nearly all eat between meals: "I come home from school and I'm *starved.*" Most parents do not prohibit this, but try to control amount and selection to some extent.

Favorites are soft drinks, cookies, fruit, milk, "cookies and milk."

A few eat when bored or lonesome, and some others eat at bedtime.

Relatively little mention by parents of children's craving for sweets, but cake and ice cream are still the great favorites.

TABLE MANNERS: Those with good manners slightly outnumber those considered bad-mannered. Parents describe the largest number as "fair," and they themselves say manners are not mentioned. A few report, "When I'm at home my manners are perfectly *awful.*"

A variety of parental complaints occur at this age, but the major ones are: poor posture, elbows on the table, eating with fingers, criticizing food, knocking things over, eating too fast or too noisily, talking too much.

Interest in own speed of eating and in who finishes first.

Most try to do better in presence of company or at a restaurant, even eating a little of a disliked food. Where Ten said, "She makes me eat things I dislike," Eleven may say, "I try to eat a little of things I dislike."

COOKING: An age of enthusiasm about this for about half our group, as many boys as girls: "Love to cook—may sound funny for a boy." Chief foods prepared are eggs, hamburgers or hot dogs or other meats, cookies and cakes, but anxious to try new things.

12 Years

APPETITE: "Tremendous" is the parents' word for Twelve's appetite. "Enormous eater—always hungry—no end to his appetite." Amount consumed may strike some parents as awesome—or repulsive. Twelve is no longer called "finicky"; no longer mentions feeling full.

A few try to diet to lose weight.

PREFERENCES AND REFUSALS: Many more likes than dislikes. May have few or no refusals; some like "everything." More varied mention of favorites (fried apples, mushrooms, watermelon, artichokes). More ability to generalize, especially about dislikes: "anything creamed—any kind of seafood—anything with fat or gristle." Wants things attractively served.

Favorites: Mashed potatoes with gravy. Steak, hot dogs, hamburgers, roast beef. Sweets—cake and ice cream. Peas and corn. Fruits. *Plain* things. ("Why have hash when you can have hamburger? Fancy food is ridiculous.")

Refusals: Fish, asparagus, cabbage, broccoli, squash, turnips, spinach, eggs.

SNACKS AND SWEETS: By far the majority eat between meals. More eating just before bedtime than occurred at earlier ages.

Favorite snacks are cookies, soft drinks, candy, "crackers with stuff on them."

A stronger age than eleven for sweets. Some are said to eat them constantly, and, next to potatoes and steak, sweets are the most preferred food.

TABLE MANNERS: Twice as many of our subjects were reported to have adequate manners as poor ones; none were described as "terrible." For most, manners are considered "fair." Parents comment less on manners.

Poor posture and elbows on the table are the major complaints, along with holding the fork incorrectly and talking with a full mouth.

Tries to do better—to eat a little of disliked foods; to "leave some for others" of favorite foods.

COOKING: Less cooking. Girls' enthusiasm continues more than boys', but less "I love to cook" and more "Yes, I do, a little bit." Favorite things to prepare are eggs, flapjacks or waffles, hamburgers and hot dogs, other kinds of meat.

13 Years

APPETITE: Our group divides between those who are still enormous eaters ("eats like a horse—anything and everything—can't fill her up") and those whose appetites are slightly less ("not three or four helpings anymore—only two, and sometimes only one"). Even the relatively small eaters usually come back for seconds, and mothers seldom worry now about how little is consumed.

Food, however, even for some of the bigger eaters, is not the absorbing interest it was earlier. Less enthusiasm and more matter-of-factness about eating.

Unevenness of appetite—hearty eating in spells, or only of favored foods.

Some comment about dieting (some girls at this age look potbellied), but little actual dieting.

PREFERENCES AND REFUSALS: Fewest likes mentioned, and thirteen is the only age at which more different dislikes than likes are named. Some odd dietary notions prevail—one girl "balances things inside" by eating sour apples, then sweet cake. More generalized expressions of preferences—fruits, vegetables, meats, starches, fats, chocolate things.

Favorites: Steak (by far). French fries, hamburgers, hot dogs, chicken, fruit, ice cream, desserts, beans, carrots, peas, corn.

Refusals: Liver. Vegetables—cooked celery, beets, cabbage, spinach, stewed tomatoes, turnips, squash, parsnips, asparagus, broccoli, onions, and (by many) beans—baked, lima, and "those awful string beans."

SNACKS AND SWEETS: Between-meals eating is almost universal, and with some is almost constant—"I'm always hungry, every minute of the day." Pre-bedtime snack is very common, and often eating just before and just after meals. Favorites are soft drinks, cookies, fruit.

In general, there is less eating of sweets than at twelve, but great variation. Some crave sweets; others are not much interested and prefer fruit. Some would like sweets but are "pretty good" about not eating them.

TABLE MANNERS: Said to be improved. Less trouble at the table and much less fuss and confusion. Chief complaints are talking too much and poor posture. Fathers may complain more than do mothers.

COOKING: Only about a third of our group now express interest in cooking. Interest seems less experimental and more practical than earlier. As in athletics, many show interest earlier, then later interest narrows down to those with some ability. Most frequently prepared are eggs, hamburgers, hot dogs, cake.

14 Years

APPETITE: Appetite again (or still) is very large in the majority: "Eats everything—great quantities—never full—endless appetite." Considerably interested in food: "Food was the best thing about the party [or the movies]."

Again, some try to diet.

PREFERENCES AND REFUSALS: Likes again exceed dislikes and are more generalized ("seafoods," "starches," "all the protein foods"), while dislikes are more specific. Some say they like "everything" or just "food." Some are becoming critical of meals served, type of food, how it is cooked, and report that disliked foods "nauseate" them. Liken their tastes to those of others ("I dislike good old spinach. Did you ever hear of anybody who liked it?" Or, "Liver—all kids dislike that").

Favorites: Ice cream and steak (by far). Fruit, milk (much relished by many), turkey, chicken, seafood, potatoes (all kinds, mashed best), sweets, cake. Also hamburgers, roast beef, sandwiches, pie. Some strong-flavored foods—catsup, horseradish, sardines.

Refusals: Similar to thirteen—liver, fish, hash, spinach, turnip, cabbage, broccoli, brussels sprouts, artichokes, cooked onions, celery, squash. "Odd-tasting" things—caviar, French pastry, headcheese, sauerkraut.

SNACKS AND SWEETS: Nearly all eat between meals, some constantly, especially right before or after meals, after school, before bedtime. Some eat when lonesome or sad.

The social, away-from-home aspect of eating is beginning—something to eat at the ice cream shop, fast food restaurants.

Favorites are dairy concoctions, soft drinks, fruit, and milk. Some eat a lot of candy, but more, though strong on desserts and sundaes, do not. Some just don't like sweets, but many believe candy is bad for teeth, complexion, or weight, and feel appearance and health are more important than sweet tooth.

TABLE MANNERS: Many no longer mention manners, though about as many as at thirteen are still "bad" or only "fair." Poor posture and eating with fingers are the main complaints.

May contribute little to mealtime atmosphere—criticize food, either talk too much or answer in monosyllables, argue with father. Disagree if he says they should be forced to eat disliked foods or complains of their manners. Argue as to whether elbows are permissible on table or not.

COOKING: An increase again, nearly half doing some cooking—boys as well as girls. Several comment that it is important to know how to cook, but earlier enthusiasm is largely lacking. Some say they can if they must but don't enjoy it much; others have to cook—like it or not—especially breakfast. Some like the social aspect—like to cook *for* others.

Foods prepared most are meats, eggs, cookies, cake. Some can make simple meals. Criticize their own cooking rather specifically.

Their statements may contradict themselves ("No cooking. Well, I might just make some cookies or something like that") or may conflict with mother's statement (mother reports no interest in cooking; girl says she likes to cook, prepares whole meals).

2. Clothes

10 Years

BUYING CLOTHES: Mother and child shop together. Though to some extent consulting child's taste, mother decides which clothes to buy, and most children accept this. Some hate trying on clothes in the store. But in general not too many arguments.

DAILY SELECTION: Most select their own clothes for wear in the morning, but mother usually checks and may even lay clothes out. Some battles over what is "suitable" clothing. Several hate the idea of wearing new clothes or dressing up. Though some might mention that they are fat or thin, most are not particularly concerned about their own appearance.

CARE OF CLOTHES: The majority are extremely careless about the care of clothes. Outer garments are flung down anywhere. Other clothes are dropped where they are removed, "just slung around," or at best piled on a chair. Most don't notice or mind if their clothes are dirty and do not report tears.

11 Years

BUYING CLOTHES: Child has more say than earlier. Most accompany mother for buying the more important clothes. Girls may go alone to buy less important things, while boys more often let mother buy them. Some complain about stores: "too confusing," "awfully hot," "got all mixed up."

If disagreement with mother occurs, the decision may go either way. The extremes range from: "Mother goes with me, but I decide" to "Sometimes mother makes me get something I don't like. I get used to it though."

DAILY SELECTION: About half our group decide what to wear (except for special occasions); half still ask what to put on.

Children are beginning, if they did not earlier, to have very definite ideas about what they will or will not wear and may refuse clothes they dislike. "If I don't like them I don't wear them, period." But a few show only glimmers of this interest, and many prefer old clothes or would wear "all colors of the rainbow."

CARE OF CLOTHES: Interest in care of clothes lags far behind responsibility in buying or selection. Eleven drops them on the floor as he removes them, "just steps out of them and leaves them," throws them at a chair or hamper, or piles them on chair or bed, but does not hang them up. A few put dirty clothes into the hamper.

12 Years

BUYING CLOTHES: Fewer issues occur than did earlier, and shopping is a more cooperative venture: "We pick clothes out together." If real disagreement occurred, mother would probably win, but most work it out together. Each has more respect for the other's taste: "She knows if it's a good thing or not, but I know what the kids wear." Some respect mother's taste in general but are stubborn about a few things.

At the extremes, some boys still allow mother to do all the shopping; some girls shop alone. Most prefer to have mother along. A stronger need than earlier is felt about trying things on before buying.

Wanting clothes like everyone else is at least beginning, and in many is very strong.

DAILY SELECTION: A marked change appears. Most girls and some boys take great interest in their own appearance, though blue jeans are a great leveler. Many girls dislike wearing dresses.

Many still consult mother about what they plan to wear and whether clothes are clean enough. Girls are generally quite responsible about changing underwear and socks frequently. Boys more often like dirty as well as clean clothes; old as well as new.

CARE OF CLOTHES: Interest in looking nice seldom extends to *care* of clothes. Some can take responsibility for putting dirty clothes into the hamper, and a few hang up outdoor clothing; but mostly clothes are just piled on bed, couch, or chair.

13 Years

BUYING CLOTHES: For many, this is the last age when mother generally makes the final decision. Mostly there is good agreement and appreciation of each other's taste, especially if mother recognizes the child's need to wear what others are wearing. Often shopping goes more smoothly with girls than with boys.

Less important items are frequently bought alone. Some mothers allow the child to go and scout around, then go along for the final decision. If mother brings things home, it is definitely on approval.

Girls, especially, are showing more specific taste: color, style, what friends wear.

DAILY SELECTION: Most select their own clothes for daily wear. Interest in personal appearance increases, some becoming quite narcissistic. Many girls and even some boys are described as "meticulous."

CARE OF CLOTHES: Though the extremes range from "has never hung up one garment in his life, to my knowledge" to "even presses his own clothes," carefulness has generally begun, especially in girls, to extend to care of clothes as well as of self. Best clothes more often are hung up on hangers, other clothes on doorknobs or backs of chairs. Shoes still under the bed or "right where he took them off."

Some are good about selecting clean clothes and putting dirty ones in the laundry.

14 Years

BUYING CLOTHES: Many girls and boys are now allowed to make the final decisions but nevertheless prefer to have mother along when shopping, and in case of serious disagreement will try to compromise. More disagreements occur with boys, who may speak of "winning out" or "losing," where girls more often speak of agreement or compromise.

A few shop alone, and some have a clothes allowance.

DAILY SELECTION: Both sexes "love" certain clothes, and boys take pleasure in looking "sharp." Girls may have reached the "clean stage"—cold cream, deodorant. Boys may now be careful about shining shoes and changing shirts daily.

CARE OF CLOTHES: Many, but not all, hang up their clothes fairly consistently (though not always on hangers—may all be hung on same hook). Girls are more often careful than boys, and some are "fastidious" about care of clothes as well as about their own appearance. Some show inconsistency—hanging things up one day, not the next; meticulous, then sloppy.

Many are very careful about clothes—dirty ones into hamper or to cleaner's. Some girls take all responsibility for clothes, wash out their own underwear and sweaters. Responsibility ranges from a few (including girls) who do not even report tears in clothing to a few (including boys) who sew on their own buttons.

3. Care of Room
10 Years

Rooms, on the whole, are very messy. Clothes just slung around all over everything, shoes on floor, desk piled high. Many say they *prefer* rooms this way. May dislike "a made bed."

Spasmodic cleaning, parent-instigated.

Some pennants or pictures on walls but most rooms are not "fixed up" very specially.

11 Years

Room is still very messy: clothes piled on bed or left on floor, desk piled high. "A terrible mess, awfully untidy"—parents express great dissatisfaction.

A few children say that they *try* to keep rooms neat. Most apparently do not try very hard. Many report they want things left messy: "I don't like my mother to move stuff without telling me, whether it is on the floor or not."

Many now have room fixed up elaborately: banners, posters, stickers; pictures on the walls of athletes, rock or movie stars, or horses.

Occasional spurts of cleaning, parent-instigated.

12 Years

Little improvement. "Messiest room in the house"; "A shambles. Top of the desk littered—can of worms, half-eaten apple, candy wrappers, dirty socks." Clothes still all over the room; litter of collections, systematic or otherwise.

With some boys, mothers have given up and clean room themselves. With others, and with girls, a weekly cleanup is usually instigated.

Much "fixing up" of room: pennants, pictures of rock stars, athletes, horses, bulletin boards, wildlife posters.

13 Years

The bedroom—"my own room"—was important earlier; but now is even more so. Many spend most of their spare time in it. In some cases it is a little neater, but mothers still complain: "cluttered," "careless," "sloppy." Some Thirteens try to clean up spontaneously but complain that it gets messy again right away. Child may be satisfied, but parent rarely is.

Some rooms fairly tidy except inside bureau drawers and closet and on desk.

Decorations (banners, pictures, etc.) still very important.

"Hermits" who live in their rooms may have them quite elaborately equipped with food and provisions for entertainment.

14 Years

Care of room usually lags far behind care for own appearance and clothes.

Children themselves are mostly satisfied with their care of room; parents are less so. Our group is about equally divided between those who keep their rooms reasonably neat and those who do not. Girls are a little more often in the neat half than boys are.

Some are beginning to want their rooms to be neat, though they do not always achieve this. They may forget from time to time, or only parts of the room are kept tidy.

4. Work
10 Years

Most are not good about helping at home: "I hate it"; "I'm tired and I don't want to help"; "Not too good at it." Parents say, "Never does a thing without groaning." Slow about responding to requests for help: delay, object, dawdle. Most do not openly rebel.

Most work best away from home. Boys do better outdoors than indoors.

Some are paid for work; others are expected to work in return for allowance. Among regular tasks: set table, do dishes, make bed, clean room, take out trash or garbage, mow lawn, garden, shovel snow, sweep, dust, feed dog. Some care for younger siblings, but most do not yet baby-sit outside of home.

11 Years

Most are even worse about helping than at ten. Nearly all have to be reminded about tasks. Some merely sigh, fuss, groan, delay. Others resist, argue, rebel: "Like heck I'm nice about working. Quick and prompt? I'm just the opposite!"

Mothers say that tasks formerly accepted now become major issues and many wonder, "Is it worth it?"

Tries to get out of tasks if possible. Works slowly, resentfully, messily. "In a minute" stronger than at ten. Also, "Do I have to?"

Home tasks about the same as at ten years.

As at ten, better away from home. Some do a little baby-sitting away from home, in the afternoons mostly. Boys do outdoor work away from home.

12 Years

Still reluctant about helping but most now resigned: *"Might as well do it the first time she asks. Have to anyway,"* Or, "If she wants to, she can make me." Most don't volunteer but will help if asked or if they have a schedule. Resistance may be silent: "I do it, but I pout to myself."

About one fourth of our subjects do baby-sitting. Almost as many boys as girls do sitting, and Twelves sit at night as well as in the afternoon.

Boys' tasks at home include: mowing lawns, shoveling snow, odd jobs, burning papers, raking leaves, clearing out the garage, errands, washing car, making own bed, emptying wastebaskets, washing dishes. Usually better at outdoor than at indoor work.

Girls' tasks at home include: doing dishes, making beds, cleaning own room, vacuuming, dusting, a little simple cooking and ironing, baby-sitting. Their chief work outside of home is baby-sitting.

If no boys in the home, girls do some outside work. Boys often do some inside work, but in most families the tasks of the two sexes remain differentiated.

13 Years

Most are now much better about helping. Not enthusiastic but at least willing. "Quite good about helping though I may say, 'In a minute.' " May say, "I do it voluntarily"; "I'm responsible for my room"; "I'm determined to improve about helping"; even, "Some of the things I like to do." May even offer to help when not asked or required.

Parents say, "She can do her share without resisting, dawdling, getting in the way."

Many, boys as well as girls, now do steady baby-sitting at home. Tasks are about as at twelve, except that girls now often prepare a simple meal, and boys are starting to do caddying.

14 Years

Helping around the house is now less of a problem. Tasks are taken for granted by many: "My responsibilities are . . ." May not be enthusiastic about helping but do it more or less routinely; less delay and fewer objections than earlier.

Most do not take as much responsibility as parents think they should. But some mothers feel that Fourteens are very busy with school and outside activities, and actually make fewer demands on them than earlier.

Nearly half of our subjects supplement allowance with earnings from outside work. Paper route, caddying, baby-sitting, and working in stores are the most common activities. Most are very responsible about such outside work.

chapter eleven
EMOTIONS

Adolescence is for many a time of emotional storm and stress. This opinion is disputed by some (probably nonparents), who argue that if society behaved in a supportive way the adolescent ages need not, after all, be particularly difficult for all concerned.

Margaret Mead's (now questioned) *Coming of Age in Samoa* to some extent supported the environmental notion—that children could grow up easily and comfortably if only society did not throw roadblocks in their way. With all respect to Dr. Mead, we do maintain that in our American culture, at least, the teenage years in even the best of families tend to be a time of substantial discomfort for both family and child.

No single aspect of behavior totally determines what we may expect at any age. But in the years from ten to fourteen, it seems fair to say that the young person's sense of self, relation to parents, and emotions may be at least among the factors which most determine and define the behavior climate.

There are those who, like Piaget, define "cognition" or mental processes as somehow separate from the rest of behavior. We at the Gesell Institute do not make this differentiation. As Dr. Gesell often remarked, "Mind manifests itself in nearly every aspect of behavior."

It is the same with emotion. Though Benjamin Spock at one time criticized our work because, he claimed, we did not deal with emotion, to us emotions, like the mind, permeate every aspect of behavior. The calm, serene, well-adjusted individual who is not behaving "emotionally" in the dramatic sense of the word is nevertheless expressing one—very positive—aspect of emotional behavior.

Not only is each individual characterized by a certain kind of emotional makeup—calm, violent, well-adjusted, confused, even, uneven—but the ages themselves have their own emotional characteristics. As we have pointed out earlier, ages of equilibrium tend to alternate, as the years go by, with ages of disequilibrium. Ages of outwardized, ready-for-anything behavior alternate with in-wardized ages of withdrawal. Obviously, environmental factors play their part.

But allowing for the almost infinite number of possible variables, there appear to be certain rhythms of emotional change that are more or less inevitable in the years from ten to fourteen. Some of these have already been mentioned in the earlier chapters on the specific ages from ten to fourteen. Here we will highlight our find-ings on outstanding emotional characteristics of these years in boy or girl brought up in today's American culture.

Thus the abiding and pervasive goodwill of the ordinary ten-year-old colors everything about the child of this age. We have de-scribed ten years as a Golden Age—a time when child and environ-ment come into mutual harmony. This harmony is unquestionably a result of the extreme goodwill projected by the typical Ten on to others. It is hard to be unhappy in the face of Ten's belief that mother and father are just about perfect in every way, and that he or she loves them best of anything in the world. Ten is an age when many boys and girls may be described as "simple," "direct," "sin-cere," "confiding," and "friendly."

Not that all is serene. Ten is not a great worrier, but does still express a fair number of fears—some rational and some possibly less so. On the other side of the coin, Ten likes his or her little jokes—jokes often rather labored and obvious and not tremendously funny from the adult point of view. Punning, riddles, and many "corny" jokes make up the bulk of Ten's repertoire.

Ten, as we have observed it in most, is one of the least sad and the most happy ages. Almost anything seems to bring a smile and a good, warm response from the typical ten-year-old. The majority of our subjects describe themselves as being "really happy," and as simple a thing as going out after supper to play can be the cause of that happiness.

Ten is not a particularly competitive age, nor is it characterized by jealousy or a desire for revenge when things go wrong pervasive.

But all of this doesn't mean that every Ten is peaceful and happy all of the time. The best of children will be unhappy, upset, angry, resentful, rebellious at times. And when things go wrong with or for Ten, he lets you know it in unmistakable ways.

More just plain physical violence is expressed now than at any age which follows except for eleven and twelve. Nearly half of our ten-year-olds admit that when they are "really mad" they express this feeling in clearly physical ways. They stamp around, hit things, "break the place up." And more than one third admit to exploding and crying. Such explosions tend to be brief and only occasional, but they do occur.

Eleven, emotionally, is quite something else again. It is sometimes hard to believe that gentle, glorious, friendly Ten could turn, almost overnight as it sometimes seems, into often monstrous Eleven. Boy or girl of this age has good points, as we are quick to admit, but most parents will tell you that, at least much of the time, Eleven is not an easy age emotionally.

We think of Eleven as an age of tremendous emotional disequilibrium. Behavior seems to fly all to pieces in every direction. The child tends to be rude and resistant to parents, especially to mother. He or she would rather say "No" than "Yes," would rather reject than affirm. This age reminds us, in many ways, of that earlier time between five and a half and six when it was almost impossible to elicit any cooperation or assent from boy or girl. Scorn, refusal, negation, and criticism are basic emotional responses as well as rudeness and quarrelsomeness.

Parents describe their eleven-year-olds as sensitive, proud, egocentric, selfish, cooperative, belligerent, jealous, argumentative, contrary, uncooperative. Quite an indictment!

Eleven is given emotionally to vast exaggeration. And, characteristically, much of this exaggeration is negative. Things are "horrible," "dreadful," "the pits."

Bold as Eleven may seem on the outside, especially when he or she is telling mother, "No I won't," this is an age of rather considerable vulnerability. Both worries and fears—in this seemingly bold girl or boy—are rather excessive and can be the source of much unhappiness.

Even humor, of which there is a good deal, is not particularly amusing from the grown-up point of view. It tends to be corny, silly, and unattractively smutty, with bathroom humor high on the list.

Outside the home, especially at the homes of friends perhaps more than at school, the child of this age is reported to be polite, energetic, cooperative, and downright good company. Unfortunately, there is something about home and Eleven that does not bring out the best in a child's emotions.

Though Elevens tell us that they are already trying to conceal hurt feelings and touchy emotions—they say that if hurt they might just go away by themselves—when the emotion felt is anger there seems to be little effort to cover it up. Markedly more violent emotion tends to be expressed than at the age which just preceded. Sixty-one percent of our boys and girls admit to sheer physical expression of anger—hitting, kicking, stamping; and forty-one percent admit that if really angry, they cry or explode.

More on an even keel at Twelve and more positive toward the world, girls and boys alike are described by their parents as emotionally stable, accepting, smooth, tolerant. Hostility is diminished; cooperation and tolerance are vastly increased.

Emotions are characterized by more enthusiasm and vigor than by definition, though the child makes a good effort to control them but not always with success. Fifty-three percent of subjects still admit to outright physical expression of violence when angry, and twenty-six percent—more than at succeeding ages—admit that they still explode or cry when things go wrong. But Twelve, unlike an earlier self, can go quite far in the direction of violence and then rather quickly pull back into acceptance and equilibrium. Emotions are definitely coming under better control.

There comes a big, big change at thirteen. Twelve, happy or sad, tends to go out to meet the world emotionally. Thirteen is an age of withdrawal. Many spend much of their time in their own room—a complete physical withdrawal. Others simply withdraw emotionally —they look right through you. Even if their eyes are focused in your direction, they seem to film over with a cloud of not seeing you.

When your child is thirteen, you may become aware all of a sudden that you seldom see him or her around the house. And even when you do catch a glimpse, this child may not touch you much, emotionally, or allow himself or herself to be touched.

Thirteen may be best described by such words as "sad," "moody," "aloof," "withdrawing," "negative," "uncommunicative." Even when your child does something as positive as to become angry at you, the typical response now is to withdraw from the room. Forty-five percent of our subjects report this as their usual response when things upset them.

Thirteen, when he or she does reluctantly come into contact with others, seems to be emotionally sensitive and vulnerable, easily hurt, and easily angered. Though boy or girl of this age is certainly not without his or her happy hours and days, his hours of friendship, her hours of "fun" things to do—especially giggling with girl-friends—this is, in most, a less than happy, friendly, comfortable age.

And then if you are lucky, your typical fourteen-year-old really blossoms, "comes out of that temporary shell and looks around," as one mother put it—and for the most part likes what he or she sees. Emotions are once again not only on an even keel but are often highly positive.

Sunshine definitely follows rain at this point: emergence takes the place of withdrawal; cheerful contact replaces sullen, critical with-drawal. One may fairly describe the fourteen-year-old as expansive, outgoing, energetic, enthusiastic, positive, ready for anything.

This is neither a worrisome nor a fearful age in most, and humor abounds. Fourteens love the ridiculous, the incongruous, and when things go well seem able to see the funny side of almost anything. And almost any of the many, many new things they experience can make them happy.

Fourteen is, of course, not without his stormy moments, but even when angry, girl or boy may at least attempt to "sit and take it" without crying or exploding. Or they may try to "laugh it off."

When really angry, at least according to their own reporting or their parents' account, about an equal number just leave the scene or make some verbal retort. Physical violence or exploding or crying are at a minimum.

Our emphasis here, as in other chapters, has been primarily on the expected emotional characteristics of the various ages; that is, the expected developmental changes in emotions. It should also be em-phasized, however, that emotions vary not only with age but also from one individual to another.

Our own approach to individual differences follows that of Wil-liam Sheldon, whose system of Constitutional Psychology is based on the assumption that behavior is a function of structure and that, to a large extent, we behave as we do because of the way our bodies are built.

Thus the roundish, well-padded individual whom we call an *endo-morph* tends to be friendly, easygoing, and comfortable to be with. Unlike people of other physiques, children of this type tend to wear their hearts on their sleeves. They want people to know how they feel and will tell anyone all about everything. They give way, at all times, easily and naturally to their feelings, whatever these may be, and make no attempt to hide them. Emotions, though easily expressed, are not deep. Above all else, the endomorph loves peace. He or she will do anything to avoid an argument or trouble, is not competitive, and almost seems to prefer to keep out of the limelight. As a rule, the endomorphic child does not have temper tantrums.

Not so the heavily muscled *mesomorph*, who even when rather young is characterized emotionally by a love of power. Girl or boy loves to compete, to dominate, to command, and to conquer. Mesomorphs have great push, drive and energy, are not sensitive to the moods or feelings of others, and seem almost insensitive to pain. They are in fact usually highly courageous, like to be leaders, out in front. If angry or upset, they like to take it out on somebody, often on mother.

The sensitive, thin-skinned *ectomorph* is entirely different in his or her emotional expression from either of the others. The ectomorph overreacts to any emotional situation and may become quite nervous in even quite ordinary social situations. He or she is shy, aloof, and withdrawn. Doesn't want other people to know how he feels; suffers in silence. Much as they want to cry, if they break down in public they are terribly embarrassed. One of their greatest problems (but also one of their greatest assets) is their sensitivity and vulnerability. It causes them to suffer, but it also makes them aware of what other people may be going through. If miserable, they suffer inside themselves. Ectomorphs tend to be oversensitive to pain.

Thus, regardless of age, one may expect, in general, that some teenage girls and boys will be more outgoing and exuberant or more quiet and reserved than others. Some will quite normally have rather good control of their emotions and some will not.

A third variant which must be considered is the effect of the environment. In years past, the environment which has been considered has been chiefly that provided by other people. Clearly the boy or girl who has been raised in a happy, comfortable home has a better chance for happiness than the one raised under adverse circumstances.

Today we are also considering a quite different type of environmental stimulus which can affect emotions—that produced by the physical environment. Much consideration is now being given to the effect of foods we eat, the air we breathe, the allergens which often affect behavior adversely.

It is now appreciated by many that food can have an especially strong and often adverse effect on emotional behavior. Typical of the many informative books available on this subject is Lendon Smith's *Improving Your Child's Behavior Chemistry.*[15] Smith explains much of the violent, aggressive behavior which disturbs so many households as resulting from improper diet.

EMOTIONS AFFECTED BY FOOD CONSUMED

Most of us have experienced irritable feelings when hungry. The sudden change in feelings that comes with eating is especially striking in the infant, who may go from a desperate, angry, irritable howling to a mood of blissful tranquility within minutes of being fed.

The teenager is usually expected to achieve more or less adult control over anger or sadness provoked in part by hunger. Self-control is expected, but access to food is also easier. Helping oneself to what can be found in the refrigerator, being able to do one's own cooking, and, especially, having some pocket money to spend on food provides the young person with the means to avoid the very insistent hunger that dominates a rapidly growing body.

Now comes the question whether the emotions are affected by what we eat. Does it make a difference whether Thirteen, already moody and vulnerable, withdraws nutritionally to a diet of saturated fats, white flour and sugars, cheeseburgers, soft drinks, ice cream and candy?

Deficiencies of minerals, vitamins, and essential fatty acids are prevalent in large numbers of teenagers. These deficiencies tend to affect the overall equilibrium of a person long before they result in typical patterns of disease. The lack of equilibrium tends to be expressed in different ways in different individuals. The skin, the intestinal tract, and the nervous system are the busiest systems of the body and tend to be early indicators of nutritional stress of all kinds. But the specific symptoms of this stress may be dandruff and oily skin in one person; bumpy, patchy dry skin in another, and acne in a third; or depression, fatigue, restlessness, and hyperactivity in another; or diarrhea in one and constipation and gassiness in another. The nutrition-emotions question can be stated quite clearly and answered without qualification when it is applied to the individual: If a given child is showing extremes of emotions, could his or her diet have a significant role in making the situation better or worse? Yes!

JERRY

After hearing us lecture on the subject, a psychologist who was a colleague in an institution for young people where we served as consultants asked us about his fourteen-year-old son, Jerry. Jerry was doing good work in school, had good friends, smoked a little pot, had experimented with alcohol but claimed to his parents not to like the taste. He slept well and looked healthy to his father. We asked about his hair (long and well-tended), skin (a few "zits"), and nails (bitten), but our "consultation" took place in a hallway outside a lecture room, and we never actually met Jerry. The problem was his moods. Like many typical late Fourteens, Jerry had ups and downs—hard on his parents when he was up and on himself when he was down. And he had a particularly irritable (and irritating) quality about him, as if, as his father put it, "one of his motors was in high gear."

Jerry's father's question was, "Could Jerry's being a junk food junkie have anything to do with his emotional pitch?" The answer, yes, had already been presented in our lecture, but the real question was how to find out, especially since Jerry was somewhat famous for his intake of sweetened, processed, colored, preserved, and thoroughly dead food. Except for sweet rolls, ice cream, and soft drinks, which were available at home, most of his junk intake came from outside sources, purchased with his own hard-earned money. Our lecture had overwhelmed Jerry's father with possibilities: food allergy, vitamin deficiencies, mineral deficiencies, essential fatty acid deficiencies, the chemical effects of natural and artificial food substances—and it seemed hopeless to get a basically healthy and maybe even completely "normal" fourteen-year-old to make major changes in his diet or undergo a lot of expensive laboratory tests.

The answer could only take Jerry's father to the first step, to see if Jerry would be willing to go off junk food for five days. Jerry's willingness to do so for five days (in return for a modest cash bribe) was evidence and support of the notion that he was basically "a good kid." And the results were spectacular. Jerry himself declared that even the withdrawal symptoms—insomnia, achiness, and profound fatigue—were worth the discovery that he could be "a different person" by avoiding junk food.

GROWTH GRADIENTS

1. Emotions in General

10 Years

Ten is seen by his parents as direct, matter-of-fact, simple, clear-cut, childish. Generally easygoing and balanced.

Some fears persist, but Ten is less anxious, exacting, and demanding than he was at nine. Seldom cries and reports that he or she is "real happy."

Anger is not frequent, but is violent, immediate, expressed physically, and soon resolved. Humor is broad, labored, not generally funny to adults.

11 Years

Eleven is described by parents as penetrating, sensitive, proud, selfish, competitive, belligerent, jealous, resentful, argumentative, contrary, rude, uncooperative.

Yet with other adults the child can be polite, factual, serious, honest, sincere, confiding, unguarded.

Dramatizes and exaggerates his expressions ("never had a decent Christmas"; "worst mother in the whole school, and everybody says so").

Response to anger is frequent, violent, physical, emotional, and verbal. Humor is lively, "corny," often smutty. Many fears, many worries, many tears—yet most think of themselves as happy.

12 Years

Twelve is viewed as expansive, outgoing, enthusiastic, overgenerous. Described by parents as good company, friendly, understanding, thoughtful, likable, reasonable.

Relatively uncomplicated—many fears, but fewer worries, less jealousy, little crying. Great enthusiasm for things he likes; utter hatred for things he dislikes. *Loves* or *hates;* no middle ground.

Deals with others and can be dealt with through humor, which is now funnier to adults, though drawing on insult, sex, and practical jokes.

13 Years

Thirteen is described by parents as thoughtful, inwardized, quiet, self-contained. This may go to extremes, and then the child is described as withdrawn, morbid, morose, moody, secretive, lethargic, indifferent, sullen, reclusive, "in a minor key," "a regular hermit."

Extremely sensitive and vulnerable—easily hurt, irritated, or annoyed. In anger, wants to go off alone to his or her own room. Many cry on occasion. Humor is less frequent and leans on sarcasm, but is more amusing to adults.

14 Years

Fourteen is expansive and outgoing, energetic and enthusiastic. He is much less withdrawn and appears much happier than at thirteen. Loves competition. Anger is less frequent and is manifested verbally rather than physically or by withdrawal. Humor (other than parents') is much appreciated.

Fourteen actually may experience more inner confusion and turmoil than his or her independent, self-assured manner might indicate.

2. Anger

10 Years

Ten is not a characteristically angry age. Tens say they try to keep their tempers and, more than at following ages, say they don't get mad or don't do anything about it when angry.

But response to anger, when it comes, is violent and immediate. Most commonly its expression is physical: "beat them up," "sock them," "hit and kick and bite," "kick the place around." Next most common is some kind of emotional violence: "blow up," "explode," "boil over," "get so *mad* I could kill people." More cry in anger than at any following age.

Already a few leave the room or go away by themselves when angry. Even this is usually preceded by some token of violence: "stamp my foot and go to my room," "boil over and go to my room." Responding merely verbally also occurs, but less often than at following ages. Though verbal, the responses are nonetheless violent—Tens yell, screech, call names: "You're a bitch!" They shout back if sent from the room. A considerable number plot revenge, though they seldom remember to carry this out.

Most say their response depends on whom they are mad at. If at parents, some can't do much; some boil over. If at friends or siblings, there is usually physical violence. If at teachers, they "can't do anything" or "just tell the other kids."

In summary, *physical* and *emotional* violence predominate at this age.

11 Years

Eleven's anger is aroused far more often than Ten's. (Nearly twice as many anger responses are reported at eleven than at any other age in our range.)

Physical violence is even more prominent than at ten and is, by far, the most common response. Children fight, hit, slam doors. Emotional violence too reaches its high point, and the angry eleven-year-old is likely to "blow his top." Nearly as much crying occurs as it did at ten.

Violent retorts are also common: yelling, swearing, calling names, saying mean or sarcastic things, or snapping back. Leaving the room, though a less common response for Elevens, still occurs more than at ten or twelve, and occurs violently as "stamping" or "slamming out of the room." Pouting, sulking, and planning revenge are also characteristic.

When angry at a teacher, the majority say they just sit and take it, "just burn up inside," or else write notes about her and pass them.

Thus, *physical violence,* some *violent retort,* and *leaving the room* all occur conspicuously, in that order, at eleven.

12 Years

This is the last age when immediate physical violence is the most characteristically reported response to anger. Twelve still may fight, strike out physically, or take some less common action such as throwing things (for which this is the leading age).

Verbal response to the situation is now more common than earlier. Twelves talk back, "tell her off," "just talk nasty." They may call names, and some mutter under their breath.

Boiling over or exploding occurs, but less commonly, and there is less crying than earlier. Some just "sit and seethe." Some, though fewer than at surrounding ages, simply leave the room. Most can now do this without slamming the door.

If angry at a teacher, Twelve reports, "I tell her to shut up in my mind"; "I say, 'Shut up, you old mole,' or, 'Drop dead.' "

Thus *physical violence* and *angry verbal retort* are the leading types of response.

13 Years

Thirteen brings a marked change. By far the most characteristic response is to leave the scene, often to go to their own rooms and close the door.

Some kind of verbal response is the next most common. This retort is less violent than earlier—there is little shouting and screaming, and even less talking back. For the most part thirteen-year-olds merely say mean or sarcastic things. A few swear or argue.

Sulking is a common response and quite a number do cry, but

there is much less "blowing up" and "boiling over." Scowling, frowning, and making faces are characteristic of thirteen.

Behaviors not easily reported are deflected responses to anger—taking it out on someone else (especially on mother) or even getting mad at themselves for getting mad at others.

A large number say that they never get mad, or that even when they do there is nothing they do, or can do, about it. Some say they "just sit and think about it."

Anger at a teacher most often results in practical jokes or making faces. In general, leaving the scene is the most common response at thirteen.

14 Years

Anger responses, as reported, are greatly reduced in number at fourteen. Highly characteristic of the age is the remark, "I just sit and take it."

The usual responses at fourteen, and following, are verbal ones. Physical violence seldom occurs, and emotional violence, including crying, is much less frequent than formerly. However, verbal responses may be quite violent. Fourteen may yell, swear, call names, or just say mean or sarcastic things. Talking back and snapping back often occur.

Leaving the room when angry—often to go to own room—occurs as often as a harsh retort. Some may mutter, slam the door, even lock themselves in.

Quite a few take it out on someone else (especially on mother) or try to make the person at whom they are angry feel uncomfortable. A few now do nothing immediately, but later talk the situation over with some friend or with the person himself.

Fourteen, if angry at a teacher, will "grin and bear it" or "talk to myself."

The leading responses at fourteen are leaving the room and making some verbal response.

3. Worries and Fears

10 Years

WORRIES: Fewer worries than fears. The main worries at all ages from ten to fourteen concern school, and nearly all worries at this age center around homework, lessons, and being late. A few worry about family finances and the cost of food—a concern which lessens in later adolescence.

FEARS: Many different kinds of fears are reported, but fewer than in the age immediately following. Animals, especially wild ones and snakes, are mentioned most; the dark is feared by many. Also high places, fires, criminals, "killers," burglars.

A few are spontaneously beginning to mention things they are not afraid of—chiefly the dark, dogs, and being left alone.

11 Years

WORRIES: The most worried as well as one of the most fearful ages. As usual, the most fears deal with school, homework, and lessons. Money, mother's welfare, and own health are other frequent worries. Several also mention family relations, father's driving, and world conditions.

FEARS: Eleven and twelve are the most fearful ages in this age range. Animals are the most feared—snakes, bugs, cows or bulls. The dark, especially being left alone in the dark, is next most frequent, and high places are often mentioned.

More at this age than any other spontaneously tell what they do *not* fear—chiefly the dark and snakes.

12 Years

WORRIES: Fewer worries than at eleven, with school still the main source. Money and health have dropped out in favor of social worries—family relations, that people may not like them, or that they may make a bad impression.

FEARS: Another relatively fearful age. Being alone in the dark or being out in it are mentioned most. Next, some animals, especially snakes; then crowds and high places.

Some say their fears are "silly" or "disgusting," but they still have them. Again, many spontaneously list things not feared—chiefly dogs and heights.

13 Years

WORRIES: At thirteen and fourteen, more worries are reported than fears. Most worries still center around homework and lessons, with more concern over grades than at any other age. Other main concerns are mother's welfare, own appearance, and, for girls, their relationships with boys.

FEARS: Much less fearfulness (our group reports about half as many fears as at twelve). The dark definitely leads, followed by fears of crowds and of high places. Animals are less feared than formerly, though snakes are still mentioned by many.

New social kinds of fears are beginning: "people," "applying for a job," "performing in public," "family quarreling," "gossip," "going out on a date."

Fewer children need to mention spontaneously the things they do *not* fear. However, quite a few make such modifying remarks as, "not exactly afraid of it, but don't like it very well."

A few enjoy scaring themselves with frightening thoughts.

14 Years

WORRIES: As at thirteen, worries exceed fears. School is still the chief source of worry, though less so than earlier. World conditions are now a source of worries, though these are exceeded by more personal social worries: "my appearance" or "that people might not like me, or I might make a bad impression."

FEARS: The fewest fears are reported at this age. Animals (especially snakes), dark, high places—all are feared about equally. As at thirteen, social fears are mentioned: applying for a job, performing in public, gossip.

4. Humor

10 Years

Humor is mostly obvious, often heavy and labored, and not usually funny from an adult point of view. Cannot understand why no one laughs. Asks, "Get it?" Explains joke.

Most cannot take a joke on themselves or any kidding; are afraid someone will make fun of them.

Practical jokes. Jokes about each other's names. Considerable punning. Riddles.

When repeating jokes of others, apt to tell them badly, omit salient parts, miss the point. May repeat dirty jokes to mother, often not understanding them.

11 Years

Humor is now lively, "corny," and often smutty. The majority are reported by parents to have a good sense of humor; and many like to amuse others, adults as well as contemporaries.

Eleven shows spontaneous interest in whether others, especially teachers, have a good sense of humor. Parents' humor, especially father's, is usually much more appreciated now than it will later be.

Most like practical jokes, laugh at misbehavior in school ("Throwing apple cores and erasers is funny"), clown, say silly things, mildly insult each other ("Say it, don't spray it").

Cartoons and funnies, movie, radio, and TV comedies are much enjoyed. Puns and limericks are also appreciated. "Deadpan" humor (girl sees picture of microscope in book on biology and says, "Oh, it tells how microscopes have babies").

Smutty humor chiefly concerns elimination ("A blizzard of birds"; "Aren't you glad elephants don't fly?"; "European—Oh, no I'm not." Boys laugh coarsely at mention of horses and start to say, "Sh . . ."). Girls often object to the dirty jokes of boys at school and say they like clean jokes.

12 Years

Humor is becoming funnier from an adult point of view. Most Twelves appreciate adults' humor, and many can carry on quite humorous banter with adults.

May criticize parent under guise of humor ("What a physique!" to father, or semisarcastic jokes about father's reported athletic prowess when younger).

Practical joking continues (calling for taxi to be sent to other people's houses) and increases in many, though a few start to outgrow this. Clowning around and insulting friends runs high ("You look like Frankenstein. Anybody looking at you would die"). Some "kid" each other about the opposite sex—may even "kid" a dog about *his* girlfriend.

Less interest in funnies, but much enjoyment of magazine cartoons as in *Mad* magazine. Some still pun, but some already groan "Oh, no!" if others do.

Some make dry, humorous remarks against themselves or their own products if praised (sarcastically, "Great!"; "Genius at work—I could sell this idea for a million dollars").

Smutty humor is now more about sex (butcher's sign in boy's room: "Legs and breasts, $1.99"), though some elimination humor continued. Much sex humor at school—notes passed, poems and jokes told when teacher is out of the room. Some quite uninhibited.

13 Years

A less humorous age for many, though what humor there is may be very good from an adult point of view. Sarcasm is an important element of Thirteen's humor and is enjoyed by most, though a few are much against this.

Others' mistakes in action or speech (especially parents') are enjoyed. Some are still amused by parents' efforts at humor.

Cartoons are much enjoyed: even quite sophisticated cartoons in *The New Yorker.*

Less practical joking in many, except in school. Clowning around and loud, foolish horseplay is still considered funny, especially by boys.

"Kidding" each other about the opposite sex occurs often, and some are beginning to take kidding better, though great individual differences exist.

Smutty humor continues and can be very advanced and direct. Thirteen is the last age, for many, for enjoying such jokes freely in mixed company.

14 Years

Some of Fourteen's humor is excellent from an adult point of view, and many spontaneously comment that they like a sense of humor in others. But most are much distressed by any attempts at humor on the part of their parents, especially before outsiders.

Humor may be used against parents or teachers. (The "Mary Helen Fan Club"—all girls called in by school principal for misbehavior.)

The incongruous is especially appreciated. Many themselves pun, though they dislike any punning on parents' part. Still much enjoyment of magazine cartoons.

Practical joking is definitely on the wane in most, except at school. Here, boys (more than girls) play many crude practical jokes on each other and on teachers.

Insult and ridicule are still favored humorous techniques. Fourteen's loud, "corny" humor in public places (especially buses) can be very tiresome to adults.

Some are unwittingly humorous. (One boy remarked, "I like people—most every kind except girls.")

Smutty humor is definitely on the decline in group situations: dislike of "off-color jokes in mixed company."

chapter twelve
THE GROWING SELF

The search for self is, in some ways, what adolescence is all about—finding oneself, learning to identify, count on, and depend on oneself. And to do this, one must get free of one's earlier dependence on and veneration of one's parents.

The task is not easy. It involves much trying on of different personalities, much slavish following of the crowd, and, later on, having the courage to be different from the crowd. It involves much trying of new hair styles, new facial expressions. (As one mother commented when her son left for college, "I don't think of it as losing a son. I think of it as gaining a mirror.")

Long (or short) hair on boys, as style may dictate, and other aspects of grooming and dressing which are most irritating to parents, are part of this search. A sad, glum face (which the owner may optimistically think tells an interested world that she harbors a secret sorrow) is a part. Making friends with boys and/or girls considered unsuitable by parents can also be a part.

It is extremely important for a parent or teacher to keep in mind that when a young person is behaving in what may seem an extremely peculiar or unattractive way, this behavior may not actually be related to you or to the child's feelings about you, but rather to the strong, long, difficult, and often exceedingly painful search for an inner self.

Even college-age individuals nowadays talk a good deal and make a good deal of fuss about their problems with "finding" themselves. This search in most begins very early, and in some continues very long.

This search for self, if it has started at ten, is initially painless at worst and probably quite superficial. Your typical ten-year-old is too satisfied with self and the rest of the world to worry very much about "self." Ten seems to take himself or herself pretty much for granted; in fact, "unselfconscious" pretty much describes both girl and boy.

Tens like themselves and they like other people, especially their parents, whom they describe as "just about perfect in every way." They accept their directives, and even the punishments they hand out, as fair and reasonable. They like their teacher. They like their friends. And most seem quite contented with themselves.

If children of this age search for self at all, it may be through activities. They like to try new things; like to see what they can accomplish. In fact, Tens often seem to evaluate themselves in terms of specific abilities: "I'm a pretty good skater." The typical response —"Sometimes I do and sometimes I don't," when asked a question, suggests that however things turn out it is okay with them. (That is, if a boy or girl did not skate too well, it really wouldn't matter.)

The ten-year-old, like his or her younger and rather similar five-year-old self, lives very much in the present, doesn't worry about the past, does not project very much into the future. Life, and particularly self and family, seems highly satisfactory to most. Why worry about the future?

And yet, touchingly, well over three fourths of our Tens plan to marry and have children. Slightly more girls than boys express these intentions. By far the majority say they hope to go to college, and most girls as well as boys plan to have careers.

Eleven is quite something else again. Though the child of this age does not verbalize special concern about self as such, the vigor of his or her rebellion against mother or teacher suggests a strong need to make his presence felt in his own small world.

The child seems to be trying himself or herself out against all of those in authority; seems to find self through conflict. "He makes a horrendous fuss about tasks he has done willingly for years," as one mother put it. Girl or boy seems to find it difficult to accept even the simplest directive. "What do you mean my rude outburst?" one girl asked her mother after an all-too-typical explosion over some minor matter.

School, as well as home, tends to report a marked change for the worse; and even Eleven herself may report that she seems to be changing, and not for the better. "Now everything I do is wrong."

And though girl or boy does not delve deeply into the reasons, Eleven does tend to be as critical of self as of others. Your ten-year-old seems, for the most part, pleased with self and with you. Eleven, much of the time, is satisfied with neither.

Any evaluation of self at this age tends to be specific rather than general: "I swear," "I have bad table manners." However, a few do generalize, describing themselves as "sloppy," "careless," "stubborn."

Though we suspect that most do not ruminate much about their future, by far the majority, girls as well as boys, plan to go to college, then marry, have children, and pursue a career. As at ten, the percentage of girls who express positive plans in all these directions is somewhat more (over eighty percent) than the percentage of boys (over seventy percent).

And then comes Twelve, a happy change. Twelve is an outwardized age and, pleasantly, an age of reasonably good equilibrium. The twelve-year-old girl or boy tends to be rather explosive, interested in coming into contact with every aspect of the environment.

Fortunately, most that he or she contacts pleases. And most seem reasonably pleased with themselves. Many are so secure in themselves that they can even forgive mistakes in others, even in mother. "Oh, you know you, Mommy," a girl will say when her mother behaves in a, to her, especially eccentric way.

Twelve is an expansive, enthusiastic age, though there is often more vigor than shape to activities. Fortunately, most tend to be even less critical of self than of others, so they are not disturbed by their own minor faults or failures. Girl or boy of this age is much less egocentric than just earlier, fully as interested in and generous to other people as to self. Everything no longer must be for them. Now they can share.

Twelve is enthusiastic as well as positive. He "can't wait" for Christmas or summer vacation. Even when a boy tells us of his hates, he does so in an interested way: "I just *love* tomatoes but I *hate* broccoli," he will tell you, eyes dancing.

Though twelve is in most respects a positive and outgoing age, perhaps increased maturity brings caution in planning for the future. Whatever the reason, fewer girls than earlier (only seventy-eight percent) plan to go to college. And for boys, this is a low point in the entire age range for college plans—only sixty-six percent say they expect to go.

Twelve is also a low point for interest in matrimony in girls, only seventy-four percent saying that they hope or expect to marry. Boys, on the other hand, though often in everyday life less than interested in girls, shoot up to a high point of eighty-three percent who say they plan to marry. Interestingly enough, and rather negating the validity of young people's responses at this age, slightly more girls and more boys say they plan to have children (eighty-one percent of girls, seventy-five percent of boys) than plan to marry.

Twelve is a low point for girls for planning to have a career. Only sixty percent say they expect to work after they get married.

Now comes age Thirteen, quite unlike the years that have gone before. The search for self is really on now, and it takes the form of withdrawing from other people. We assume that this withdrawal, though presumably to a large extent instinctive, serves a real purpose in the economy of development. Certainly it gives time for rumination, for thinking about the world and the people in it. But perhaps most of all for thinking about one's self.

Thirteen is not one of the more cheerful ages, so one may guess that the usual thirteen-year-old is not supremely satisfied with what he sees and feels about himself.

It sometimes seems as if the typical Thirteen is hoarding every experience, adding it to his or her meager store of selfhood: "Oh, I'm not going to tell them too much," girl or boy can be heard to mutter. At no age, except perhaps at fifteen, are the young person's responses to adult questions more monosyllabic. "How was the party?" a mother may ask her daughter. "Okay," responds the daughter. "Who was there?" asks mother. "The kids." "What did you do?" "Played games." And then daughter slumps out of the room, muttering darkly, "Prying into a person's private affairs."

Yes, Thirteen insists on total privacy, not only mental and emotional but also physical. It is not unusual for boy or girl of this age to withdraw almost completely from the family group. "He lives like a hermit," says mother. "And he has enough things—food, drink, books—in his room to last him all winter."

Twelve conducted his or her rather superficial search for self in contact with other people. Thirteens look within and do not necessarily like what they see. Their "personality" is not particularly appealing to them. Nor do they like too much better what is revealed by the mirror: "too fat," "too thin," "that horrible nose."

Brains as well as looks are important, and because thirteen is on the whole a rather minor, melancholy age, many are discouraged even on this front. They are afraid they "just can't cut it" intellectually.

Some play secret roles. Some try out, in imagination, what it would be like to be a successful actor or athlete, or what it would be like to be a person suffering bravely from a horrible tragedy.

College, matrimonial, and parenting plans are all rather high at this otherwise somewhat withdrawn age. More than eighty percent of both the boys and the girls have positive plans in all three directions. Though most girls, as at other ages, report rather definite work or career plans (teaching, law, veterinary medicine), only two thirds say they plan to combine a career and marriage.

Almost as rhythmic as the tides, the teenage boy or girl swings, as he or she grows, from inwardized to outwardized behavior, from times of disequilibrium to times of rather comfortable equilibrium. And so, in response to this seemingly rather predictable rule of Nature, at fourteen the more or less typical girl or boy swings into a time of outwardization and equilibrium.

Fourteen is an age of exuberant exploration of the world. It is as if at thirteen the person withdrew from the world in order to discover, build up, and strengthen the sense of self. Now he emerges from his room, even from home and neighborhood, and tries self out in contact with other people and other things.

Friends are numerous, appetite for activity enormous. The average fourteen-year-old fills his or her days to the brim, often with more activities than a twenty-four-hour day will encompass. Parents often feel that the school goes too far in piling on "outside activities." If the school does this, it is because the fourteen-year-old demands it.

Fourteen's strongest source of information about self, his or her strongest confirmation of that self, comes from comparisons with other people. And perhaps because the sense of self is still unformed and tender, boy or girl seems to feel more secure and comfortable if he or she dresses, acts, and thinks as nearly like his or her chosen friends as possible. Parents tend to resent this slavish imitation. We believe that it represents a highly important stage in the young person's search for self.

Your usual Fourteen has rather large plans for the future, at least so far as college is concerned. However, though seventy-eight percent of our girls, eighty-four percent of the boys, say they plan to go to college, this is the low point for girls for planning to marry (only seventy percent) and one or the two low points for boys (only seventy-two percent). Fourteen is also a low point for girls in planning careers—only sixty-seven percent say they will continue to work after marriage. As at some other ages, more boys and more girls say they plan to have children than say they are going to marry.

For the most part, Fourteen tends to be an outgoing age, a time when boy or girl finds much to enjoy and much to share. However, an outstanding characteristic of the age, and one assumes one which is necessary as the younger teenager tries to establish a sense of self, is a driving need to separate oneself from the adult world, especially from parents.

It is almost as though Fourteen cannot feel like a successful and complete person unless he equals or exceeds his parents. And since this is a difficult thing to do, boy or girl seems to need to build self up by pushing parents down. But aside from reaction to parents, Fourteens' search for self, intense as it may be, particularly as they talk with friends and compare their selves and their reactions with those of others doesn't seem particularly painful. In fact, one might say they enjoy it.

GROWTH GRADIENTS

1. The Growing Self
10 Years
Ten shows no great concern about self, tends to take self (and life) as it comes. Parents report that child is much happier and easier to get along with than at nine.

Easygoing and matter-of-fact. Very specific; doesn't generalize.

Shrugs off responsibility; can usually toss off criticism and bad grades. If asked a question, replies easily, "Sometimes I do, sometimes I don't."

Much interested in own future parenthood and in how he will treat his children.

Still describes self as "pretty good."
11 Years
Often describes self as changing for the worse since ten: "Now everything I do seems wrong." Parents tell a similar story.

Seems to be engaged in an active search for self and finds it in conflict with others—parents and friends. Responsive to outside forces, but against mother. Jockeys for position with friends.

May oppose whatever is going on in the home; works against what is expected of him. Little sense of wanting things to be smooth for others. Described as egocentric and selfish.

Hypochondriacal. Clumsy. Very talkative, but cannot generalize. If asked a question, temporizes: "Well . . ." Then "amplifies, glorifies, clarifies" even the simplest statement. Tells plots of movies in endless detail.

Supercritical of both self and others, but resentful of others' criticism.

12 Years

Twelve seems to search for self by trying to win approval of friends and by assuming (at times) new roles of more mature behavior. Very insistent about not being "treated like a baby."

Has much better perspective. Can stand off and view parents a little objectively; less embroiled with them. May even be able to view self more objectively, to realize that he or she is not in all situations the center of the world.

With less egocentricity and better perspective comes a smoothing out of interpersonal relationships. Most are said to be much "better" than at eleven.

Enthusiastic and impatient; "can't wait" for all the wonderful things anticipated. Often seems shapeless in thought, action, and posture.

Very uneven: very childish and then extremely mature. Responsible, helpful behavior, which seems to be on a whole new level of mature, smooth functioning, may alternate with childish, obstreperous, "bratty" behavior. Shapes fingernails but forgets to clean them; fusses with hair but doesn't wash face.

Very critical, at times, of self and own appearance. Cannot accept praise gracefully—clowns or comments ironically ("exquisite!") if praised.

13 Years

Thirteen seems to search for self within himself; tries to understand himself—contemplates his own looks, thoughts, moods. Beginning interest, in many, in own personality (though may scorn personality tests—"What good are they?"). Agonies of concern about personal appearance: too fat, too thin, bad complexion, poor features. Great insistence on outward conformity with others; generally better groomed than at twelve.

Inner life important; "brains" an important concept. Some Thirteens imaginatively play secret roles: great actor, athlete, tragic figure whom nobody understands. Some pretend to great sophistication; try to appear very jaded and worldly. Often self-absorbed—indifferent, absentminded, dreamy, "doesn't hear."

Often an age of withdrawal in one way or another. Quieter outside the home than at twelve or fourteen. Many comment that they like the feeling of being alone. Like to be in own room with door shut, even locked. Withdraw from family group, sometimes even from friends—may be considered "a regular hermit." Generally much less sharing and confiding with adults: "I don't want to be close to anyone." May construe a normal interest of others in his or her affairs as prying.

Many are thoughtful not only about selves but also about more remote problems: underprivileged people, women's role in the world.

14 Years

Searches for self by comparing and matching self with others. Wants to be just like the others. Directed toward other people (rather than away from them, as at thirteen). Very anxious to be liked by friends.

Great interest in personality of self and friends. Interest in results of personality tests, concern as to whether or not he or she is "normal." May be quite dissatisfied with own personality, behavior, and appearance; may comment, "That's me" when he sees someone very fat, or very thin, for example.

May understand that she behaves much better away from home than at home. Parents describe Fourteen as selfish and lazy—yet also as busy every minute, trying to do much more than time allows, "just squeezing things in." Extremely preoccupied with own activities, friends, life. Independently establishes relationships with adults outside the home as well as with contemporaries.

Much interest in appearing grown up and in having freedom. But very uneven again, as at twelve: very mature one minute, babyish the next.

Often has a concept of age changes in behavior of self and of friends. Spontaneously resolves to "do better" next year. Many seem to feel that "something wonderful" is right around the corner.

2. Likes and Dislikes

10 Years

LIKES: "My mother and father, of course" is the outstanding answer to the question "What do you like best in the world?" "Horses" comes next in frequency.

Other leading preferences are activities (skating, drawing, playing) and possessions (own stereo, house in the country). Holidays, travel, money are also named. Some likes are really wishes: "to be a missionary, doctor, or actress"; "to be a hunter."

DISLIKES: Things mentioned as dislikes tend to be either quite broad or quite specific. Most often mentioned are war and work. Also reported as disliked are school, teacher, "people who treat me badly," staying in on a rainy day, and specific foods such as peanut butter.

11 Years

LIKES: As at ten years, "my mother and father" are mentioned most often when asked who or what are liked best and, again, "horses" is second in frequency. Few other likes are mentioned, except eating and travel.

DISLIKES: School now holds first place as the thing most hated. Eleven's more specific hates often seem more pointed, less bland than those mentioned at ten, and include cruelty to animals, losing friends, going to bed at night, poison ivy, snakes, things that cause injury.

12 Years

LIKES: Mother and father still lead as best liked of anything and animals of some kind—cats, dogs, horses—are next in frequency. Sports have come in strongly, and eating, dancing, and reading are other favored activities. Nice clothes and "my home" are among the things most liked.

DISLIKES: School, homework, "my friends," "my brother and sister," and "people who boast" are now mentioned as most hated. New twelve-year-old hates are being sick, someone scratching on the blackboard, and eggs.

13 Years

LIKES: A real change appears at thirteen years—great variety of likes occurs, and parents have dropped out in status as best liked. Friends of the opposite sex are now most often mentioned and are followed in frequency by eating, "my home," and automobiles. Items mentioned for the first time at thirteen include a good time, the United States, peace and quiet, luxury, and music.

DISLIKES: War, as at ten years, now leads the list of hates, which includes cruelty to animals, losing friends, going to bed at night, poison ivy, snakes, things that cause injury.

14 Years

LIKES: Fourteen's likes seem to be broad-ranging. Sports and friends of the opposite sex now lead in frequency, followed by travel and music. Likes first mentioned at fourteen include knowledge, art and literature, just living, and shelter.

DISLIKES: War is still most often mentioned as the thing most hated. Work, as at ten, is again hated, and certain friends are mentioned. The personal, intense feelings of anguish which some Thirteens had from *thinking* about things are replaced by more objective, external kinds of hates. New fourteen-year-old items, for example, are: off-color jokes in mixed company, "things I don't understand"; ungodliness; being afraid of things at night; "bigger boys bothering me"; and "people who come to your house and say, 'I don't care' when you ask them what they want to do."

3. College, Marriage, Family, and Career Plans
10 Years

By far the majority (eighty-four percent of girls, seventy percent of boys) say they plan to go to college. After college, girls plan mostly to be teachers, nurses, or veterinarians. Boys plan to be doctors, carpenters, construction workers, sports figures, or truck drivers.

Nearly all (eighty-seven percent of the girls, eighty-two percent of the boys) expect to get married. Boys name rather specific traits they desire in a wife—that she be smart, pretty, blonde, tall, economical. Girls also seek specific and practical qualities in a husband —that he be a good father, good provider, good-tempered, easy to get on with, honest, and have a liking for horses.

Eighty-four percent of the girls and seventy-nine percent of the boys plan to have children. Two is the favored number, though fifteen percent of both sexes plan four or more. The majority of girls plan to combine work or a career with marriage, though eighty percent expect to take time off when their children are young.

11 Years

College attendance is still planned by the majority (eighty-two percent of the girls, seventy percent of the boys). Girls plan to be teachers, nurses, doctors, or dentists; boys, sports figures, doctors, policemen, or truck drivers.

Nearly all (eighty-nine percent of the girls, seventy-two percent of the boys) expect to get married. Attributes desired in a wife include that she be blonde, and that "she likes me and I like her." Attributes desired in a husband include being handsome, good-tempered, and "making money enough to support me." These lead, but girls also mention sense of humor, brains, understanding, nice personality, helpful around the house, ambitious, unselfish, gentlemanly, a careful driver, good father, and "not too important so he won't be too busy."

Eighty-five percent of the girls, seventy-two percent of the boys, plan to have children. Two is still the favored number, with only six percent planning four or more. Sixty-nine percent of girls say they plan to combine marriage and career, but eighty-three percent plan to take time off when their children are young.

12 Years

Slightly fewer now plan to go to college—seventy-eight percent of the girls, but a low point of only sixty-six percent of the boys. Career plans are very varied, but teacher, doctor or dentist, and veterinarian still lead for girls. Boys plan on being sports figures, carpenters or construction workers, lawyers, doctors, or businessmen. This is a high point for planning to get a job after high school (forty-five percent of the girls, forty-two percent of the boys). In many cases this is so that they can help out with their college expenses.

This is one of the low points for girls in planning to marry (only seventy-four percent). But eighty-three percent of the boys, after a falling-off of interest in matrimony at eleven, now expect to get married. Boys want a wife who is pretty, smart, blonde, a good cook, with a nice personality, and "not be always fooling around with other boys." Girls want a husband who is kind, smart, "able to support me," good-looking, understanding, tall, helpful around the house, has athletic figure, character, same religion, and "loves me."

Now eighty-one percent of the girls, only seventy-two percent of the boys, plan to have children. (More girls plan to have children than plan to marry). The preferred number continues to be two. Only ten percent plan four or more.

This is a low point for career planning in girls—only sixty-six percent expect to work after they get married. But, again paradoxically, eighty-six percent say they plan to take time off from work or from their career when their children are young.

13 Years

College plans are strong once again, with eighty-four percent of the girls, eighty-eight percent of the boys, planning to go to college. Career choices for girls feature teaching, law, being a veterinarian; for boys, sports figure, author, and doctor lead. Fourteen percent of girls but fifty percent of boys cannot say what they plan to be.

For all the withdrawal that is characteristic of Thirteen in many areas, this is a high point for marriage plans. Now eighty-six percent of the girls, eighty-eight percent of the boys, say they expect to get married. Attributes desired in a wife include being pretty, a good housekeeper, smart, and having a nice personality. (Being blonde is no longer a requisite.) New qualities mentioned now include being good-natured, cheerful, affectionate, able to follow leadership (!) and liking to have a good time.

Girls want husbands who have a nice personality, "something in common with me," are good providers, good-looking, same religion, well-liked, neat, well-educated, a good dancer, nice, tall, and insist "we love each other."

And this is a strong age for planning to have children, with eighty-six percent of the girls and eighty-two percent of the boys expressing this interest and intent. Two continues to be the number planned for, though fourteen percent of girls plan four or more.

Sixty-six percent of girls say they plan to combine a career and marriage, though as at other ages more (eighty-two percent in all) plan to take time off for babies than plan to work in the first place. This inconsistency suggests that, for many, plans for the future are actually rather vague.

14 Years

College plans at most ages are strong, with seventy-eighty percent of girls, eighty-four percent of boys now planning college attendance. Career plans for girls include, chiefly, veterinarian, teacher, nurse, doctor, or dentist. For boys, doctor, sports figure, carpenter, or businessman lead as choices. Girls, though their plans are very varied, for the most part can say what they want to be, but fifty percent of the boys cannot tell what they plan to do when they finish school.

This is the low point for planning to marry for girls (only seventy percent so plan) and one of the low points for boys (seventy-two percent expect to marry.) As to characteristics desired in a wife, personality rather than physical characteristics are now most often named: smart, economical, good personality, same tastes, good disposition, "understanding the way I think," "doesn't want everything just so."

Girls want a husband who is, above all, a good provider as well as a good father, smart, good-tempered, tall, helpful around the house, has a sense of humor, and "something in common with me." Personality, religion, politeness, education, background, and love are also mentioned. Several comment that looks, money, and race don't matter.

This is also a low point for girls for planning careers, since only sixty-seven percent say they plan to work after marriage. Interestingly enough, more say they plan to have children (eighty percent of girls, seventy-eight percent of the boys) than plan to marry. It is not likely that they actually intend to be unmarried parents—more likely they are not thinking clearly as they respond to questioning.

Two remains the preferred number of children, though almost as many of both sexes say "two or three." Seventy percent of girls say they plan to combine career and marriage, and slightly more (eighty percent) intend to take time off when their children are young.

4. Sandy

At some point, usually shortly after twelve, boys and girls become open to a landmark experience that can act as a focus for gaining (or losing) self-confidence. Around the developmental age of twelve and lasting through sixteen, a sense of self-permanence comes into being in the growing child. "I am not only 'me,' but I am stuck this way" is how Sandy put it to us when he described his own discovery of self-permanence when he was twelve years old. He had a twinkle in his eye when, at age fourteen, he recalled his discovery of self-permanence as being "stuck this way," and it was clear that he was not displeased with this self-imposed prophecy.

He, a freshman, had just won a regional high school wrestling tournament. He described his permanent self in terms of the way he *felt* about people and things, but connected his confidence in his insight to a single experience that happened in September of fifth grade. At that time he was ten and a half years old but was mature for his age and, developmentally, perhaps two years ahead. The previous year had been "the worst year of my life," he said. His family had moved from New Hampshire to Georgia in the middle of the school year. They rented a house for six months and then moved, again, to their own house in another school district in the same town, a suburb of Atlanta.

The second half of the fourth grade had been miserable for Sandy. A New Hampshire accent in Georgia is enough to make a kid conspicuous without joining a class in the middle of the year. A huge bully had been transferred to his class at the same time and the bully's search for self-esteem put Sandy, the other new kid, in the path of trouble. The bully's gang and a club that formed among the other boys both picked on him, and by the time the summer move came he was friendless and feeling depressed.

At camp that summer he grew in all directions: two inches in height, and in frame he showed himself to be a typical mesomorph —broad-shouldered and muscular. He began fifth grade with a new body to house the same battered self that had survived the second half of the fourth grade, listening to sad songs on his stereo and walking alone on the golf course, where grownups might rescue him if he was bothered by his antagonists.

The gym teacher in his new school had set up a fitness evaluation test measuring speed and strength. All the fifth grade girls and boys gathered around the high bars in the playground to watch each one squeeze out one or two or three chin-ups—the first of several tasks. No one was more surprised than Sandy when he did eleven. His nickname became "Muscles."

By the time he had won a high school wrestling championship at fourteen, he had become aware of a connection between his self-confidence—realized in that moment of chin-ups in the fifth grade —and his consciousness of his self as a permanent personality within. He speculated that feeling good about his body at an early age allowed him to feel especially confident that he was "normal." It is as if the years from ten to sixteen are a kind of vigil for signals that one is "normal," and when the signals came in loud and clear for Sandy they gave him an early and strong sense of himself.

We asked him if he remembered the time when he recognized that his personality was formed so that, as he put it, "I will still be basically the same person when I am forty." He said this recognition occurred within a month of his first ejaculation. "I had masturbated regularly for about a year—with orgasms, and all—but nothing came out. When, one day, something did, I thought I should remember when this happened. I was twelve. Right after that I had a sense of thinking ahead a lot, and now I know that that was the time I sort of became me—or at least realized that I was the same person I will be when I grow up—you know, the same feelings, and beliefs, and stuff."

Sandy was probably closer to a developmental age of fourteen when this self-realization occurred. Whenever it occurs, it doesn't usually happen with the same awareness and specificity. Many people, however, attach their consciousness of themselves as permanent to the appearance of a permanent physical feature. For girls, it is often the attainment of mature breast size that brings the full dawning of the feeling that they have become fully themselves.

chapter thirteen
INTERPERSONAL RELATIONSHIPS

Interpersonal relationships are really what adolescence is all about. If boy or girl could grow up alone, with no need to gain independence from parents, no need to put up with ever-annoying siblings, no necessity to fit in with social groups made up of boys and girls who often seem (to him or her) so much more attractive, worldly, knowledgeable than he or she, the early teenage years might not seem so excessively difficult to many.

True, there would be school. And there would be the need to accept one's own changing body, moods, and personality. But it is in contact with and often in conflict with others that the growing boy or girl finds his or her greatest challenge and difficulty. And as dating becomes less of a novelty and hazard, it can become his or her greatest pleasure and happiness, even reason for living.

PARENTS, SIBLINGS, AND FAMILY: Family perhaps comes first as a source of conflict. Friends come first as a source of effort and pleasure. Siblings, though a source of problems and of many squabbles and fights, are not the main conflict source and certainly not a main source of pleasure. Their importance as someone to compete with and fight with tends to lessen as boy or girl moves into adolescence and moves emotionally, at least to some extent, beyond the confines of the family.

Family relationships change as the sense of self changes. Ten takes self and family for granted. Eleven finds self in conflict with other people and most especially with family members. Twelve, to a large extent, can live and let live, can even permit other family members to make an occasional mistake. Thirteens, though they would probably miss their family should it suddenly disappear, spend much of their time at home trying to escape from other family members.

Fourteen, alas, puts family close to the bottom of any list of those who give satisfaction and pleasure.

Parents tend to look upon the teen years with a certain apprehension. And quite rightly so. These years between ten and fourteen can be difficult for all concerned. The major task of childhood is to get free of one's parents and to stand on one's own feet—that is, to move from a state of dependence to one of independence. This transition is seldom accomplished smoothly and comfortably. At no time are its difficulties and tangles more evident than in the adolescent years.

This is in part because the young person is struggling against parents for independence. But at the same time he is struggling within himself. The drive toward independence is very strong, but independence itself can at times be frightening. And so the struggle for autonomy goes on not only with the outside world (parents and other adults) but also within the soul of the youth, who wants at one and the same time to be free and yet to enjoy the benefits of dependence.

Before we give more details about family relationships and other interpersonal associations in the years from ten to fourteen, just a few words about the great amount of disagreement with and disaffection toward other family members which we shall describe. It may seem that we take an unnecessarily gloomy view of what goes on in the average family.

However, recent research by Murray Straus and colleagues makes our own descriptions seem bland indeed. According to Straus, the average American home is a place of extreme violence. And it is in the home—not, as so many insist, from television—that children learn violence.

Children learn, as their parents punish them physically, that it is those who love them who hit them. And since physical punishment is used to train the child and to teach him about dangerous things to be avoided, it establishes the moral rightness of hitting other family members.

In a comprehensive survey of acts of violence in a nationally representative sample of more than two thousand American families, Straus found the following numbers of acts of violence per year in every one hundred families:

Between spouses—16
Parent to child—63

Child to parent—18
Child to child—79

Though as children grow older their violence rate goes down, it far from disappears. According to Straus's figures pertaining just to major acts of violence, the rates go from seventy-four per hundred three- and four-year-olds, to sixty-four per hundred five- to nine-year-olds to forty-seven per hundred ten- to fourteen-year-olds.

He points out, probably correctly, that within the confines of the family we accept a great deal as normal, or at least as inevitable, which we would absolutely not tolerate outside the family. We tend to accept the fact that violence in the family is just a part of life—not necessarily a good part, but one that is to be expected.

He notes that "parents react differently than if it were someone else's child who had been punched or kicked by one of their children, or someone else's child who had done this to one of their children. If it were someone else's child there would be cries of outrage and possibly even legal action if the violence persisted. But between their own children, parents, in effect, tolerate such behavior for years."[16]

And unfortunately this violence continues into the late teens. In one of Straus's samples, sixty-two percent of the high school seniors hit a sibling during the year, but "only" thirty-five percent had hit someone outside the family during the same year.

However, patient and tolerant as most parents may be, admittedly some teenagers do get out of hand. Their behavior may simply be intolerable of itself or it may actually reach the point where it distorts or even threatens to destroy family living.

When this occurs it is not particularly useful to tell oneself that fifteen or seventeen, or whatever the age may be, is normally a difficult age. In some such instances the so-called "geographic cure" —sending boy or girl away to boarding school or to live with some other family—may turn the trick. Or if that is not desired or practical, family therapy in which the whole family as a group seeks help may save the day.

Now in a little more detail, here are some aspects of the changing relationships of boys and girls with their families in these rapidly changing years from ten to fourteen.

To the matter-of-fact, comfortable, easygoing ten-year-old, his or her family is *just about right.* Children will tell you very sincerely that they love their mother and father more than anything else in the world. What "Mommy says" is the ultimate authority. Mommy gives or withholds permission, and Ten seldom questions. Father is perhaps even more admired—"the shining light," "best father in the world," "knows everything." Grandparents are still, as earlier, much loved and much admired.

Siblings? Well, that's something else again. There is much fighting, bickering, squabbling. "That spoiled brat. I'd like to smash her face in." Tens get on much better with older than with younger siblings, but even with those younger they can on occasion be tolerant.

Eleven, in contrast to Ten, is a disturber of family peace, much of the time in very special conflict with parents, especially mother. With typical egocentricity, girl or boy tends to object to anything she requests. Eleven is quick to criticize, very slow to praise. Siblings displease almost as much as do parents. Grandparents—especially if they live outside the household—may be the only family members the child approves of.

But dissatisfied as Elevens may be with family, they want to be right in the thick of family activities and are anxious that there be a good many of these activities. They love trips, vacations, family get-togethers, little as they may add to the smoothness of these occasions.

Twelve is much easier to live with, though he or she is beginning slightly to pull away from parents and grandparents. "I'm not quite as much interested in doing things with my family as I used to be, but I take that as natural," girl or boy will tell you in his or her reasonable way. Happily, Twelves may be getting on a little better with siblings, at least with those under five and over fifteen.

Thirteen, probably self-protectively, definitely withdraws from other people, especially from parents. A thirteen-year-old girl may tell you, "My mother worries that we're losing our close relationship. *But I don't want to be close to anybody!*" Another, probably very truthfully, may say, "I yell at her if I'm mad. But the way I treat her is not a part of what I think of her."

This may be the first age at which grandparents notice that the child is withdrawing from them. If they are calm and not too dependent on what is, to them, an important relationship, all can go well. If, however, out of their disappointment they press, they may be in for further disappointment.

The fourteen-year-old has a hard time with family because parents seem so embarrassing and inadequate. Fourteen measures them against his or her concept of what "everybody else's" family is like. And, for the most part, they fall miles short. Parents and what they have to offer in terms of house, cars, privileges, youthfulness—just do not measure up. And they are so embarrassing. Since in Fourteen's mind they represent him in public, they are just not what he would wish for. And they do such awful things!

Our interpretation is that there is not room under the sun for both the fourteen-year-old and his or her parents. It is necessary for Fourteen to push them down in order that he or she can come out on top.

Siblings are, in the child's estimate, as awful and embarrassing as parents. And this is a hard age for grandparents as well. It is hard to shift suddenly (when actually you are the same person, for better or worse) from being adored to being ignored. Fourteen has many criticisms of his or her grandparents: "Always telling the same old stories over and over."

Clearly, relating to one's ten- to fourteen-year-old can have all the joy and comfort of a roller coaster ride. One shifts, reluctantly, from Ten's adoration of parents to the antagonism of Eleven, the tolerance of Twelve, the withdrawal of Thirteen, the embarrassment of Fourteen, the disdain of Fifteen to, finally, the kindly acceptance of Sixteen. These are tricky years.

FRIENDS AND ASSOCIATES: Making, keeping, losing friends is a big part of what the teenage years are all about. Some boys and girls during this period are loners or prefer a single "best friend." And if they lose that single friend may have considerable difficulty in finding another. Others are totally gregarious.

In spite of these marked, and often lasting, personality differences, there are certain things we can tell you about age differences in friendship.

The casual, easy-come, easy-go friendships of the typical ten-year-old are quite different from the all-consuming friendships of mid-adolescence. Ten year-olds, girls as well as boys, tend to play with anybody who is available. Boy-boy friendships, however, are as a rule more harmonious and less intense than those of girls. Most boys, in their own words, "get on good" and it almost seems with some that friends are interchangeable. If Frank is not available, Fred will do.

Ten-year-old girls tend to be very cliquey with their friends and also very jealous and often even spiteful. There is much ganging up of any two against a third. "Are you speaking to Nancy? Okay then

I'm not playing with you." Also, there is much emphasis on secrecy and on who can or cannot "be trusted." Boys seem to gang up together to have somebody to play with, but for girls friendship tends to be a much more personal matter.

The majority of both boys and girls are not as yet much interested in the opposite sex.

By eleven, boys—here as so often about a year behind girls in their maturity—are developing more intense friendships, with both the good and the bad results that intensity can bring. Many now have a best friend, "a true pal." At the other extreme are those who, like the girls earlier, are very critical of friends: "He brags." "He blames me." And considerable fighting and making up goes on.

Girls continue, though even more so, with the emotional intensity of friendships characteristic of ten. There is much getting mad, not speaking, threatening "all right for you" or waiting for the other to give in. Friendship means a lot at eleven, but it is not always smooth or easy.

Some girls now express strong dislike of boys: "pests," "disgusting," "just horrible all over." Others, more mature, express mild interest but explain that they don't play with boys because "they won't let us." Two thirds of the girls interviewed say they are not dating yet, though more than half say they would "just as soon" or would like to. More than half the boys say they are not dating, though two thirds say they would like to. Some say merely, "I haven't gotten to girls yet."

Friendship at twelve, for girls, is expanding in numbers and tends to be less emotionally intense than just earlier. Many now have a "whole gang" of friends, "go around with anybody," "try to be nice to everybody." Some friendships break up when one girl moves into dating and the other does not. Boys too, for the most part, have rather a large number of friends and get along well with all or most of them. "No special friends. Different ones at different times."

Many girls now are on the verge of dating. "We're sort of interested in boys but don't go out with them yet." The majority of the boys, as well, are not yet dating though many say they would like to.

Some thirteen-year-old girls still have a whole group of friends, but many seem less well supplied than earlier, and their own temperamental natures at this time often make friendship difficult: "I have spells of liking her and then I don't." Thirteen's preference for being alone often cuts into friendship time. Boys too are often less sociable at thirteen than at surrounding ages and, like girls, may tell you, "Well, I had a friend but he moved away."

As to relations with the opposite sex, about a third of our girls say that they do date, but others still characterize boys as "idiots." The majority seem to be about halfway between. They like boys and like to talk about them but are not as yet doing much dating.

About a third of our boys too say that they date, but perhaps the majority are just on the verge. "I'm interested in them, but I don't *actually* take them out."

However, when asked if they have friends who "make out," ninety percent of each sex answered in the affirmative. Thus though fewer than half admit to dating, almost everybody seems, according to their own reporting, at least to have friends who not only date but "make out."

At fourteen, girls' friendships are an extremely important part of their lives. Alienated from their families or at least not looking to their old-fashioned parents for guidance, many girls look to their girlfriends for confirmation of their personalities. And, of course, for sharing their feelings about boys. Their friends are so important that even when separated physically they seek contact by interminable telephone conversations. Through shared confidences friends help them to understand their own budding sexuality.

Boys, like girls, are interested in their own and their friends' personalities. Many share details (often exaggerated and somewhat untruthful) of their friends' sexual interests and activities. But friendships are generally less intense than those of girls. Shared interest in sports may be the common bond.

Dating is now a big thing for most. More than half do date or at least have dated. Dating may be quite bland or, for a few, very intense. More than half of both girls and boys whom we interviewed say that at least some of their friends have "gone all the way." The shocking number of fourteen-year-old pregnancies in this country affirms that this estimate is no mere boast.

GROWTH GRADIENTS

1. Mother-Child

10 Years

The relationship between Ten and his or her mother tends to be straightforward, uncomplicated, sincere, trusting. The child throws himself or herself wholeheartedly and positively into it. Many say that they like mother (and father) the best of anything in the world —"My mother's just about right!" Criticism of mother's behavior and embarrassment about it in public does not occur to Ten. Mother is important as a final authority: "Mommy says . . ."; "Mommy doesn't like me to . . ."

Girls are very confidential with mother and like to confess to her not only bad deeds but even bad thoughts. Both boys and girls are extremely affectionate and physically demonstrative, sometimes embarrassingly so. Boys especially like to snuggle and to have mother tuck them in at night.

Several boys are described as having a "mother attachment"— "trails mother everywhere, depends on her." But boys also seem more ambivalent than girls: "Trails mother, but you don't dare give him an inch"; "Wants to give mother things, but much turmoil— shouts and loses his temper."

Ten is aware of mother's criticism and may try to improve. But some—boys more than girls—feel that mother is always trying to improve them.

The beginning of some eleven-year-old resistance and "yelling" appears in some.

11 Years

Eleven, in sharp contrast to Ten, tends to be rude and resistant to mother, seems to "work against" her and may argue about "everything," the main purpose being to prove her wrong. Some seem to feel there is nothing right about mother. Girls may observe her closely, then criticize. And both boys and girls may resist or object to any suggestion that she makes, vetoing it practically "before it comes out of her mouth."

Eleven strikes out against mother, verbally and even physically, "takes things out on" her. Great scenes can occur: stamping feet, yelling, talking back, calling names—"dope," "stinker," "liar," "old meanie." Mothers are sometimes reported to "get mad and yell in return."

Much exaggeration and dramatization—"You're the meanest mother in the whole school, and all the kids say so!" Very mocking in reporting privileges denied by mother.

Many report that mother is trying to "improve" them, and mothers do feel that both girls and boys should help more with housework, pick up room better, get on better with siblings. But though they expect a lot from mother, eleven-year-olds are very reluctant to give any help, and to any request are apt to reply, "Do I have to?" Many mothers give up trying to get Elevens—especially boys—to help around the house.

Eleven seems extremely unappreciative of "treats" and always wants more than is provided.

At times, a much more friendly, cooperative relationship does prevail, with girls described as confiding, as "pallish." Some boys are very affectionate with mother. Girls may feel much better after confessing even minor misdemeanors to her. But, in spite of this, more things are kept from mother than earlier.

12 Years

Twelve seems to have emerged from the eleven-year-old battle with parents. Many now express considerable humor and friendliness toward mother. They have themselves better in hand and so can often be quite patient and tolerant, tactful, sympathetic, and objective with her. May even "handle" mother with humor.

Twelve is easier to reason with, less ready to fight, argue, shout, or rebel openly. Many do feel that mothers are overly critical about their not helping with housework, keeping room neat, getting on with siblings, and about table manners. Some are reported not to hear mother's commands and comments. But Twelve generally seems reasonably helpful, and some boys, who might earlier have cooperated with mother's suggestions, may now even take the initiative in improving a situation—"Don't say a word, I'll fix this."

Some feel that mother does not give them enough privileges, doesn't full appreciate them, or "treats them a little younger than they are." But, in general, Twelve is much less demanding. He or she is more willing for mother to live her own life in her own way. Many show that they really care about her opinion and approval. Twelve's outlook on the parent-child relationship is shown by his or her still speaking in terms of "minding" and "not minding."

Twelve generally feels quite friendly, confiding, and companionable toward mother. Though most are less openly affectionate than earlier, they like to be chummy. But their behavior is very uneven—babyish one minute, very mature the next.

Among many girls, there appear the beginnings of feelings that mother is "not very modern" in dress, makeup, hairdo, and deportment.

13 Years

Thirteen brings a withdrawal from mother. Mothers often worry that they are losing the close, confiding relationship they used to have, but thirteen-year-olds comment that they don't want to be close to anyone—just want to be left alone.

Thirteen is very reticent, gives grudging, one-word answers to questions. Some (especially boys) are reported to behave as though mother were persecuting them. The simplest questions or show of interest from her may be construed as prying. But some Thirteens can enjoy occasional thoughtful discussions with her if they instigate these themselves.

Most are much less influenced by mother's directives than earlier. If disagreement arises, girls may sulk and openly express resentment; boys may argue and talk back. Boys report, "Often she gets mad and gives me a big talking to." Still more violent friction can occur: "We yell at each other"; "Sometimes we brush it off, but sometimes it's terrible." Some boys are quite openly rebellious and hostile, and speak rudely, even profanely, to mother. A few boys, however, may be starting to try to influence her through use of techniques other than direct demand or rebellion. And, fortunately, Thirteen's descriptions may give more hope than his behavior: "I yell at her if I'm mad. But the way I treat her is not a part of what I think of her."

If reminded to help around the house, Thirteen responds with less open rebellion, but more "in a minute" than earlier. Many know and list parents' criticisms but have no intention of changing. Most feel criticized too much, and some mimic mother, "Why do I always have to tell you, blah, blah, blah?"

Criticism of mother is often quite extreme; there are times when nothing is right. Boys are most likely to be critical of the way things go around the house: "What! My egg isn't cooked yet?" Some feel that she knows nothing, and there appears the beginning of the complaint, "She just doesn't think the way I do." Girls more often criticize her makeup, hairdo, clothes—"for her own good." They may also criticize her personality and may be as faultfinding (though not as embroiled) as at eleven. Beginning to be embarrassed by mother in public. With all this, Thirteen may nevertheless worry about mother's health.

14 Years

Fourteen's basic attitude generally seems to be that mother is hopelessly old-fashioned, that she doesn't understand him or her, that they "have nothing in common." Complaints at thirteen were more specific and minute. Now they are more general: mother is just too antiquated.

Mother often feels put on the defensive, trying to please a child who demands everything, appreciates and gives little. From girls especially, the typical comment at any remark or activity of mother's is, "Oh, Mother!" Fourteen seems much embarrassed by mother in front of friends—by her actions, her remarks, her humor; walks at least several paces behind her in public. May criticize one parent to the other.

Most feel that mother restricts them too much. "Parents tend to make children of our age much younger than they really are." But they can slip back into quite childish behavior with mother: "I'm *not* a good girl!"

On the other hand, Fourteens often react passively toward maternal criticisms of them: "I just sit there when she criticizes"; "Don't like to be preached at because usually I know what the person is going to say before they say it."

Fourteen generally has much more difficulty with mother than with friends or the outside world. Boys often feel freer to express anger, displeasure, or disagreement with mother than they would with father. Some may be unsympathetic if she is tired or ill. Many know they wouldn't want friends to see how they treat her.

However, many are companionable. Some feel on an equal basis with mother, and boys may tease her affectionately. Girls can be reasonable and good company for mother, and most girls report, "I confide in her." Many boys too may confide if allowed to do so spontaneously, though most mothers wouldn't dare to probe or ask questions—would be "so squelched." Some may even enjoy times alone with mother, may find her a good listener. Both boys and girls may apologize to her after rude retorts or shouting in a rage.

2. Father-Child
10 Years
Both boys and girls, for the most part, are said to get on extremely well with their fathers. Girls are described as "adoring" their fathers, being "wonderful pals." "He's the shining light." And many boys are described as "admiring" or "idolizing" father. "Thinks his father is the answer to everything." May say, "He's strict and if you're bad he spanks you. But that's a father's privilege." Children themselves spontaneously report. "We have fun"; "I think he's just about right"; "Best father in the whole world." "He's a doctor and he's so busy, but he just sits there drinking his coffee as if he had all the time in the world."

Many girls believe that they are more like their father than their mother. Several mothers say that they leave the disciplining of daughters to the father because he is more effective.

A few boys do not get on well with father—he loses his temper at them.

Some of both sexes complain that father doesn't have time to do things with them. However, most spend a good deal of time alone with him—at ballgames, movies, on walks, playing games, reading, or wrestling.

11 Years

Some Elevens continue great admiration or even adoration of father, but in many this attitude is becoming much more matter-of-fact. Most do get on reasonably well, and there is still much companionship between fathers and children (in addition to "whole family" activity). Fathers take sons or daughters rowing, swimming, walking in woods, shooting, to games, movies, the zoo.

Father's role in many cases is now that of disciplinarian. Many Elevens say their fathers are *very* strict and get angry with them. Fathers are generally less patient with the arguing and talking back of Eleven than are mothers, and particularly feel that girls do not help enough around the house. Fathers are apt to lose their tempers, and several Elevens complain that they are impatient and irritable.

Both boys and girls have less to say about fathers than at ten. Most do not directly criticize their fathers yet, but many have some complaints, and there is some resistance. The majority complain that fathers do not have enough time to spend with them, and a few suspect that fathers don't *want* to spend time with them. Several feel that father gets on better with some other sibling because his personality is more like theirs.

Several are, mothers report, definitely afraid of their fathers. Some fathers are quite harsh with sons: "He's not a fierce man, but if he's tired and you do wrong he'll hit you." At the same time, a few boys are beginning to talk very roughly to (or about) fathers: "Old so-and-so."

Girls, especially, are often better with father than with mother at this age, even though father may be less patient and tolerant than earlier. Girls report (with some pride) that when father speaks, "He means it!"

12 Years

Most Twelves get on well with their fathers. With boys and with most girls the relationship is now less adoring and more companionable than formerly. The earlier strong relationship is "toned down": "I'm on good terms with him, but arguments come up"; "We get on normally, but I hardly ever see him." A few girls develop a flirtatious or hero-worshipping attitude toward father and get along extremely well on this basis. And some, boys especially, who before had trouble, now get on better with him.

Fewer activities are shared, though in some cases—*if* Father has the time—sailing, sports, reading, shooting, playing ball, watching TV, and discussing (sports, politics, war) are enjoyed together.

Most boys as well as girls are good about minding father. Some resent prohibitions but still accept them.

Children of both sexes are likely to report that they resemble father more than mother.

Twelves are quite aware of father's criticisms: that they don't help enough around the house, are too lazy, don't treat siblings well, are not prompt or neat. Fathers are said to scold or "blow up" or be irritated about these things. Quite a few say that father is stricter than mother.

Some Twelves now start to evaluate father's behavior as they never did earlier. "He has an awful temper, but he's nice"; "He's not henpecked, but he doesn't assert himself." Many feel that father (as well as mother) spoils siblings. Some (boys especially) begin to criticize father's treatment of mother or mother's belief in what father says.

Some boys begin to criticize parents jokingly. Some also compete with fathers in feats of wit, skill, or endurance.

13 Years

Thirteens do not show a "typical" pattern to the extent that the earlier ages did. Great individual differences exist: some get on better with father, some with mother; some think father is more strict, some think mother is.

A few girls are still very affectionate toward father or are affectionate now for the first time. The majority take father for granted more than earlier. Some, especially boys, are described as resentful of him, but they do not flare up at father as much as at mother.

In general, thirteen-year-olds mind father better than mother, and his discipline is usually more effective. Thirteens are more afraid of him and also feel that he doesn't nag so much, so they pay better attention. Less out-of-bounds rebellion occurs with father than mother. Some Thirteens are saucy and snap back, but most still do not. "I plan to, but then I don't dare."

Most confide in father less than in mother. They admire and respect him more, criticize him less, and behave better with him, but feel less close to him.

Often behavior in father and child seems to be complementary. Children themselves withdraw and, at the same time, think that father is too busy for them. Father thinks boy is too interested in sports, and boy is disappointed because father is not more interested. Or, more positively, when homework goes better, girl says, "Daddy's easier to work with now," and father says, "She's beginning to think."

"Doing things together" tends to decrease. About half our Thirteens still do companionable things with father: ballgames, swimming, sailing, movies, discussions. Others report that he is too busy or that he is cross and irritable because he works so hard. Father's help with homework may be accepted better, and with less bickering, than mother's. Some fathers take only occasional interest in Thirteen, and their timing may not be good: "When he does try to talk and take an interest he asks different things, and you don't feel like talking, and then that makes trouble."

Nearly all Thirteens feel that father is critical of them in some ways. "He says I don't stick to anything, I'm messy, and selfish." Some know that father criticizes them to their faces but praises them to outsiders.

Thirteen's criticisms often include the complaint that parents favor or pamper younger siblings. And a few boys criticize the way father treats mother.

14 Years

Many Fourteens, both girls and boys, state that they get on better with father than with mother. (There are, however, many exceptions—father is too busy, too unreasonable, gets mad too easily.) Mother's estimate of the father-child relationship does not always agree with what son or daughter reports.

Some think that father is hopelessly antiquated, though this is more apt to be thought of mother than father. Fourteens seem a little more likely than earlier to think of parents, together, as "they" and to think that "they" are pretty hopeless. Especially in public, Fourteen *is* embarrassed by "them."

But many Fourteens feel that father does understand them better than mother, is more reasonable, does not have to have everything just so, does not nag, and is not so oversolicitous and fearful of their welfare. Even then, his standards may be felt to be hopelessly high: "Anything I do makes him criticize"; "He tries to improve me in almost every way." And father is still less confided in than mother, though he might be consulted, depending on the problem.

Fathers are usually firmer than mothers and may be unduly restrictive about their daughter's dating. Fourteen admires, respects, and fears him more, and minds him better. Girls quarrel with fathers much less than with mothers, and boys are more respectful to fathers. With boys, fathers seems to know "when to put the pressure on" better than mother does.

Some criticize father to mother and mother to father, and are quick to play mother's authority against father's if the two do not agree.

Boys and girls resist any physical show of affection or even too much verbal concern. Some fathers are annoyed because sons and daughters show so little appreciation or because they do not fully answer direct questions (which are not always well timed). Fathers' complaints suggest that Fourteen is rude, insolent, selfish, messy, lazy, and ungrateful.

A few Fourteens still attend sports events and other activities with father, but much less of this occurs than earlier. Many prefer father to mother for help with homework. And some enjoy discussions and arguments together.

3. Parent and Child in Conflict—"I'm Going to Destroy You"

When her parents returned home at eleven-thirty, Cynthia was gone. On her bed was a neatly folded note and on the floor was a crumpled "first draft" which read as follows:

Dear Franklin and Suzanna,

I have left home to find someplace where someone understands me and can communicate with me. I know you will be relieved to get rid of your little bitch of a daughter.

I hate you and I cannot stay in this house another day. Your stupidity and hypocrisy are driving me crazy, and I only wish you could feel the pain that I have felt just trying to live in this awful family. If only the world knew how screwed up you and our whole family really are.

I'm going to destroy you, and I'll do it by destroying myself. Then everyone will know what horrible people you are. I hate you. I hate you. I hate you!

Someday you will understand the mistakes you have made and regret that you didn't get a divorce before you had me or at least last year when I said you should. Good-bye and good riddance!

(signed)Sin

The neatly folded final draft of Cynthia's note went like this:

Dear Mom and Dad,

Don't worry about me. I have gone to stay at Gloria's house for a few days to try to sort things out. I will be safe there and I need a grown-up friend like her to talk to about things. I have been very unhappy at home, and I think that if we put some distance between us it will work better for everyone. I know you care about me, and I want you to know that I care about you. I am not "running away." I promise to take good care of myself. I will be able to do it better if I have some space. Thank you for understanding.

Your daughter, Cyn

At thirteen Cynthia is experiencing the strong unbalancing forces of rounding a sharp bend in her path. The way she handles this stage of her development has to do with many factors, including her inborn temperament as well as all the other complex environmental factors that contribute to a particular behavior. The factor we wish to emphasize in this example has to do with the way in which her behavior is reinforced by the fact of her father being in a similar place in his developmental path.

He was turning forty-two as she headed toward fourteen. A change in jobs had given him a new view of himself. His focus was away from home. Legal work took him on trips where he experienced a sense of success that contrasted with the way he felt at home, where things did not seem to him nearly as manageable. Cynthia's anger at his absences from home heightened his sense of contrast between his "home self," and his "away self." He renewed his old interest in skiing; drank excessively; and had an affair, which Cynthia got wind of. His behavior and his wife's anger influenced Cynthia's behavior in many direct ways, but it is probable that the impact would have been different if its timing had not coincided so perfectly with Cynthia's developmental crisis. The fact that they experienced similar struggles at the same time tended to make Cynthia's behavior more extreme than it might have been if her father had been well settled while she was going through her up-heaval.

Take, for example, Cynthia's pushing divorce in her crumpled letter. It is an expression of her own worst fears—the loss of a stable family platform from which to launch herself. It is also the ultimate expression of her hope that dividing her parents would increase her own power. Her fears and hopes are intensified as she goes through her developmental crisis. Her father, going through his own turmoil, is even more vulnerable to the reinforcing influence of his daughter's behavior. Picture them each on the sharp turn of a pear-shaped path. Each is on his or her own level, but they influence each other in ways that tend to increase the outward forces for each of them.

Consider the effects of Cynthia's crumpled letter on her father's path. By signing her name "Sin," she reawakened a thirteen-year old disagreement between her mother and father that had to do with the giving of a name that could be shortened in this way. Cynthia had decorated several school notebooks and a pair of jeans with her name spelled "Sin," but had done this so artfully that the letters were concealed by the design. This was the first time she had used her name that way openly, to her parents. Unaware that she was striking an old wedge, her aim was as true as if she had practiced for years.

In a way she had. Learning where to drive wedges that separate parents is a skill many young people develop to a precise accuracy because it helps them get their way. Cynthia benefited regularly from divide-and-conquer tactics with her parents. They were usu-ally united on major issues about curfews, school, and grades, but she took pleasure in finding little ways that divided her parents: her messy room, her habit of borrowing clothes, and her hairstyles and dress. Her instinct led her to clothes that would feed little feuds her parents might not know they had except for her incisive reminders.

When she detected a lack of unity in important matters, she usu-ally came out best when her parents were the most divided. The tendency to get the benefit of doubt and disagreement led to her expectation that divorce would be a kind of ultimate victory for her. From her close range, and considering the impact of her behavior on their peace of mind, she didn't think her parents got along very well anyway. More important, she felt that she would be the main bene-ficiary of their splitting up and, if they had, she would have taken a good bit of credit—or blame. Her insight and power would have been confirmed while some of her worst fears were realized.

4. Grandparents

10 Years

Ten may love mother and father more than anything in the world, but grandparents come not too far behind. A boy loves to show his grandma a special exhibit at a museum: "You'll love this one, Grandma." Or may say, "Just about the best grandfather in the whole world. He'd even make a good father." And the love affair is quite mutual.

11 Years

Though the child of this age may seem to be conducting a never-ending feud on every front with mother, grandparents are as a rule exempt from the effects of this "turn for the worse" which so often comes at eleven. A girl of this age, when asked by her grandmother how come she was so good when visiting her grandparents may reply, "You want me to be good and happy, so that's the way I am."

12 Years

Twelve, though good-natured and friendly with other family members, except perhaps siblings, much of the time is beginning to pull just a little bit away from family involvement. He or she confides a little less, shares a little less, cares a little less. This is true of the relationship with grandparents as well as with parents, and grandparents may feel a faint shadow falling over what may have been for them up to now a perfect relationship.

13 Years

Thirteen tends to withdraw from all other members of the family, grandparents included. If grandparents can accept the basic nature of boy or girl of this age and can accept the lessening of their formerly close relationship, all will be well. If they push and pry and ask unacceptable questions such as "What's the matter?" they are apt to be met with cold aloofness, which is extremely disappointing to some.

14 Years

Grandparents had best tread softly now and for several years to come. The typical fourteen-year-old's chief method of reaching the place in the sun which he strives for is by knocking down and criticizing his elders. Grandparents are no exception. If well brought up, young people may still be polite to them, but time with them is no longer treasured as it used to be.

5. Siblings

10 Years

The majority of ten-year-olds fight with their brothers and sisters —at least younger ones (except infants), at least part of the time ("sometimes we get on and sometimes not"). Most say they would not want to be an only child, but several comment, "Once in a while I wish he'd just disappear" or, "Sometimes I'd just as soon go live somewhere else for a while."

A minority express stronger antagonism: "That spoiled brat! Sometimes I feel as if I hated the sight of her"; "I'd like to smash her face in!" Whether or not there is real rivalry and jealousy seems to be more a matter of individual temperament and situation than of age.

Fighting is more frequent with younger siblings. The usual pattern is that the younger one teases, "needles," taunts, or pesters until Ten retaliates physically. Then the younger calls for help, or parents step in. Then Ten thinks parents are unfair. Most feel that younger siblings are favored and also that they "get away with a lot of stuff I never got away with."

With younger siblings close to Ten's own age, though there is much good-natured playing together, fighting and bickering are very common. Fighting involves name-calling ("pig," "fatty," "dope"), "wrassling," and real physical fighting intended to hurt— pushing, kicking, hitting, biting. Good-natured "wrassling" becomes real fighting when someone is hurt. Much fighting occurs over possessions—"We both want the same thing."

Younger siblings feel that ten-year-olds are too bossy and try too hard to keep them in line. However, Tens do at times play nicely with younger siblings. In fact, younger ones often tease Tens to play with them. And many Tens are very good about caring for or helping with siblings who are under five. These younger ones are often reported to "adore" the ten-year-old. Some Tens know they are not good to younger siblings: "If I want to play with him I'm nice, but if I want to be alone he's a *goner!*"

Tens get on better with older than with younger siblings and report that older ones sometimes play with them or take them places, but that there is still a lot of fighting. Many think that older siblings consider them a nuisance or tattletales because they seek protection from parents.

11 Years

Eleven gets on badly with younger siblings much of the time (except with the very young ones). Fighting varies from "occasionally" to "about half the time." And though physical fighting is giving way to argument and name calling, violence still often occurs—hitting, kicking, biting, pulling hair. Much "needling" occurs, both physical and verbal: "She can't go by without touching him—just a little poke or jab. Then he reciprocates. Then there's a real physical battle."

Eleven's chief complaint is, "He gets me into trouble!" The younger one "starts something." Eleven "pays him back." Parent punishes Eleven. Elevens resent parents' idea that because they are older they should put up with the younger one and not retaliate, feel that this is "siding with" the younger one.

Eleven is very critical of the faults of younger siblings—thinks they are lazy, messy, careless, untruthful—and tries to correct and boss them, which is resented. He often yells at younger siblings, even though he complains that older siblings yell at *him*. Possessions too are the cause of much difficulty: "He gets into my things."

Some lock the door to keep out very young siblings and "try to ignore" those nearer their own age. They feel that young siblings tag along too much and sometimes don't mind this, but often do. Occasionally, however, Eleven plays well with younger ones and may be glad of their company, especially when away from home.

Most Elevens get on reasonably well with siblings who are much older than they—eighteen years or older. About those just a few years older they say, "We fight some, but not as much as we did." Fighting with older siblings may now be more verbal than physical: "We don't hit each other, but we argue about everything." They still tease older ones and are teased by them.

Some play with older siblings—especially sports. But older ones feel that Elevens tag along too much and don't want them around when older friends are present.

Many say they miss older siblings who have gone away to school but are partly glad they are away.

Eleven may worry that brothers and sisters prefer each other to her or are ganging up against her.

12 Years

Twelve seems to get on a little better with younger siblings than he did at eleven, though relations are usually less than the parents' ideal. Mostly, Twelve expresses a great lack of enthusiasm for younger siblings: "Oh, I guess he's all right"; "Guess I have to *say* I like having a sister." His expression may be as positive as, "We get on about as well as most, I guess—squabble some, have some fun together" or may be more negative: "We get on awful"; "He's a pest"; "She's terrible."

The amount of fighting admitted to ranges from "occasional quarrels" to "always fighting." One girl says, "Once in a while we have a break and don't fight. On the average we fight once a day—sometimes three times, sometimes not at all."

Having the last word is very important.

Chief complaints are that younger ones tease and taunt them (especially in front of friends and particularly about boyfriends or girlfriends), hang around too much, pester them to play games, get into their "stuff." "He hits me but I'm not allowed to hit him" is common, as is, "He gets away with things I never got away with."

Relationships between siblings tend to improve with increasing age. Many Twelves are quite good with brothers and sisters who are four or under. These are described as "okay" or even "fun." Relations with brothers and sisters sixteen and over also is mostly good: "idolizes her," "admires him." This is a recent development with most. Their own statements about the improved relationship reflect considerable docility: "He teases me all the time but only in fun. He never beats or hurts me"; "Get on fine now—she doesn't seem to dislike me as much as before."

Most, however, get on very badly with thirteen- and fourteen-year-old siblings, at least part of the time: "We're always fighting—sometimes with words, sometimes with fists." When not fighting, they get on "fairly well." Boys enjoy wrestling.

Several at this age say they like being an only child: "I don't know if I should say this, but I have a dog and I like him as well as I would a brother or sister."

13 Years

Most Thirteens, as earlier, get on quite well with older or much younger siblings, sometimes expressing real affection for the latter. Most still have trouble with those just a few years younger, but this trouble is usually less constant than earlier and often is just general trouble. Rather than listing specific complaints, as earlier, they say, "Don't know exactly what it's about." Fighting may also be less bitter: "We fight a lot. We enjoy it, but my parents don't like it." Real hatred for a younger sibling is rare, but occasionally is reported by parents. Younger siblings in these cases may like, even "adore," the older brother or sister.

Worst difficulty seems to be with the ten- and eleven-year-olds, with whom some "argue and fight all the time" and with six- and seven-year-olds, whom they describe as "pests," "nuisances," "awful," "impossible," "spoiled brats." Thirteen is critical of younger siblings: they lie, are messy, ask stupid questions. The younger ones resent this and give trouble when Thirteen tries to "boss" or discipline them.

Fighting now is more verbal than physical. Occasionally Thirteen says very mean things to younger siblings: "Who could like that stupid so-and-so?" "She's just a queer." And these younger ones definitely talk back ("Oh, mind your own business") or mimic and mock. A few Thirteens are mature enough to control younger siblings, but most still just try to boss.

In several families, Thirteens are punished for mistreating younger siblings by taking deductions from their allowances. But parents may be beginning to side with Thirteen a little more, recognizing faults of the younger children. This helps out.

Insight into relationships with siblings is shown increasingly: "Probably partly my fault; he wouldn't pester me if he didn't get any reaction"; "Later she won't find it such fun to bother me, but right now I'm sort of touchy." And some use humor: "We get on fairly well. For instance, when he's asleep."

Some admit the advantage of siblings as playmates if nobody else is around. And several comment spontaneously that they are glad not to be an only child because if they were they might be spoiled.

A marked improvement occurs in relations with older siblings, even with those close to Thirteen in age. Not only may they not fight but they may even express affection: "We do a lot of palling around together"; "She's definitely my sister now"; "I can tell her things and she understands—definitely convenient."

Thirteen is described by parents as "devoted" to older siblings, admiring, proud. And though parents often report the relationship as being better than the children say it is, Thirteen herself may say, "Get on better than we used to—real improvement this last year." Quarreling with older siblings is now only occasional in most.

14 Years

In his relations with siblings, Fourteen usually shows some improvement over years past but generally still leaves much to be desired by parents, especially in his relations with those closest in age. Most trouble is with eleven-year-olds.

With much younger siblings—five or under—most Fourteens get on well: take care of them, play with them, even buy them things. But the trouble that occurs with those between six and thirteen is suggested in Fourteen's comments: "nuisance," "pain in the neck," "that face of hers—it kills me!" And some simply say, "I just don't like her as well as I used to."

Fourteen's chief complaints about siblings are: "argues all the time," "gets into my things," "tags along," "makes noises and moves around so," "when she isn't talking she's singing or dancing," "shows off and wants to be the center of attention," "wants me to do everything for her but doesn't want to do a thing for me."

Fourteen may recognize and comment that if one member of a family is out of sorts it spoils things for all. But, nevertheless, a great deal of arguing takes place. And though physical violence occurs less than formerly, it still does occur. Some merely threaten to hit, but others actually "get mad and hit him," "slug him whenever I get the chance."

Most parents feel that Fourteens should treat younger siblings better and try to improve their own behavior. Frequently parents step in to prevent ill-treatment of younger ones. Some Fourteens, on the other hand, occasionally protect young siblings from parents.

Marked individual differences exist in Fourteens' relations with older siblings. Some get on very well—go to dances and sports events together—but many get on badly. Fourteen especially criticizes the way older ones treat him or other members of the family. Many say they get on better than they used to with older siblings because they don't see much of each other.

Fourteen sometimes comments that in families of three children there is constant pairing off of two against one. Many of both sexes say they would rather have brothers than sisters.

6. Family

10 Years

Tens feel a much closer relationship with the family than at nine. Most accept and enjoy their family and usually participate most willingly in any kind of family activity—picnics, rides, movies, trips together. "Every Sunday afternoon the whole family goes for a ride."

Most Tens are well satisfied with both parents and do not like older siblings to criticize them.

However, quarreling with siblings may upset family harmony: "We're not a very harmonious family. Every meal something happens. We eat and scream mostly."

11 Years

Many Elevens have a strong family feeling. Though rude and quarrelsome within the family, how they behave does not necessarily indicate how they feel. Eleven likes belonging to a family, likes the idea of having relatives, appreciates his or her own family, and prefers it to friends.

Eleven enjoys family activities, of which there are often many: movies, picnics, weekly rides, the zoo, listening to music together. In fact, he can be quite demanding: "What are we going to do today?" Mothers report, "God forbid that we just stay home!"

Many are beginning to see their parents more as individuals, not just as parents, and some criticism of them occurs. Some rebellion: "I'm a free person. Why do I have to do what the family tells me?"

Eleven often appears quite unaware of the extent to which quarreling with siblings, rebellion against mother, and unwillingness to help interferes with family harmony.

12 Years

Twelve is more easygoing within the family group and shows less rebellion, but also less intense interest. The majority are still well satisfied with their families and feel close to them: "Pretty good family—I'm lucky to be in it"; "I think we do well as a family."

Family activities and excursions interest Twelve a little less than they did at eleven. Beginning of some withdrawal: "I like to spend some time with my family, but some time with my friends." Or even, "I just have to get out of there sometimes."

13 Years

Thirteen often brings a marked and sudden withdrawal from any participation in family activities. He may spend only the necessary minimum of time with family, as at mealtimes. "Just not a part of the family—withdraws and is hostile to individual members."

Thirteen has less to say about the family than earlier. Comments: "Of course we have our arguments"; "Fairly harmonious—of course everybody has their little spats"; or even, "I think I'm beginning to break away a little, but I take that as natural."

Each member of the family may be critical of others: son may think father treats mother badly or that mother is too much influenced by father; mother thinks father is too strict with son; father thinks mother is too easy.

Boys may go out with father alone rather than with the whole family.

14 Years

Many Fourteens are highly embarrassed by their families. They feel strongly the need of breaking away and establishing independence: "Sometimes if you're too close to your family it's too bad because you never can leave them."

They may be highly insulted and indignant if family does not have the very best TV, car, house, etc.

Fourteen is often less worried than earlier when parents argue and may think it's silly.

Some admit that they wouldn't want their friends to see the way they treat their families: "I don't add very much to family life. I have a very nasty disposition, you might say. Well, what have I got in common with them?"

7. Effect of Divorce at Different Ages

Clearly divorce is not a happy or comfortable affair for the child of any age. Its effect will vary from child to child and from family to family. Assuming that the age of the young person involved might be an influencing factor, we offer the following gradient.

10 Years

This might be a very bad year for parents to get a divorce. The typical Ten loves not only mother and father but the total family; loves for them to do things together; thinks (even in the face of evidence to the contrary) that he or she has "the best family in the world."

The child of this age, as a rule, has not started the normal pulling away that characterizes the teens. Thus a divorce at this time could be a terrible shock, surprise, disappointment, and all-around blow.

11 Years

The typical eleven-year-old tends to be exuberantly belligerent but may still be enthusiastic about family outings. Earlier total worship of parents is much diminished. One almost feels that so long as there is plenty of food in the house, the child might be willing to spare one of his or her parents.

12 Years

The child of twelve is definitely beginning to lead more of a life on his or her own than earlier. Twelves tend to be on a rather even keel—taking things as they come. Friends are definitely beginning to be as important or even more important than family. We would expect that a twelve-year-old might be able to accept divorce better than children of some other ages.

13 Years

Thirteen is definitely a pulled-in age. Girl or boy does not spend any more time than necessary with family. Thirteen tends to be a loner and may prefer time spent alone in his or her own room. Boy or girl tends not to confide in *anyone*. It might seem, therefore, that divorce would not make all that much difference, but we suspect that it would. The child of this age might suffer a good deal from divorce, and all the more so since he or she finds it so hard to confide. Divorce might constitute a deep inner blow.

14 Years

Bouncy, energetic, vigorous, peer-oriented Fourteens tend to find that their greatest problem is their parents, who are so old-fashioned, peculiar, restrictive.

Boy or girl of this age also tends to have same-age best friends who can be a great support in a crisis (especially if they have experienced divorce in their own families.) A child of this age might not suffer quite as much from a divorce as a just-younger or just-older boy or girl.

8. Responses During a Personal Interview

10 Years

INTERVIEW: Extremely friendly response to interviewer. Generally trusting, confiding, frank—but also seems shy and vulnerable. Sits near interviewer or actually leans on her desk. Asks questions about interviewer, compliments her.

Very active—moves about room, asks about nearly every object in it. General bodily wriggling, much fiddling with things. Sits on end of spine or all over chair. Pushes chair around on floor. Swings legs. Comments on typing, examines typewriter. Wants to read own responses.

Inclined to go on and on with plot of story or details about his life. Tends to answer, "Sometimes I do and sometimes I don't." May not understand questions; needs examples to choose from. Asks "how much more?" Short attention span; needs diversion.

11 Years

INTERVIEW: Friendly and polite, frank and confiding response to interviewer. Gives information freely, candidly; tells all. Quite factual and detailed.

Leans on interviewer's desk, manipulates typewriter. Comments about typing, interviewer's speed, number of pages. Wants to read interview questions and own responses.

Is all over his chair; feet over chair arm, lifts buttocks, bounces up and down, pulls arm of chair, pushes chair around on floor. May roam around room inspecting things, asking about them. Hands constantly active, swings leg, kicks at desk, knocks knees together, fools with shoe.

Interrupts interview with questions about objects in room or things in general. May request something to eat. Tires and wants to know how much more. Hard for some to give clear-cut answers: "Well, yes and no," "Hard to say." Prefaces many responses with "Well . . ." But once started may go on and on in endless detail. Dramatic emphasis on key words. Much grimacing—either ticlike or to express disgust. Much laughter; may tell jokes to examiner. Not much generalizing; just lists things.

12 Years

INTERVIEW: Generally friendly, cheerful, enthusiastic, outgoing, cooperative, frank, and honest. Comments, "This is fun!" But less communicative than at eleven and also less interested in interviewer (though still makes such comments as "quite a place you have here!"). Comments on typing, reads what has been written. May instruct interviewer which remarks to record and which to disregard.

Most do not leave the chair now. Instead, *look* around room from chair, commenting on books and other objects in room. However, very active in chair—much wiggling; may move chair around on floor. Hands very active, much fiddling. Jiggles leg, swings foot.

Groans, makes faces, dramatizes if questions are difficult, or just to illustrate points. Jokes with interviewer. Asks if he is going to learn about self.

Though some find it difficult to make clear-cut statements, answers are generally more cut-and-dried with less embellishment than at eleven. And some can now generalize, not just list as they did previously.

13 Years

INTERVIEW: Though most are friendly, they often appear withdrawn, look rather sad. Not spontaneous or communicative. Even when rapport is good, interview not very revealing. No secrets are told; answers are brief and guarded.

However, many seem to examine own thoughts and try to answer accurately. Some do become warmer as interview proceeds.

Most sit quietly, with little general movement. Hands are active, fiddling with things. May hold foot or swing leg. Few mention typing or ask to see what is being typed.

Some interest in what tests show about their personality. Listen to interviewer's comments and may question her. Interviewer feels need to phrase questions carefully.

Little humor expressed. Not too explicit in responding: "It varies"; "It depends."

14 Years

INTERVIEW: Again friendly and outgoing. Conversational and humorous. May spontaneously comment that they are enjoying themselves, "like it here."

Enthusiastic and energetic, but energy now directed to expression of ideas rather than moving about room or in chair. Most sit quiet and relaxed, with only hands slightly active; some occasionally move foot or swing leg.

No attention to recording, but some do express interest in what they have said earlier or what others their age have said.

Volunteer information spontaneously. Usually quite frank but not as confiding as earlier. Many try hard to express themselves accurately but may have trouble in saying a thing just right.

Most are interested in interviewer's comments, frequently ask her opinion, but may wish to leave for other engagement before interview is finished.

9. Same-sex Friends

10 Years

GIRLS: Most have a best friend, often several. Relationships among these friends are extremely complex and intense—much getting mad and not speaking. ("We just don't speak for a while—and then she'll come back with some ice cream cones and we'll make up.")

Much anger, jealousy, and fighting if friends associate with other, disliked girls ("Laurel spits fire if I go out with Nancy"). Very possessive of friends and very demanding.

Apt to be very cliquey and purposely say things to pit some girls against others. "Let's go against somebody."

Much emphasis on secrets and whom they can trust: ("I can trust her never to tell *anything,* no matter how mad at me she is"). A few describe the personality of friends ("We're very much alike except that she hates to read and I love to read"), but most emphasize trustworthiness.

Considerable spending the night with each other.

BOYS: Some ten-year-olds have one or two "best" or "trusted" friends. Others have a whole "gang" whom they seem to like about equally: "To me they aren't best friends. They're *all* my friends."

Groups may be fluid. Or one boy may have two definite groups which do not mix. Some, though they have many friends, often prefer to play with just one friend at a time.

Most "get on good." Not as much fighting and getting mad and not speaking as among the girls. However, some ganging up of two against one.

Boys, in telling of their friends, usually tell their full names, ages, where they live, and what games are played together. Some will shift kind of activity to suit the taste and abilities of the companion of the moment.

Chief activities seem to be baseball, football, wrestling, electric trains, riding bicycles, building tents or huts, going to the movies, computer games.

11 Years

GIRLS: A few have just one or two best friends; others have many. Some just loosely have "a whole gang" of friends; others arrange them in a definite hierarchy ("My best friend is Lollie. Then next comes Ruthie, and on the same line with Ruthie is Eve"). Some may list all friends, criticizing each. One typical Eleven asks, "Could I just say who *isn't* my best friend?"

Relationships continue to be very emotional, intense, and complicated. Much getting mad, not speaking, threatening. "All right for you" or waiting for the other to give in. All this is probably enjoyed, at least by some. ("Whole gang of friends and I like everybody. But we have to quarrel to break up the smoothness.")

Considerable verbal, emotional, and physical conflict among girls: "She's always trying to strangle me"; "She's just plain nasty—mentions my braces and asks why I lisp." Very vulnerable to mean remarks by friends in front of others; very limited ability to laugh it off.

Some are strongly under the influence of a best friend and try hard to please her in everything. May, for instance, neglect practicing at friend's behest. A few very warm or even sentimental about friends: "She's awfully nice" or, "I'd never get mad at my pal." A few take up with some unpopular or unattractive child and are very loyal.

Jealousy about who else their friends play with; quarreling about very small, unimportant things. Much jockeying for position: insisting on paying for own treats, or on treating friends; too compulsive and insistent to be mere generosity.

Beginning of specific criticism of friends: "She's really too tough for me" or, "She swears a lot."

Spending the night with each other is a continued interest.

BOYS: As at ten, some concentrate on one or two best friends, some are part of a gang, and some have both.

Relations in many are described as "okay," but in others are much less smooth than at ten, though not as complex as among girls. There is much quarreling and making up, getting mad, not speaking. "I let them start speaking, but if they won't then I have to."

Rather specific criticism of friends: "he brags," "he blames me." And, conversely, warm compliments: "one real friend, a real pal"; "my greatest friend. Interesting to talk to and we both have the same ideas"; "about the same temperament as me."

Baseball, bicycling, sports, movies, and hut or tree-house play are enjoyed by the gangs.

Beginning to spend the night with each other.

Several report that they have plenty of children to play with ("roughly about ten good ones"), whereas their mothers say that they are lonesome, don't have many friends, or don't have much social life.

12 Years

GIRLS: Expansive in friendship at this age. Many no longer have a single friend but now "a whole gang." ("Go around with everybody. Try to be nice to all"). Sometimes just two or three separate off from the group, but it's "not against anybody." A few now have real trouble making friends, but these are in the minority.

Relationships less intense. Some getting mad and not speaking, but less than before. Less under influence of friends. However, "telling her off" is important.

"She lives near me" seems to be an adequate reason in many cases for friendships. Most report that they have a good time together or "get on pretty good."

Some friendships break up when one girl suddenly moves over into great interest in boys, leaving the other behind: "She goes around with older kids now"; "All she talks about is boys and clothes." Or, conversely, "She seems so goody-goody. I've changed. I was like her."

Spending the night with each other is strong, as is telephoning.

BOYS: The majority now seem to have a rather large number of good or best friends: "I have four best friends," "three different buddies," "quite a few friends, maybe twenty; of these, eight are my best friends."

With the diffuseness of Twelve, several report that, though they have many friends, they have "no *special* friends" Or, "A lot of special friends—like them all alike." "Different ones at different times."

Neighborhood play with whoever is available has somewhat given way to telephoning or specially inviting certain friends.

Some dissension and some complaining about friends: "Some of them annoy me"; "We quarrel some"; "Some are silly—they brag and fool too much." Most, however, with considerable shifting from friend to friend, get on reasonably well. They are beginning to mention dependability of friends.

13 Years

GIRLS: Some still go around with a "whole gang" ("Four of us fool around together"). But many thirteens seem less well supplied with friends than earlier: "Marcia was my best friend but she left"; "This year I don't seem to have many friends." May also be less close with friends than earlier: "not really intimate," "nobody close now."

Unevenness seems to mark friendships now: "One day I'd love to do something. Next day I don't feel like it"; "I have spells of liking them." However, confiding secrets to friends is important: "I don't have any definite friends, but I do trust those I have"; "I do tell her my secrets."

In a group of three, any two, then the other two, may pair off and talk about the third "just to decide how we want to do."

Beginning interest in discussion of own and others' personality and behavior. Girls classify other girls as the "fast" set, the "intellectual" set, and so on.

Some now said to treat friends much better than family.

Still a good deal of spending the night and telephoning.

BOYS: Some still play with a "whole gang" or have several "best friends." But most are less sociable than at twelve. Many have only one best friend. "Had a best friend but he moved away." Many have plenty of friends at school but say that, because of where they live, they have nobody to play with at home. In several cases, groups of gangs of three or four break up, and all members withdraw to more or less solitary activity.

Those who still have a group of friends may nevertheless prefer to play with them separately.

There seems to be more "getting mad" than at twelve. One boy reports, "The guys at school are awful. All hate each other and hate everything. Act awful. Not wise to themselves. Juvenile. A few good ones. If anybody hates your guts, just look out. They really get you."

Boys do some telephoning but usually less than girls.

Can now keep up friendships with out-of-town friends by writing and visiting.

14 Years

GIRLS: Preferred friends may now be schoolmates who live in other parts of town. May associate with girls in the neighborhood because of proximity, but may not consider them best friends.

Friendships not so intense and quarrelsome as earlier. But much interest in each other's personalities and may try to change friends' personalities. Much talking about activities, boys, emotions. Typical comment: "Last year we used to talk about horses an awful lot, and the boys didn't come into it; but now they're the main topic."

Each school class seems to have its "gang" (not club) of the more popular and successful girls. Those outside very anxious to be accepted by them.

Girls very active with friends: movies, sports events, band or orchestra, baby-sitting, picnics, parties, hikes.

Perhaps the high point for telephoning: "as much as mother can stand"; "as much as we can get away with." They giggle, gossip, do homework, listen to records while phoning.

Some girls at this age go out of their way to be nice to unpopular or unattractive girls.

BOYS: A few have a single best friend. But the majority have "a whole gang of friends."

No longer choose friends on the basis of availability. Thus preferred friends may be school friends who do not live nearby: "quite a few friends at school but they don't live near me." The majority of boys mention sports as the thing they have in common with their friends. A few choose friends who are "smart." Or they may have several different friends to share different interests.

Most seem to get on reasonably well with friends. "Everybody pretty harmonious."

Boys, like girls, are becoming interested in the personalities of their friends.

10. Opposite-sex Friends

10 Years

GIRLS: Perhaps the majority are "not interested in boys yet or are "against" boys: "Oh, we don't like boys. They can be plenty mean." Girls complain that boys pull their hair, chase them, push them down, act rough, and throw food at parties. But some are said to dream about boys.

Some girls are willing to play with boys but are not personally interested in them: "I like to play with boys, but that's all."

However, about a third of our ten-year-old girls express positive, personal interest in boys or in one special boy: "I fool around with boys. They walk home with me. I like some of them"; "One boy that I admire from a distance"; "Two boys I like. They like me. We fool around when the teacher isn't looking."

Most consider girls who kiss boys to be extremely forward.

When asked if they have started dating yet, eighty-five percent of the girls say they have not. But fifty-four percent say they would like to. Sixty percent of the girls say they have adequate information about sex and dating.

BOYS: The majority of ten-year-old boys express either no interest in or active dislike of girls: "I don't like girls. Period. Tattletales"; "We sort of hate girls"; "They're tiresome because they always get mad at you." But some do like to "bug" girls.

Some say they used to have a girl, but now she likes someone else and they "haven't bothered to get another." Some still let girls play baseball or other games with them. A few express friendship, but nothing warmer, for girls: "I like girls, but I don't love 'em"; "The nearest I do is *like* a girl. That's all. I haven't told her yet. I'm not all that interested in girls."

11 Years

GIRLS: Many girls are now in an extremely anti-boy stage: "they're stinking," "disgusting," "all pests," "some of them are very queer," "just horrible."

Some, however, are neutral. "I don't think we've got to boys yet."

May emphasize the nonromantic aspect of any relationship: "I don't like those who go around saying they love you and you love them. All thinking about love. Not an interesting topic at this point."

Others, more advanced, are on the verge of heterosexual interest: "A little interested. We talk to each other about boys. But we don't play with them. *They won't let us.*" Or, "We each have ones we sort of like. I don't know if they like us, and I don't know if they know we like them."

Some girls are now very aggressive about boys—chase and annoy them.

Seventy percent of girls have not yet started dating, but fifty-seven percent say they would like to. Fifty-seven percent say they have adequate information about sex and dating.

The whole relationship, if friendly, may still be very peripheral: "Boys I like. I'm not sure whether they like me. They might. My sister finds out for me. She asks their sisters."

Boys do pester girls considerably. They trip them up, throw spit-balls or snowballs, hit them, pretend to strangle them. Girls, as a group, tend to feel that boys, as a group, are fresh, rude, and disobedient at school.

Beginning of calling up and "kidding" over the phone—either boy or girl may initiate this. Usually do it when a whole group is around to enjoy the results.

BOYS: Most boys now express a neutral feeling about girls. "I don't hate girls but I don't like them yet"; "We don't mind girls, but we don't usually play with them. I guess we would if we had to." However, nearly a quarter of our boys are warmer than this. They are either "interested in" some certain girl or even "have a girl-friend," though this latter may be "just to keep in step with my friend." Interest is usually reported very matter-of-factly and without the self-conscious, pleased smile which comes in later.

Several boys "had one but she moved away." A few, perhaps more mature, emphasize, "I like them as *friends*. Not as girlfriends."

Reasons for liking certain girls include: "She walks lightly"; "She's pretty."

Most feel that girls are no good at sports: "They have no judgment at all. Even a dumbbell could do better."

The boys in a school class are, as a group, rivals of and hostile to the girls.

Just over half the boys say they have not started dating yet, but seventy-one percent say they would like to. Fifty-nine percent of boys say they have adequate information about sex.

12 Years

GIRLS: Many now are on the verge of being interested in boys. Typical is the statement: "Yes, we're sort of interested in them and have ones we like." Or, "Well, I have one boy that I like. Just kind of like him, but we don't go out together. He doesn't seem to know it." A few think that the boy of their choice does "know it" or believe he likes them because he calls them "stupid."

Others don't have a particularly favored boy but say, "I think boys are okay"; "They're all right"; or "Nobody I like. I just have my eyes open at the moment."

Even now the majority of girls do not yet date, but thirty-four percent say they would like to. Of those girls who do date, about equal numbers double-date or single date.

Though the majority are friendly and even enthusiastic, some still express hostility. And even more than at eleven, girls may be very aggressive and teasing with boys.

Interest is fairly general. What dating occurs is usually in relation to planned parties or dances, and parents usually provide transportation.

A few admit that they flirt or are "boy crazy," but these are somewhat advanced for their age.

Girls are often larger than the boys, which seems to present a problem.

BOYS: About a third, whether accurately or not, report that they used to have a girl but they lost her or gave her up and haven't bothered to get another. About a third "haven't gotten into girls yet." The remainder say that they do have one girl or more. However, some of these girls do not know it yet.

Thirty-eight percent of the boys have already started dating, and fifty-two percent say they would just as soon start.

Enthusiasm of most boys for the girl of their choice is not excessive: "Just got her for something to do"; "Got one just to keep up with my friend. Then he gave up his, so I gave up mine."

Some, however, seem quite enthusiastic about marrying and even mention it spontaneously—some current choice or just someone eventually. But others still speak of going over to a girl's house "to play."

Probably it is the somewhat immature boy who is now strongly anti-girl. "All you can picture them as is tattletales and squirts" or

"They're useless. Every time you want to do something, there's always some stupid girl in the way. Like if you throw a spitball, there's some stupid girl has to stick her head right in the way."

Regardless of own status, the majority report that "most of the boys have somebody," even though she may not know it or they may not actually be taking her out.

Many of the boys say they do enjoy parties.

13 Years*

GIRLS: Only about one third of our girls say "Yes" to the question "Do you do much dating?" though, somewhat contradictorily, forty percent say they go steady or have gone steady. Even more, fifty percent of girls, "believe in" going steady. ("If you're in love," they add.) Ninety percent of girls say that either they or some of their friends "make out."

Some girls, however, still say that boys are idiots and they don't like them. The typical thirteen-year-old seems to be between these two extremes. She likes boys and talks about them to other girls but is not yet "boy crazy." Several say they don't *necessarily* like boys but guess they're all right.

Many say there is one (or several) they like, but these preferred boys may not know about it. In fact, a good deal may go on in the girls' minds with no actual contact with the favored boy. Apparently, to many thirteen-year-olds, boys in the flesh are too much trouble, but they love to talk and think about them.

Many girls are more withdrawn from boys than at twelve—more critical of them: "Last year I liked boys terribly much. But now I don't like them as much. Oh, they're bad! They like to play kissing games." Also, girls seem to get less attention than earlier. They often prefer just to invite other girls to parties; call each other "darling!"

Most association with boys occurs at school, at parties, or still in "playing together." Parents may still transport girls to and from parties.

A good many girls say cheerfully that they have no one now but seem to look forward to more success in the near future. Some admit that they giggle, talk silly, and act silly when boys are around. Explain that this is because they are excited and embarrassed.

Girls still have the difficulty that many boys their age are shorter than they.

---

* Note that our subjects are, for the most part, middle-class young people. The whole story is, of course, often quite different in the inner cities.

BOYS: Less interest is expressed in girls than at twelve years. More than half the boys say they have no girl of their own. The majority of these say, "No girl yet." A few have tried having a girl, but it hasn't worked out very well: "I used to have a girl, but I got bored." And several express neutral feelings as at eleven: "Don't find them repulsive"; "Like some as friends, but not as girlfriends. Don't like that kind of stuff too well."

About a third of the boys respond "Yes" to the question "Do you do much dating?" and forty-four percent say they go steady or have done so, even if only once or just for a few weeks. Even more (sixty-eight percent) say they "believe in" going steady. And ninety percent say that either they or their friends make out.

A few say either that they have a girlfriend, or at least "sort of like" girls. But with most, this has not gone as far as dating. Boys "play with girls," "sit with them at the movies," "kid" on the phone, dance with them at dances, but don't "really" take them out. Might get a friend to invite a girl out for them, but won't take a chance themselves.

"Interested in them. Don't actually take them out" is perhaps as typical a statement as any. Or, typical of Thirteen's negativism: "I wouldn't say I don't like girls." A few, however, are "woman haters" or "don't give a snap about girls."

Qualities liked in girls are "a good personality," "manners." Or, "She's quite special for a girl. She's a tomboy and quite interesting. Good mind. Pretty. At some things she can lick any boy in school—skiing, for instance."

At school, between classes, boys pour sawdust in girls' hair, grab their books, and pay other such attentions.

BOTH SEXES: The question "Have you ever had a friend who made out?" was first asked of thirteen-year-olds. Apparently we began asking this question too late, since ninety percent of each sex answered in the affirmative. As one thirteen-year-old girl replied, "Yeah! Everyone does." (This does not entirely agree with information given by individual children.)

However, only twenty-five percent of girls and thirty percent of boys claimed to have a friend who had "gone all the way." For the few who, by report of their friends, had had sexual experience, the condom or pill was the main contraceptive measure used. Twenty-five percent of girls and forty percent of boys claimed to have a friend who at one time or another had gotten "into trouble," but the actual age of this supposed friend was not indicated, and it may well have been an older (or even a mythical) friend.

14 Years

GIRLS: Now thirty-two percent of girls say that they do much dating; fifty-six percent say they believe in going steady; sixty-eight percent go steady or have done so. Most, however, have gone steady, if at all, for only a few months at a time.*
Other girls report, "Not any boy right now"; "Haven't started dating yet." Several say, "Just started recently." There is much individual variation here from girls who still have a secret crush on some boy who doesn't know it to those who do quite a lot of dating.

Many girls are considered to be quite boy crazy. Think boys are "simply wonderful," "absolutely divine." Spend a lot of time talking about boys though, for some, enthusiasm may exceed actual activity. Girls often ask boys to arrange dances. Many girls at this age seem suddenly to blossom out and become very effective and sure of themselves with boys.

BOYS: More than half our boys (fifty-six percent) answer "Yes" to the question "Do you do much dating?" Seventy-four percent believe in going steady, and fifty-four percent go steady or have done so. The largest number of boys who have gone steady have done so more than four times.

Boys are now interested in whether their friends do or do not date. Their estimates vary. One boy says, "No one in our class goes out with girls. More interested in sports and our future." Another estimates, "Less than half the boys have girls. But only a couple of boys don't have an interest in girls." Still another comments, "I think the girls are much more interested in the boys than the boys are in the girls."

Dating is just beginning for some, as for the boy who describes

---

* Terminology is important here. Different communities have different ways of speaking about dating activities. One fourteen-year-old girl explained to us, patiently, "You don't 'date.' You either are going out with somebody or not." Another put it, "You don't 'go steady.' You just go out with someone." But in other cities, "dating" and "going steady" are still acceptable descriptions of boy-girl relationships. (Whatever the topic, as one mother says, it is not useful to try to keep up with teenage terminology. However you, the parents, phrase it, you are most likely to be out-of-date and thus subject to ridicule.)

his friend as "*actually* going out with a girl." Some don't date yet do enjoy hanging around and "kidding" with girls.

Some boys who did like girls earlier are now less interested than they were. Others have just not yet become interested, like the boy who says, "I like people. Every kind except girls." Some report themselves as being more popular with girls than their parents say they are.

BOTH SEXES: The question "Ever had a friend who made out?" is, interestingly enough, answered in the affirmative by slightly fewer Fourteens than Thirteens—eighty-two percent of girls, seventy-five percent of boys. However, this is balanced by the increasing number who, reportedly, have had a friend or friends who "go all the way"—fifty-seven percent of girls, fifty-five percent of boys. This is the first age at which more than half our subjects answered this question in the affirmative. Contraceptives used continue to be primarily the condom and the pill. Now thirty-nine percent of the girls, fifty percent of the boys, say they know somebody who has gotten "into trouble."

11. Parties
10 Years
There are not too many boy-girl parties at this age. At any which are given, games and food are the main interests. There is not much interaction between girls and boys, though some girls report that boys are beginning to tease them.

Twenty percent of our boys say they "kiss" or "make out." Except for kissing, which might occur only in kissing games (and most Tens are not too much interested in this), this report may be more fantasy than fact.

11 Years
This is not a strong age for parties. Those given are mostly for just girls or just boys. However, as was the case at ten, if boy-girl parties are held, dancing is definitely beginning to come in. Interestingly, girls and boys whom we interviewed report somewhat different activities. Girls say they play games, dance, talk—in that order. (Twenty percent of girls now say that they "make out.") Boys report dancing (forty-two percent) and making out (sixteen percent) as their main party activities and interests.

12 Years
There is now much interest in having boy-girl parties, but they often do not turn out too well. The boys may still, as just earlier, all

gang together and ignore the girls; or they may act very disruptively, throwing food and acting rough. There may be a good deal of turning out the lights, which boys consider a very racy thing to do.

Dancing is the main activity reported by girls (fifty-four percent), with talking and playing games also important (twenty-eight percent each). Twenty percent each say they "have fun" or "make out." Boys are surprisingly reticent at this age about what they do at parties—possibly because they often throw food or roughhouse with each other. Thirty-six percent of all boys do not say *what* they do. Activities which are reported by boys include eating and making out (sixteen percent each), drinking and playing games (twelve percent each). Drug use is reported here for the first time, but at a mere four percent.

13 Years

In general, parties are beginning to be a little calmer than earlier, though some boys may still be somewhat destructive, and girls tend to become overexcited and a little silly. Thirteen may still play games or may have moved on to dancing. (Thirty-two percent of girls, forty percent of boys, name dancing as the outstanding activity). Talking, "having fun," listening to records are also mentioned frequently by girls; talking, by boys. Twenty-four percent of girls, twenty-eight percent of boys, say they "make out." Drinking or drug use are specified by only a few.

In some parts of the country, shopping centers have added huge game rooms for teenagers. These provide places where young people can walk around, play games, roller-skate, and eat.

14 Years

Parties are now going very smoothly, though they still require considerable adult supervision if they are to go well. But boys and girls are, for the most part, now quite interested in each other, and this makes for better parties.

Making out, real or reported, is now by far the leading activity. Sixteen percent of girls, but a whopping ninety-five percent of boys, say that this is what they do at parties. Also, for the first time, drug use is reported substantially—by twenty-eight percent of girls and fifty percent of boys.

Other activities listed by girls are eating and dancing (twenty-four percent each), "having fun," and making out (sixteen percent each). Sixty-five percent of the boys say they drink at parties; sixty percent say they dance; thirty-five percent talk; twenty percent each eat or "have fun"; fifteen percent like to listen to music. But clearly —for boys—making out, drug use, dancing, and drinking are the main activities.

chapter fourteen
ACTIVITIES AND INTERESTS

In few areas of behavior does growing boy or girl show as truly his or her developmental level as in recreational tastes. School demands can, on occasion, require an individual to perform ahead of a comfortable level. Family demands can do the same. But when it comes to things a person does for fun, his true level of maturity can be rather plainly seen. A girl or boy whose behavior age is ahead of or below chronological age shows it very clearly in his or her chosen pastimes.

A thirteen-year-old girl put this very clearly when she explained to us that her same-age best friend was always about a year ahead of her in the things she liked to do. First her friend was wild about horses at a time when she herself couldn't have cared less. And now that she had gotten to horses, her friend had moved on to boys.

Though most parents care a great deal about their teenager's manners and morals, their clean hands and neat room, their good grades in school, most of these things for the growing girl or boy are definitely secondary. Their prime interest is in making friends and having a good time.

What constitutes having fun, of course, changes dramatically in the years between ten and fourteen. Ten may enjoy nothing more than going out of doors to play after dinner. Fourteen's ideas of pleasure are obviously far more sophisticated.

The gradients which make up the body of this chapter provide details as to this rather major sweep of changing interests in these lively years. Here we give just a brief overview.

OUTDOOR ACTIVITIES: The outdoor activities of the ten-year-old are distinguished chiefly by their vigor and shapelessness. Ten is not so much interested in formal sports with rules as in sheer movement. He loves to run and race and chase, to "fool around," and "wrassle."

Any sort of ball play intrigues him or her: baseball, soccer, tether ball, or just throwing a ball against the side of the house. Sandlot baseball is extremely popular with girls and boys alike. In fact, girls and boys often play together. Other sports are popular in season: sledding, skating, swimming, skiing. Or hide and seek or bike riding or the current year's version of Cops and Robbers.

Girls more than boys enjoy jump rope, roller-skating, hopscotch. Anything, so long as it involves whole body movement, goes well at this age. And most play relatively amicably.

Eleven's play is not too different, except that it is calming down and shaping up a trifle. They enjoy most of the things that Tens do. A few more games with rules come in and a little less just plain "horsing around." Running and hiding games as well as all sorts of ball play are still popular. But some Elevens have calmed down to the point where simply walking in the woods with friends gives pleasure. The play of boys is still rather more active than that of girls, and the two sexes play a little less together, but both sexes enjoy the seasonal sports.

Though to the uninitiated eye a group of twelve-year-olds playing out of doors is still rather active, the keen observer will note a lessening of sheer animal vigor, an increasing casualness in at least some of the young person's outdoor activity. There is a lot of "hanging around" or "just fooling around."

Though all but the most bookish of boys still maintain a generalized interest in sports, girls seem quite divided between the athletic and the nonathletic. Some of the latter while outdoors are content simply to walk and talk. (In fact, at all ages from now on, indoors or out, talking will for most girls be a major interest.) Seasonal sports are strong: baseball, football, basketball, hockey, swimming, and skating. Also tennis, badminton, boxing, bicycle races, fencing.

Horseback riding, which begins around eleven in horse-loving girls (of whom there are many) continues strong at twelve. Though some boys ride horseback too, many have moved on to a beginning interest in hunting and fishing.

By thirteen, at least in many communities, boys and girls take quite different paths to enjoyment. Many boys are described as being "all wrapped up" in sports—basketball, football, hockey, as well as their possible continuing interest in hunting and fishing. Bicycling, horseback riding, roller-skating, are big with many girls, though except for the more athletic, walking and talking (about boys) continue to be the main activity.

Fourteen is not too different. Boys continue to be more physically active than all but the more athletic girls, and also to have more different outdoor interests than do girls. Dating is for many, especially girls, becoming a major and time-consuming interest, whether active dating itself or just talking about dating.

INDOOR ACTIVITIES: These interests are so many and so varied that it is difficult to compress a listing into a simple summary.

Collections, of almost anything, are very strong at ten, eleven, and twelve. Card games and table games, puzzles and models are also dominant interests in the early part of the ten to fourteen period. Pets, of course, even though young people may not do a very good job in taking care of them, are a constant source of comfort and pleasure. Secret clubs cement friendships and ostracize enemies.

Dolls and paper dolls, important to many girls at ten, are considered babyish by some Elevens and nearly all Twelves. Girls who earlier sewed doll's clothes, even though somewhat clumsily, may be beginning to sew and knit for themselves by twelve.

Boys by twelve are showing considerable skill in drawing, making gadgets, putting together models. Chemistry sets, electric trains, and, in the more intellectual, the beginning of chess are enjoyable time-passers. Both sexes, if talented or pushed by parents, may also play musical instruments.

By thirteen, and even more so at fourteen years of age, such generally popular activities as reading, talking on the telephone, and dating usurp many of the young person's free indoor hours. At thirteen, many are much involved in their individual hobbies, of whatever nature, but by fourteen, personal hobbies for many are losing their charm, and relationships with contemporaries—of either sex—are taking over first place.

A fourteen-year-old girl will tell you, when asked, that her main activities are "talking, playing cards, going to a friend's house, hanging around." Many boys by fourteen have adopted the all-consuming interest in sports, active or spectator, which for many will continue throughout their adult lives.

CLUBS AND CAMP: The ten-year-old's club, whether small and secret or large and nationally organized, can mean the world to him or her. Children who belong to the Brownies or Cub Scouts for the most part think their group, and its leader *wonderful,* and would do almost anything for it.

The same is true for most Elevens, though some, in typical eleven-year-old fashion, do behave badly at group meetings and are a little hard to control. At both ages secret clubs, as well, may be a child's be-all and end-all. Friendship seems so much more exciting if it involves a clubhouse, a secret name, and secret rules.

Private clubs continue in some at twelve, though interest in them, as well as interest in Scouts, may drop off very sharply at thirteen. Secret clubs are considered babyish, and Scouts, unless very well run, boring.

The nature of clubs changes, for most, by fourteen. Now Scouts and Campfire are out with many. Their place has been taken by 4-H, "Y," or school or church activity clubs. There may be the beginnings of secret sororities and fraternities in those schools which permit them.

Response to camp, as Dr. Gesell has phrased it, "spans the nadir and the zenith of emotional satisfaction for the young camper—the nadir if the child succumbs to homesickness and doesn't like camping away, the zenith if he or she gets the right counselor and a good bunch of campmates."

Parents will be wise to consider their own child's personality and preference about camping. A little pushing may be in order, but if a boy or girl has tried camp and hates it, as some do, parents may do best not to insist. Some young people are born campers. Others are neither born nor made.

READING: Reading too is a highly individual taste. There is many a teenager whose "nose is always in a book"; there are others whose reading remains at the barest minimum required by school and family.

One of the fears that has not proved realistic was that television watching would do away with, or at the least seriously interfere with, reading. Most parents today agree that true readers read as well as watch television; that nonreaders merely watch TV.

However, parents observe that even nonreaders will often read paperback books or magazines which deal with their own special interests and hobbies. Some parents have discovered that attention to possible visual problems which make reading uncomfortable can increase enthusiasm for books and for reading.

Despite parental prohibitions, comics, even today, are avidly read by many ten-year-olds, but there are signs of decreasing interest. Ten does not use his spending money as freely as before to increase his collections; there is less barter and borrowing. A few Elevens, however, may still read comics with moderate interest. At twelve, interest is definitely decreasing in most, and at thirteen it may be merely spasmodic.

The reading of magazines and newspapers is marginal and is determined chiefly by what is available at home. Ten, Eleven, and Twelve read chiefly for pictures, comics, cartoons, and perhaps sketchily for headlines and sports. At thirteen and fourteen, there is much more extensive and selective reading. Boys read scientific, technical, and sports magazines. Girls may elect a woman's magazine. A few at these ages frankly say that they read only magazines, preferring them to books.

RADIO, PHONOGRAPH, TELEVISION, AND MOVIES: The age trends in our group for television watching by girls are as follows: Ten-year-old girls seem to do the most TV watching, the largest number averaging sixteen to twenty hours a week. Even by eleven, the amount decreases, the largest number averaging (at least according to their own reporting) no more than fifteen hours a week. From then on, the largest number report either only five hours a week (possibly an incorrect report), or six to ten hours a week, with a slight increase at sixteen years to eleven to fifteen hours. Only a very small number at any age watch more than twenty-five to thirty hours a week.

Boys, according to their own report, watch considerably more than do girls. To include fifty percent or more of subjects at ten and eleven years, we must go up to twenty-one to twenty-five hours a week. By age thirteen, fifty percent or more watch fewer than twenty hours; at fourteen, the majority watch fifteen hours or fewer.

For girls, cartoons and comedies lead as favorite types of program at age ten; comedies and situation comedies at eleven and twelve; comedies at thirteen. Fourteen branches out and is more varied, preferring, in this order, comedies, movies, family shows, crime and police programs.

Boys too at ten prefer comedies and cartoons. Eleven likes comedies, cartoons, and sports. Twelve branches out to comedies, police or detective shows, and situation comedies. Thirteen likes comedies, sports, police or detective shows.

In brief, cartoons are out with girls after ten, with boys after eleven. Comedies lead at every age; mysteries diminish. Family shows, never strong with boys, are mostly out with girls after fifteen. Detective or police shows are strong at all ages. Interest in movies increases. Soap operas increasingly attract girls, are never too strong with boys. Boys are enthusiastic about sports; most girls don't watch sports programs.

By far the majority of both boys and girls say that, in their opinion, TV violence does not harm them. In fact, the majority of both sexes at all ages, except girls at twelve, say they think TV benefits more than harms them.

Radio and television seem to be used for somewhat different purposes—TV for entertainment, radio often more for background. We do not have current figures for the actual amount of time spent with the radio on.

Interest in the phonograph has undoubtedly decreased with the availability of television. Nevertheless, in many it starts very early —very simple phonographs which even a preschooler can manage are now available—and steadily increases in many till, and past, sixteen years of age.

By fourteen, approximately one fourth of the boys and girls whom we interviewed played their phonographs, their parents felt, almost constantly.

Movie attendance, once the ultimate entertainment for young people aged ten to fourteen, is for many less of an all-consuming passion than it was a decade ago. The somewhat diminishing appeal of cinema is probably due to two major factors. One is, of course, the increasing availability of movies on television, and VCRs. The second is the substantially increasing cost of a movie date—parking, the price of the ticket, and the cost of the food which normally follows the movie. Movie attendance seems very variable—depending on community custom and pocketbook.

Thus despite tremendous individual variation, our observation is that the kinds of things a boy or girl prefers to do "for fun" gives us one of our best possible clues as to his or her maturity relative to contemporaries. The girl who is still playing with dolls after her friends and classmates have given them up tells us very clearly that she is immature for her age. The girl or boy who is already actively dating while friends and contemporaries are still merely fantasizing about it, speaks clearly of his or her relative maturity.

GROWTH GRADIENTS

1. Reading

10 Years

Great personal variation in interest in reading appears. Some are "not much for reading." Others "love reading," "my favorite thing," "nose always in a book."

Amount of reading varies from less than a book a week to five or more; and for many, reading time equals the amount of time spent on radio and TV.

May get books from library, school, or may own them.

Quite a number are good about reading to younger siblings.

Prefer: animal (especially horse or dog) stories, mysteries, girls' and boys' adventure series, biographies.

COMIC BOOKS: A good many read comics, some avidly; and some still collect them avidly, though there is less collecting, swapping, and borrowing than earlier. Mothers mostly object, and some forbid.

MAGAZINES: Very little magazine reading, except for looking at pictures and cartoons in family's magazines. May subscribe to special children's magazines.

NEWSPAPERS: Minimal in most. Funnies and headlines are read most. Many just skim through pages.

11 Years

Great individual variation, but most read at least some, even if only comic books. Range from "never read," to one book a month, to eight a week. More girls than boys "love" to read.

In some, it is the chief spare-time pursuit. Others claim that they don't have time to read.

Quality of book important: "Like it if it's something real good."

Like to tell in great detail plot of stories they have read.

Prefer: animal (especially horse) stories, mysteries, sports, science, history, biography, Westerns, information books, classics *(The Adventures of Tom Sawyer,* and others.) Some read "just horse books"; others, "anything that's a book." Several say, "No romantic stories" or "No love!" Boys, especially, like scary stories.

COMIC BOOKS: Two thirds of our subjects read comics, some still avidly. Most read moderately, but in some the interest is definitely falling off. Comic reading is under cover for some. A few still collect and barter and may have two hundred to five hundred titles stacked around. Some do not buy but do read them. Favorites are about as at ten years.

MAGAZINES: *Mad* magazine a favorite. Also *Dynamite, Ranger Rick, Sports Illustrated, Right On.* As at ten, many just look through or read cartoons. The favored adult magazine may be *The New Yorker.*

NEWSPAPERS: Some never read newspapers, but the majority at least look through them. Comics, news, and sports are read most, in that order. Many say, "Just the funnies." Preference for "articles about planes crashing" or "crimes and murders and robbers." A few boys express mild interest in politics.

12 Years

Great variation. Some never read or "just look at the pictures"; others read five to ten books a week. Perhaps a little decline in reading, but amount read depends more on the individual than on age.

Books must be "interesting." Adult books coming in more, and ones they have outgrown them, are described as "boring" or "silly."

Many use library regularly and well. Increased interest in owning books.

Less naming of specific books liked and more mention of type of book. Beginning of interest in specific authors.

Prefer: mystery, sports, adventure, classics. "No love" and less interest in animal stories.

COMIC BOOKS: About two thirds of our subjects read comics, but few now read avidly. Some interest continues but is definitely decreasing in many. Little collecting. May not even buy them, reading only if they are available. Preferences less strong, and comics are not read and reread.

MAGAZINES: Most look at magazines which parents buy or subscribe to; some read them. Besides the adult favorites, now including *Reader's Digest,* such boys' and girls' publications as *Scholastic Magazine, Sports Illustrated, Right On, Boy's Life, Mad.*

NEWSPAPERS: The number reading newspapers increases, though the number reading thoroughly does not. Parts read most are comics, news, and sports, in that order.

13 Years

An increase in interest in reading and in amount read, though there are still many nonreaders. Many read in every spare moment, reading and rereading favorite books.

Selective—likes plot or action. Reading of adult novels is increasing, though some avoid emotional parts of books.

Preferences are varied but include classics, detective stories, adult novels, some animal stories, and adventure. Sports books and magazines very strong with boys.

COMIC BOOKS: Only about half admit to reading these at all, and virtually none read avidly or collect. Interest is generally slight and spasmodic. ("I don't buy them—I read my sister's." "No longer interested.")

MAGAZINES: Much more magazine reading, especially *Mad, National Geographic,* rock and roll magazines. Many subscribe to teenage magazines. Favorites are sports magazines, screen magazines, and some adult magazines.

NEWSPAPERS: The majority now read the newspaper, and a few read it rather thoroughly. Preference continues to be for comics, news and sports, in that order, but more read other sections too. Radio, TV, and movie news, ads, lost and found, features, society, and columns are all mentioned.

14 Years

Great variability. Some never read, while many read "all the time"—ten to fifteen books a week, some report. Others are reading less or "have no time for reading," though would like to (they say) if they had time.

Good use of library facilities. May by now be responsible about getting books back on time.

Reading of sexy books by some boys, and others will now accept romance in stories. Several mention the mood produced by different types of books.

Preferences: adult novels—especially classics, adventure, mysteries, sports (boys), books about adolescents (girls), information and science books (boys). Great interest in preferred authors.

MAGAZINES: Less reading than at thirteen, but more apt than earlier to read text and not just look at pictures and cartoons. Selective—some do not like "trashy" magazines. Science, sports, rock and roll, movie magazines all preferred besides the adult magazines favored since eleven.

NEWSPAPERS: Comics, news, and sports are still read most, but there is some reading of nearly all other parts—the most reported to date.

2. Radio, Television, and Phonograph
10 Years

This is the high point for television watching in this age range. The largest number of girls average sixteen to twenty hours a week, though fifty percent watch twenty hours or more. Boys even more. The largest number watch twenty-one to twenty-five hours. Cartoons and comedies lead as favored kinds of programs for both sexes.

Thirty-seven percent of the boys and fifty-three percent of the girls admit that there is some conflict between them and their parents as to the amount of time and/or kinds of programs watched. Sixty-eight percent of subjects feel that violence on television does not affect them adversely; and fifty-two percent of girls, fifty-eight percent of boys believe that television benefits more than harms them.

Most enjoy listening to their radios, though for many radio is used just as a background or for news and weather rather than as a primary source of entertainment. Or it may be turned on while they are studying, for many think they study better with some background accompaniment. However, some still have favorite programs, and some play their stereos long and loud.

11 Years

Even by Eleven, television watching has diminished somewhat in girls. The largest number watch fewer than five hours weekly (according to their reporting), and more than fifty percent watch fewer than fifteen hours. To include fifty percent of boy subjects, we must go up to twenty-one to twenty-five hours a week. Favorite programs for girls are comedies and situation comedies; for boys, comedies, cartoons, sports, mystery, or horror programs are in the lead.

More than one third of Elevens still say there is some conflict between them and parents about television watching. Nearly all girls and two thirds of the boys feel that television violence does not harm them; and more than half of both sexes believe that TV benefits more than harms them. One girl comments of violence, "Are you kidding? I don't like it, so I don't watch it."

Radio use continues about as at ten, often more as background filler than as primary pleasure. However, many carry their transistor radios around with them and listen as they move, and many turn their stereo up so loud that they disturb the rest of the family.

12 Years

Boys and girls are more even at this age, though boys still watch television a bit more than girls do. Fifty percent of girls now watch, according to their own reporting, fifteen hours a week or fewer; fifty percent of boys watch twenty hours a week or fewer. Comedies and situation comedies, as at eleven, are still the favorite programs for girls. Twelve-year-old boys now prefer comedies, situation comedies, or police or detective programs.

About one third of each sex admit that there is still some conflict between them and parents as to television watching. But most at this age recognize that parents do control the situation: "My parents don't allow TV on weekdays"; "When they think I'm watching too much, they tell me to turn it off."

Only twenty percent of girls, twenty-five percent of boys, think that violence on TV harms them; and forty-eight percent of girls, fifty-nine percent of boys, believe that television benefits more than harms them.

Few Twelves have "regular" radio programs. Some continue to use radio, perhaps extensively, as background. As to the stereo, we now find many are beginning to be interested in their record collections, and listening to their music (which they often turn up quite high).

13 Years

More than half the girls (sixty-three percent) watch television fifteen hours a week or fewer. Boys watch a little more. Only forty-four percent watch fifteen hours a week or even fewer, though fifty-four percent of boys watch twenty hours or fewer. Kinds of programs preferred are, for girls, comedies, soaps, family shows, drama, or movies. Boys prefer comedies, violence, sports, or movies.

Thirty-two percent of girls but forty-eight percent of boys say there is still some disagreement between them and their parents about the amount or kind of programs watched. Seventy-four percent of girls, fifty-eight percent of boys, feel that violence on television does not influence them. The majority (fifty-eight percent of girls, fifty-six percent of boys) say that television benefits them more than it harms them.

Radio may be used as background or may be kept on and listened to constantly. Use of stereo may increase, especially as boys and girls spend more time alone in their rooms.

14 Years

For busy Fourteens, television watching may be at a low point—they are just too occupied with their many other concerns. As one boy put it, rather superciliously, "I don't watch. I do not wish to live like a brainwashed American." Girls still watch somewhat less than do boys. More than fifty percent claim that they watch ten hours a week or fewer. Boys say they watch fifteen hours a week or fewer. Fourteen-year-old girls have branched out somewhat in their choice of programs, preferring comedies, movies, family shows, police or detective shows, in that order. Boys watch comedies, sports, police or detective shows.

Only twenty-six percent of girls but forty-four percent of boys say there is conflict between them and parents about amount of television watching. "If a show is too violent, I may not be allowed to watch." This conflict, if any, may be more applicable to boys because they may be watching more than girls do. As at all ages, only a small number (twenty percent of each sex) feel that violence on TV harms them. Comments about this issue include: "It doesn't influence me. If you're crazy, that's your problem"; "No, that's ridiculous!" And as at all ages, slightly more than half (fifty percent of girls, fifty-four percent of boys) believe that television benefits more than harms them.

Radio listening may be increasing in some, as does listening to the phonograph and stereo, especially for those who are "rock" fans. This interest may also lead to extensive purchasing of records, though many find listening to their radio cheaper and equally satisfying.

3. Smoking, Drinking, Drug Use*
10 Years

CIGARETTE SMOKING: Even at this young age, fifty-one percent of the girls and thirty-four percent of the boys admit that "some of the kids" they know do smoke cigarettes. This activity may still be at a purely experimental level, but it does obviously exist.

DRINKING: Some feel that it is all right for adults to drink if they don't drink too much, but others are critical of any drinking by adults. However, approximately one third of each sex claim that some of their contemporaries drink. One boy, asked if he smokes or drinks, replied, "I'm only ten!"

DRUGS: Only a minority (twelve percent) of all boys and girls whom we interviewed even admitted that "some of the kids" might use drugs. The fact that a minute fraction of ten-year-olds interviewed claimed that some of their age-mates use drugs does not necessarily add up to substantial drug use. Eighty-one percent of girls and ninety percent of boys can't tell the extent to which this drug use occurs, and sixty-six percent of girls and ninety percent of boys can't say what kinds of drugs these supposed friends use.

* See Table 5

The majority (fifty-three percent of girls, fifty-nine percent of boys) say that no friends or classmates have actually gotten into trouble with either drugs or drink, and twenty-eight percent of the girls, thirty-two percent of the boys, can't answer this question. Only fifteen percent of girls, thirteen percent of boys, claim to know somebody who has gotten into either kind of trouble.

11 Years

CIGARETTE SMOKING: Now seventy-five percent of the girls, forty-six percent of the boys, admit that some of their friends smoke. It is quite likely that boys may be less truthful in this matter than girls. Any smoking which occurs is probably, in most cases, sporadic. And the fact that some boys or girls may *know* someone who smokes does not mean that the majority actually do smoke.

DRINKING: The majority feel that it is all right for adults to drink if they don't drink too much, or if they drink "just beer" or "just cocktails." Slightly fewer than one third of each sex (perhaps somewhat more truthful and less grandiose than Ten) claim that some of their friends drink.

DRUGS: The amount of drug use by friends has increased only slightly, according to our informants. Twenty-one percent of girls and thirty-one percent of boys have friends who, at least on occasion, use drugs. The majority are not particularly clear about either the amount of this supposed drug use or the kinds of drugs used. Fifty-four percent of the girls do not know how often drugs are used, and thirty-eight percent say it is only occasionally. Sixty-seven percent of boys don't know how often drugs are used, and twenty-one percent more say it is only occasionally. Ninety-seven percent of the girls and sixty-seven percent of the boys still don't know what kinds of drugs are used.

Only nine percent of each sex report that any of their friends or acquaintances have actually gotten into trouble with either drugs or drink. One eleven-year-old girl tells us, "No. None of my friends use drugs. I have *good* friends."

12 Years

CIGARETTE SMOKING: Eighty percent of girls, sixty-eight percent of boys, now admit that either they or some of their friends smoke. We may assume that, even here, the majority do not necessarily do much smoking themselves.

DRINKING: The majority continue to say it is all right for adults, provided they don't drink too much. (Most are far more permissive about adults' drinking than about their swearing.)

This is the first age at which more than half (fifty-two percent of each sex) say that some of their friends drink. (The type and extent of the drinking is not elaborated upon.)

DRUG USE: Still only about one third of the Twelves we interviewed say that they know others of their age who use drugs. This figure amounts to thirty-two percent of girls, thirty-nine percent of boys. At this age, approximately half (fifty-two percent of girls, forty-eight percent of boys) who report this still can't tell the frequency of the reported drug use among friends. Seventy-five percent of girls and the majority of boys still cannot say what kinds of drugs are used.

A substantial but still relatively small number of Twelves (twenty-two percent of each sex) now say that some students in their school have gotten into trouble with either drugs or drink.

13 Years

CIGARETTE SMOKING: Eighty-four percent of girls, sixty-eight percent of boys, now claim to smoke themselves or to have friends who are smokers. Smoking at this age may occur just to go along with the crowd but it clearly does go on.

DRINKING: Most are now willing for adults to drink if they do not drink "too much." Sixty-six percent of girls and sixty-four percent of boys say that some of their friends do drink.

DRUG USE: Now we are moving up to nearly one half of both girls and boys who admit either to using drugs or having friends who use them. Now the figures are forty-six percent for girls, forty-eight percent for boys.

The majority either say that drug use is only occasional or can't say how often drugs are used. Marijuana is the only kind of drug mentioned frequently as being used—thirty percent of girls, forty-two percent of boys.

Thirty percent of girls, twenty-two percent of boys, now say that contemporaries they know have gotten into trouble over either alcohol or drugs.

14 Years

CIGARETTE SMOKING: At this age, all girls questioned and eighty-eight percent of boys either smoke or have friends who do. The girls who smoke tend to give justifications: "Something to do with your hands"; "People would think I was a baby if I didn't." Girls report that many of the girls at school smoke "just to show off, I'm sure, but they speak of it as if it were their very existence."

DRINKING: In discussing drinking, most now spontaneously refer to the practices of contemporaries rather than of adults. Drinking or not drinking has become a contemporary problem. By now the great majority, seventy-four percent of girls and eighty percent of boys, say that many of their friends do drink.

DRUG USE: Now we not only cross the fifty percent line, we move up dangerously close to one hundred percent. Of the girls and boys whom we interviewed, ninety percent of girls, eighty-two percent of boys, say that at least some of their friends use drugs. By now the majority of both sexes can estimate how often drugs are used by these drug-using friends. Forty-two percent of girls say that acquaintances who use drugs do so "only occasionally, or to go along with the crowd," but thirty-two percent are "really into it" and fourteen percent fit into both categories. Figures are about the same for boys: fifty-two percent, reportedly, mostly use drugs only occasionally or to go along with the crowd; twenty-four percent are "really into it"; ten percent fit both categories. (Which, of course, is rather contradictory, but that is what is reported.)

Now both sexes can identify the kinds of drugs which they or their friends use. For girls, drug use is largely restricted to marijuana (or, as they put it, "grass" or "pot"). Eighty-two percent of girls report that this is the drug preference. "Acid" (thirty-six percent) and "speed" (thirty-six percent) are the only other drugs reported by any substantial number. As to boys, seventy-four percent report the use of marijuana ("pot," "grass"), and no other drugs are used to any extent.

The number of Fourteens who say that someone in their class or crowd has gotten into trouble over drugs or drink is forty-two percent for girls, thirty-two percent for boys.

4. Individual Girls and Boys
Becky:

"I really get high on Ginger," said Becky, with a shy look in her eyes. "At school I am one of the shortest sixth graders, but when I'm on my horse I'm tall, tall, tall. . . ." "Tall" was not all she meant. She meant "high" too. That is, she meant that on her horse—usually five or six hours a day—she achieved an altered state of consciousness. She had entered a time in her development when she was capable of long, long spells of activity, such as riding Ginger for miles through familiar woods and fields, during which her mind did more than wander—it travelled.

"What do you think about when you're out riding all those hours?" we asked. "Oh," she replied, "everything."

Eleven is not the best age for direct answers. She wasn't being evasive; she just didn't have words to go with some of her experiences. When we pursued the point she explained, "Sometimes I talk to Ginger—I mean, sometimes I talk to Ginger a lot. But sometimes I just let my mind go on, and it . . . I mean, I . . . really get 'out there.' I've never done drugs, and I don't think I ever would because they're bad for you, but I think that what I do when I'm riding is similar, only it's good for you—at least I think it is." We agreed.

We think that Becky was learning to experiment with her consciousness and that she was able to talk about it in a certain way because of a knowledge about drugs (which some of her friends had tried, even though she comes from a rural area with "no drug problem").

This kind of exploration of consciousness is something that children have always been able to do from the developmental age of eleven or so—mostly in prolonged spells of monotonous activity such as riding, cycling, walking, and, more recently, watching television, listening to music, and using drugs. Before age ten, children are interested in experimenting with their senses. In the years from ten to sixteen, they tend to explore the limits of consciousness.

Twirling around to make yourself dizzy—to watch the world turn; sitting on your leg to make your foot go numb—"It doesn't feel like my foot"; pulling at the corners of the eyes to distort vision—"If I'm mad at my teacher I can make her go all blurry"—these are all tricks that children master before they have a chance, now much more accessible with the use of drugs, to alter their inner sense of space and time and their personal place in these two dimensions of existence.

Getting high on horses, on long walks, or by staring at the place where a fishing line enters the water had not been thought of much in terms of the connection between monotony and an altered sense of one's own or the world's reality. Until the emergence of the drug problem we didn't have our present frame of reference for thinking about the mental events that occur in long pensive episodes in the lives of young people. Experiencing different states of awareness was not the reason for such activity—it just happened. And we tend to learn that the capabilities of our minds are more than just plain asleep or just plain awake.

One of the tasks of the years from ten on is to achieve a dawning awareness of a permanent sense of one's self. Along the way, the activities of both mind and body help to define the limits of that self. Boundaries are found in exploring the extremes of experience and behavior and so, to a certain extent, experimenting with drugs to the point of producing extremes of consciousness is an activity consistent with the job of finding and defining one's borders. This may be one of the reasons for drug use. Becky herself may never take a single drug—but she knows about them as a frame of reference.

Derek:

Derek called at two A.M. to say that he was feeling terrible. We had been through some terrible times together over the years of trying to sort out the biochemical and psychological factors that gave rise to the major troubles this boy had had with his senses ever since he was little. His world was frequently distorted by uncontrolled hallucinations of hearing, seeing, smelling, and tasting, as well as by his feeling of really being outside his own body.

All of the kinds of experience sought by other kids who "tripped out" by using LSD and other hallucinogens had been part of Derek's unchosen experience from the time he was seven years old. By the time the middle of the night phone call came, we had shared many crises, and things had improved.

Familiar with the toxic potential of nutmeg, which can produce distortions of perception as well as nausea, headache, and a variety of mostly unpleasant symptoms, we had never (not even in Connecticut, the "Nutmeg State") heard of his current practice of sniffing it up the nostrils like cocaine. It was Derek's attempt at self-treatment. He often experienced extreme states of restlessness, anxiety, and insomnia and was looking for a remedy when he resorted to this inappropriate use of nutmeg. We cannot say whether his distress at two A.M. that morning was caused by the nutmeg or simply by the failure of the substance to produce a desired effect.

Derek was looking for a remedy for his feelings of discomfort. He had already found one in the six months preceding the nutmeg incident. It was alcohol. And it worked (temporarily). It relieved his symptoms of restlessness, and it terrified his mother. The latter effect was a dividend that would be enjoyed by many teenagers, but it was primarily the "medicinal" effect of the alcohol that attracted Derek.

"Doing drugs" is an activity for many children of ten to sixteen, and for some it is an activity, however negative, that can be understood in terms of other forms of exploration of the world inside and around oneself. The alcohol or other drug abuse of some children is an act of self-medication. A remedy for more than boredom or growing pains, it can be understood as a means of relieving pain, pain that could be better treated in other ways. Present trends among physicians and psychiatrists are leading to the more and more extensive use of pharmaceuticals to treat symptoms that a young person like Derek might try to remedy with alcohol or street drugs. We think that children in the age range discussed in the present volume are particularly susceptible to nutritional imbalance, for which nutritional remedies should be considered early in every effort to treat their problem.

Nora:

Eating, unlike riding horses or taking drugs, is one of life's necessities. Learning to feed oneself in infancy is a major milestone on the road to forming a sense of separate identity. Having control over the choice of foods to be eaten is the conscious, spoken goal of many an eight- or nine-year-old who feels the burden of parental selection of healthy foods. For many children, the years between ten and sixteen become a time of emancipation in eating that permits often secret experiments in nutrition that teach lessons too obvious to miss (potato chips and ice cream rejected by the same route they arrived, by a stomach saying, "too much, too fast") and other lessons so subtle that neither the child, his parents, nor medical, psychological, or educational advisors are able to see what has happened.

"When I was twelve," says Nora, "eating was my favorite thing. In fact, it was my family's favorite thing. Whenever we kids could decide on an activity, we chose eating. Sometimes we would choose going somewhere to do something so that it would look like we were out for more than food, but we knew we could stop somewhere and do the important thing—EAT. Even so, we had it under control. It was normal. Just ask any kid what her favorite activity is and I bet eating will be right up there. . . . Since then, now that I'm a little older, things have gotten weird about food."

First she discovered that binging—especially on ice cream—made her high. A kind of pleasant, giddy, floating feeling lasted for an hour or so after downing a "major amount" of ice cream. "Floaty and bloaty, I called it," says Nora, who went on to describe how she learned from friends at school that vomiting not only relieved the bloated feeling but intensified and prolonged the feeling of being high.

"It tasted good going down and felt good coming up—a combination that's hard to beat," she said softly, and with a note of irony, appropriate to the fact that this habit had been the reason that she and her parents had consulted us, since it had gotten to be a problem that she was unable to solve on her own. "Plus, there was the secrecy. It was my own thing. Even now that my Mom and Dad say I have bulimia, and people sort of know about it, it still is sort of my secret. Something I'm totally in control of." She smiled, knowing that from another point of view *she* had been in *its* control.

"It" in this case bears a label, bulimia, that makes it sound like a disease that attacks people in the same way that illness of many kinds is considered. "It" is supposed to have "a cause" and "a treatment." We feel that it is not especially useful to think of bulimia as a disease if it leads us to think in terms of treating the disease in some uniform fashion that ignores the unique situation of each child. The important factor that is the same for every child is that problems such as Nora's are not simply exaggerated forms of teenage activities but self-reinforcing patterns that require specific efforts at repair. A year or so of peculiar, often secret eating habits can, in a rapidly growing child, produce biochemical debts that may perpetuate the condition that gave rise to them to begin with.

It is very important, in other words, to know that Nora gets high on throwing up. It is also important to know that after a while a person who gets high a lot does so in order to avoid feeling bad. Addiction has a lot to do with the avoidance of feeling bad and the need to feel good, i.e., normal, by pursuing the addictive behavior. Normal developmental needs for secrecy, for feeling (however falsely) in control, and for exploration of the limits of one's own capacities all place the teenage girl or boy at a high risk for addictive behavior.

There is a fine line between normally exaggerated behavior in a healthy young person and a pattern of self-perpetuating or addictive behavior that is *not* developmentally productive. Estimation of a given child's place with respect to this line can be made more easily when considered in the context of his or her overall developmental status and, especially, whether or not the boy or girl in question progresses to the next stage of growth at an appropriate time. If a parent suspects that the child has a serious problem that is *not* developmentally productive, professional help should be sought without delay.

chapter fifteen
SCHOOL

The world of school is a world apart. Though our own experience in running a nursery school has been exhilarating and our experience in working in primary and elementary schools highly informative, our own personal knowledge of school in the years from ten to fourteen is less extensive. And boys and girls in these teen and preteen years do not tell the adult as much as they might about their experiences in school.

One special factor tends to restrict a developmental approach such as our own from revealing what goes on in school. During the earliest years (preschool through, say, third or fourth grade) the child's age, both chronological and behavioral, is a rather strong clue as to what he will be doing in the school situation. And age is something we know quite a lot about. But as the child grows older, two other factors play an increasingly significant role.

INDIVIDUAL DIFFERENCES become greater as the child grows older. True, even nursery school children have their own very definite personalities. But a child with somewhat modest intelligence stands out less and is at less of a disadvantage in nursery school, or even in kindergarten and first grade, than he or she will be in the later grades. The vast disadvantage of being a nonreader, or a not very good reader, is less handicapping in the very early grades than it will be later on. The gulf that exists between the slow learner and the so-called gifted and talented is not as conspicuous in the early years as it will be later on.

And though ENVIRONMENTAL DIFFERENCES always play their part, children from various backgrounds often mix well in a day-care center, and few day-care centers are places of violence. Not so in the ten to fourteen age range. The kinds of schools described in *The Blackboard Jungle* or in *Don't Push the Teacher Down the Stairs on Friday*, schools in which teachers and students are assaulted, or even killed, and those schools which still exist in a quiet midwestern suburb, for instance, are worlds apart.

We can talk of a three-year-old or a four-year-old in school with reasonable confidence and authority. Less so of a ten- to fourteen-year-old.

With this much apology for the weakness of a developmental approach as a tool for describing the school behavior of young people in the age range covered in this book, we proceed to tell you such information as we have gained from interviews with parents and teachers and with our young subjects themselves.

Your typical 10-year-old with his or her consummate good nature extends this good nature beyond home to the school. Teacher may, in his or her estimation be even more perfect than parents, and nearly all find her reasonably satisfactory. Some quote her as the ultimate authority. Others, at the beginning of the crush stage, may actually develop quite a crush on her.

If there are complaints, they tend to be not of school in general but merely of some one subject which they claim to hate. Decimals may give special difficulty to the nonmathematical student. Many Tens now show good intellectual enthusiasm for their favorite school subject. Many like to memorize; many especially enjoy geography.

Many ten-year-olds like to talk and listen more than they like to work. Many, even as later, enjoy the social aspect of school quite as much as the academics. Most Tens complain relatively little about school, and school complains relatively little about them because most respond well to school discipline.

At Eleven, especially as the year progresses, school behavior often takes a marked turn for the worse. Teachers unfamiliar with the ways of growth often wonder what has gotten into their students. Possibly nothing more or less than eleven-year-oldness. School behavior usually is not as bad as home behavior, but even in school children tend to be casual and restless, careless and forgetful, coming as close to rudeness as they dare.

Eleven tends to give the impression that he or she can take school or leave it. However, this impression which some try to give may be quite superficial. Most do care about getting good grades and also care where they stand, relatively, in their group.

Though usually bearing no lasting grudges, many at times do become quite angry at the teacher. When she does make them angry, most do not act up openly but rather, in their own words, "sit and sizzle." There is much interaction between girls and boys, though mostly at the crude level of throwing spitballs and chasing and hitting.

Twelve-year-olds, with their increased maturity, usually behave much better in school and are easier to manage as a group than are eleven-year-olds. With their tendency toward opposite extremes of feeling, they may either love or hate school, though even those who say they hate it (if they are in a school where any sort of discipline can be maintained) usually behave reasonably well, at least in class.

Most are much less challenged by the teacher than they were at eleven and seem to feel less need to react against her. In fact, most seem considerably far less embroiled with her than just earlier. The relationship is more impersonal, though if she does find favor in their eyes they may describe her as "just about the wonderfullest teacher in the world." What they especially admire at this age is that the teacher be able to teach and/or be a good disciplinarian.

Strongest feeling, as earlier, may still be expressed about math—they like it best or hate it most. As in the past, and as recent studies have confirmed, it is still more often boys who like math and girls who hate it.

There is not much social pairing off as yet, girls being at this time considerably more interested in the boys than the boys are in them. The class may think of and refer to the differences between "the girls" and "the boys."

In general, teachers report that twelve-year-olds are relatively easy to get along with and pleasant to teach. Attention span is longer than it was, and Twelve's basic enthusiasm often includes school as well as home and social situations.

Thirteen years of age is a time of withdrawal, and this extends even to school. An elementary school principal once commented that when he met the twelve-year-olds in the corridor he felt like the most popular person in the world as he was greeted with a constant flurry of "Hi, Mr. Jones," "How are you today, Mr. Jones?" Not so when he met the thirteens, for whom he might as well have been invisible.

Though most don't carry their total emotional withdrawal into the classroom, some do assume a basic attitude of indifference and report that school is "boring." Some seem so far inside themselves and so absentminded that they don't seem to hear the teacher's instructions. There is less readiness than earlier to recite or make themselves conspicuous in any way.

A definite maturity, which will be seen increasingly as the years go on, is shown by the fact that a boy or girl can admit that a teacher is a good teacher even though he or she may not like the teacher personally. The level of discipline varies greatly with the community—being still quite adequate in some, but in others quite out of hand. Drug use, and even pregnancy, may be reported in some communities.

The expansive, eager, ready-for-anything fourteen-year-old can be, if individual personality factors are favorable and the school setting reasonably disciplined, an ideal student. We have suggested earlier that, if it were feasible, fourteen-year-olds could have a glorious time in school, housed in a separate building from the other students, in a self-contained unit.

As the oldest in a twelve- to thirteen- to fourteen-year-old group, they sometimes get to be too cocky. They tend to be a bit too high-powered and domineering for these boys and girls just younger. In contrast, as freshmen in a four-year high school they are freshmen indeed, and the experience can be a bit squelching for young persons on the threshold of maturity and adventure.

As always with teenagers, the greatest respect is reserved for teachers who both maintain discipline and "teach us a lot." Complaints are as likely to be directed to the administration and the way the school is run, in general, as toward any individual teacher.

Many boys and girls are now getting better grades than they did formerly. Some are no longer using bad grades and inattention toward schoolwork to punish their parents as they may have done earlier. Many are beginning to realize that they need good grades to help them get into college or simply to get jobs when out of high school. And most manage homework better than formerly. Now, if not earlier, they are coming to appreciate that it is really their responsibility and not their parents'.

And now just a few words about discipline. School discipline, like home discipline, has always been a vital problem. Even the teacher in the one-room schoolhouse, in a time when authority was vastly more respected than it is today, faced his or her share of discipline problems. Some teachers have always been better-liked than others and some, by their very nature, are better disciplinarians than are others.

However, today new and exaggerated problems of discipline are being encountered, especially in our big-city schools. Not only is there a good deal of vandalism in after-school hours, but in all too many cities violence on the part of some students offers serious and even fatal danger to teachers and other students.

Admittedly, our own entire discussion of the school situation is rather bland, since a good many of the young people we have studied attended middle-class public schools or private schools. Figures show that in 1978-79, according to incidents reported (and of course many cases of violence are not reported), at least 110,000 teachers in the public schools of the United States were physically attacked by students. This was an increase of forty-seven percent over the figure for 1977-78.

The solution to this horrendous problem is not within the scope of this book, but we can hope that school administrations will soon become firmer and less permissive. Bills have even been introduced in the Pennsylvania legislature that would make any attack on a teacher a criminal offense, punishable with a jail sentence. But until some very firm steps are taken, it seems probable that conditions will continue to deteriorate.

We ourselves do not have a solution to these problems, which threaten the very continuation of public secondary education as we know it. We would, however, like to suggest approaches which we have found in some instances to help faltering or failing students become not only better students but also more comfortable human beings—human beings who might not need to become disciplinary problems.

DEVELOPMENTAL PLACEMENT: The first of these two considerations has to do with what we at the Gesell Institute term "Developmental Placement." It has long been our contention that at least fifty percent of school problems could be prevented or remedied by having each individual child in the grade which suits his or her developmental level—that is, level of maturity. To facilitate this correct or suitable placement, we recommend that every child be started in school and subsequently promoted on the basis of behavior age (the level of performance which he or she has actually attained) rather than on the basis of birthday or chronological age.

This means that the attainment of a fifth or sixth birthday in no way guarantees that a boy or girl will be ready, respectively, for the work of kindergarten or first grade. Our clinical service, as well as our work in schools all over the country, demonstrates clearly that many students are failing in school merely because they have been started too soon and are thus placed in a grade above the one for which they are suited.

The best solution, in our opinion, would be to provide behavioral examinations for all children so that all could be started in school at the suitable time. Failing this, the alternate solution would be to have those who need to do so repeat a grade, going back to the level where they might be expected to succeed.

POSSIBLY ADVERSE EFFECT OF IMPROPER DIET ON THE STUDENT: A second, equally important, consideration is that offered by such practitioners of medicine as Smith and Wunderlich and colleagues,[13,17] who suggest that much unsatisfactory school behavior, both academic and social, may be caused by allergic reactions to food or other aspects of the environment.

As Wunderlich puts it, "There is a growing realization that the adjustment problems of children are more often biologically based than was commonly recognized in the past."[13,17] He points out that the child who falls asleep over his desk may not be one who has not gotten enough sleep the night before. He may be one who is allergic to something in his diet or even to the fumes of cleaning material used in the school. (We have seen students demonstrate clearly allergic responses to a newly cleaned rug on the classroom floor.) Or the student may be one who is especially sensitive to electrical elements in the air in the school building.

Wunderlich comments, "Physicians need to know more about education, as educators need to know more about physicians." He himself has had striking success with school problems with the prescription of corticosteroids and megavitamins.

Lendon H. Smith,[12,15] working along similar lines, explains that much of the violence which we observe in young pupils, in school and out, may result from an unsuitable diet. He believes that the reason so many children turn out so badly, in school and in life, is because their bodies don't work right. And the reason their bodies don't work right may be because their brains are not well nourished. Improper diet, especially the consumption of too much white flour and sugar, can interfere with body function. Too much sugar, after an initial jump, *lowers* the blood sugar in the body to the extent that the forebrain does not function properly. The Dr. Jekyll/Mr. Hyde individual who is so good one minute and so unexpectedly violent the next may actually be suffering from a malnourished forebrain and improper diet. In other words, proper diet might conceivably reduce the violence and vandalism which so plague our schools to-day.

All of these considerations, as will be seen, are a far cry from the position once held by many that inadequate school or social behavior might, for the most, be a result of "home pressures" or of an inadequate home and social environment. We are beginning to suspect that it may be quite as much the physical aspects of environment (food, drink, odors) which cause unsatisfactory and even dangerous responses on the part of students as the way somebody treats them. As understanding of all these factors grows, we may look forward to an increasingly satisfactory school experience for many.

GROWTH GRADIENTS

1. General

10 Years

Most Tens say that school is "okay," and indicate that, on the whole, they like school. But they tend to be restless, and attention span is short. Most "hate" some subjects, but rebellion is passive and individual, doesn't come to a head in open revolt. They rebel by withdrawing.

Social relationships are important, but generally not intense. Fairly easy acceptance of one sex by the other. Much note passing— often about the opposite sex, though notes are passed between members of the same sex. Some plan mean things to get other children into trouble. May discuss contemporaries not as whole people but in terms of "his reading," "her arithmetic."

Beginning of a sophisticated self-consciousness in reciting or singing.

Most can get off for school on time without confusion and without losing or forgetting things.

11 Years

A turn for the worse often appears in school behavior. Elevens can be very fatigable, show uneven performance, have frequent illnesses. Many become restless, careless, forgetful, boisterous; they start daydreaming, dawdling. Attention span is very short. Still, school behavior is usually better than behavior at home.

Much interaction among children: notes, spitballs, teasing, chasing, hitting. Boys and girls very aware of "the boys" and "the girls," but gauche in their approaches: push, pull, fool around, act silly to attract attention. Their reporting emphasizes relationship with peers more than with teacher.

Many keenly interested in their relative standing in the group, work for good grades, show self-satisfaction in doing well.

Often much commotion and flurry about getting off to school in the morning. Burst out of school when dismissed.

12 Years

Many show strong emotional reactions; they either love school or hate it. Some "would like to be free not go to school." But many emerge from eleven-year-old scatter into more smoothness. Nicer in class, more cooperative, more adaptable; less lazy, aggressive, and rebellious. Sudden spurts of energy, but these cannot be sustained and child grows restless. Still needs freedom to move about.

Many act better as individuals than as a group. Group situation may foster note passing, shooting erasers and rulers, throwing chalk, hiding papers and property of others. Yet it is hard to establish a group structure because all are trying to express themselves. The group is important to them, but it is hard for them to subordinate themselves to it.

Girls stay with girls and boys with boys except for boy-girl fooling and teasing. Girls more interested in boys than boys in girls. Considerable sex and elimination joking in school; quick to note double meanings.

"Bad" classroom behavior is not necessarily a sign of dislike of school or teacher.

13 Years

Many are happier in school than earlier, think it is "better than last year," seem readier to learn. However, some go through a period of indifference to school: "Boring. No sense slaving."

Thirteen wishes to feel and to be independent. Some students may seek special projects and extra assignments. Time is now better organized, concentration more sustained, self-control and sense of responsibility more evident. But teachers and parents complain that some "don't apply themselves." Some seem so far inside themselves and so absentminded that they don't hear instructions. Less readiness to recite and perform before others.

The group acts more as a unit; less separation in class of "the girls" and "the boys." Can be boisterous in the hall but quieter now in class, though quite a bit of revolt. Group may play tricks on teacher.

Many like to get to school early and to settle in slowly.

14 Years

Many more Fourteens (in our group) say that they like rather than dislike school. Expansively enthusiastic, energetic, sociable. Fourteen may do well in school. But can become submerged and lost as a freshman in a four-year high school.

Quite a few criticize the way the school is run: the system, the administration. But may admit, "Everybody likes it, but of course we complain."

A few now admit (though this occurs more at fifteen) that they don't work as hard as they should, or don't try.

Strong group feeling. May like to sit together as a group in assembly. Group pressure strong; some "might be bad just to go along with the group."

Girls much interested in the boys. Much interaction between boys and girls.

Fourteen thrives on a variety of programs. Enjoys participation in extracurricular activities and clubs: athletic, scientific, dramatic, musical, and others.

2. School Subjects and Work

10 Years

Tens seem most interested in concrete learning experiences and learning of specifics. Generally love to memorize, but don't generalize or correlate facts, or care what you do with knowledge. May like to know what a thing is called but have little interest in mechanism or source of material. Often enjoy "place" geography—names of states, capitals, and the like—but vague about actual geographic characteristics.

Like to talk and listen more than work. Often better with oral and pictorial presentation than with printed words. Like to take dictation; like oral arithmetic.

Not able to plan own work; need schedules. Usually not much homework assigned. What there is, they can usually manage by themselves with little help and without much complaint.

Spelling at this age is not a strong point with either sex. Typical mispellings among ten-year-olds interviewed by us include: *comady, edicashanul, secraterris, receptioness, a nuf, kartuns, vilent, macanick.*

11 Years

Many Elevens are still excited about learning. Compared with Tens, may show even more enthusiasm but less organization. Seem to thrive on competition.

Most still seem better at rote learning of specific information than at generalization. Prefer a certain amount of routine. Want their work to be related to reality—may thus prefer current events to history.

Strongest feelings are expressed about mathematics—it is the best-liked subject (by many) and the least-liked by others. Most prefer the mechanics of arithmetic to the solution of problems.

Girls' favorites are art, sewing, and cooking; their most disliked subjects are (they tell us) English and math. Boys prefer science, math, shop; dislike spelling. Great enthusiasm for gym and sports.

Homework may cause much trouble. It is left until the last minute. Elevens need, but repudiate, mother's help; whole family may become involved. However, many still say they don't have too much homework..

Spelling in many has not improved. Typical misspellings include *cattoons, comidy* (or *comadey* or *commidie), secratary, syciatrist, macanic, potographer, arcatect, buty pagens, collage, vilence, of corse, diffinately.*

12 Years

Many are better able to arrange, classify, and generalize, and enjoy doing so.

Strongest feelings are still expressed about math—it is among the subjects most liked and most disliked by both girls and boys. English is especially favored by girls, French very much disliked. More are ready for social studies than before.

Boys enjoy astronomy and experiments in science; dislike spelling.

Most think they have too much homework and may rebel if they think it is really excessive. But they are a little more independent about doing homework than at eleven. Mother may need to get them started and to help some, but less of a battle and scramble than earlier.

Spelling in many is still far from accurate. Typical errors include: *commidy* (or *comity), arcatect, swegion* (for *surgeon), dix jocks, macamick, stardess* (for *stewardess), of corse, cosen* (for *cousin).*

13 Years

Thirteens may like certain subjects even though they consider them hard or dislike the teacher. Discussion periods are much enjoyed, and new subjects or new approaches are tried with interest.

Many Thirteens enjoy the broadened outlook on world affairs provided by social studies. Those who like English may prefer reading and composition to grammar.

Boys prefer math, science—especially its experimental aspects, history, shop; often dislike English. Girls more often dislike math, prefer languages, art, home economics.

Thirteens often feel that they have too much homework, but many are quite conscientious; and some would "work all night" if parents would let them. Most can accept any help needed from parents more gracefully than earlier.

Spelling is improving markedly. There are still errors: *artitec, batular* (for *bachelor), physicology, stuardess, sience.* But most spell ordinary words rather accurately.

14 Years

Many enjoy evaluating subjects and teachers. Ease of achievement is not always a criterion of interest; some like subjects even though they do not do well in them.

Less interest than earlier in the broader social studies, but more in any with a psychological slant—subjects which tell them about themselves.

Girls most often prefer art and English; boys, math and science. Girls tend to dislike math; boys, Latin.

Most think there is too much homework. Though lazy about homework, usually need less help than earlier.

Spelling is much better except in the occasional person (usually a boy) who still just cannot spell.

3. Teacher-Child Relationships
10 Years

Most Tens like and respect their teachers. May pay even more attention to teacher than to parents. "Teacher is God," one parent reports.

Critical analysis of teachers is just beginning. Most describe teacher as "nice" or "okay." Describe in terms of physical characteristics: "A little bit fat and not too tall"; "Dyes her hair and small." Like to compare one teacher to another. Main demand is that teacher be fair. Beginning evaluation of methods of teaching: "monotonous" or, "makes sense."

Express affection for and accept affection from teacher. Can be easily hurt and upset by criticism. However, respond well to firmness; seem to appreciate it. If there is to be punishment, they want it to be on the spot; can't stand long-term punishments.

11 Years

Elevens are often resentful and rebellious against teacher; may be quite difficult to manage. Very restless and active, though they say that if they are angry at a teacher, all they can do is "sit and take it" or "sit and sizzle." Or may mutter under breath or write and pass notes about her.

Describe teacher less by appearance, more by behavior characteristics. Attributes they like: She is fair, is patient, has no favorites, doesn't yell, is understanding, cracks jokes. Most disliked traits: She is unfair, is too strict, is crabby, yells, or flies off the handle.

Some have a crush on teacher; like to do things for her. Though Elevens don't want to be held with an iron hand, they do prefer a tough teacher, one who can challenge them.

12 Years

Less dependent on teacher and less embroiled with her than at eleven. About equal numbers in our group say they like and dislike teacher.

Great enthusiasm for those they like: "just about the wonderfullest person I ever met"; "perfect in any way that I can figure." They like it when she is nice, humorous, understanding, "doesn't treat us like babies," "is a good teacher" (i.e., can communicate subject matter). Attributes disliked are that she is "not a good teacher" (in techniques and knowledge), not a good disciplinarian, unsympathetic, yells, plays favorites.

Can be challenged by teacher—ready to be held in line and demanded of. But much uproar in room if teacher is not a good disciplinarian. Teacher needs also to have patience with the considerable heterosexual interest and activity which appears.

13 Years

Less embroiled with teacher than earlier. Will give in on small points to keep the peace. Many Thirteens report that teacher is "better than last year." Most like some teachers, dislike others.

Many can now recognize a teacher as a good teacher, even though they may not like her personally. Much interest in whether teacher is not too strict. Discipline varies greatly with the community—is reasonably good in some schools, very difficult to maintain in others.

Attributes liked: interesting, good personality, humorous, understanding, can keep discipline. Disliked: too strict, doesn't know how to teach, too critical. Especially dislike criticism of their work.

Want to be free of teacher, but actually need considerable help.

Some actual revolt against teacher in the form of practical jokes. "We try to get away with things with the teacher. That's only human nature." May make faces at her if angry.

May now be quite critical of the principal.

14 Years

As at thirteen, most have several teachers—like some, dislike others. In general, quite a tolerant attitude toward them: "Most are pretty nice. They can be unreasonable, but on the whole they're pretty nice."

Evaluations now quite detailed: "She doesn't have much personality; doesn't know how to keep us in order"; "Too dominating. I don't agree with her politics at all, and I can't get a word in edgewise. Don't know if she realizes it or not."

Reasons for liking teachers: "friendly," "kidding," "wonderful personality." Appreciate teachers who "try to figure out your personality, don't just think about your work."

Dislike teachers who are unsympathetic, unreasonable, too strict, unfair markers, indifferent, not worldly, "scares you." May be very critical of the way teacher conducts class.

Principal also comes in for criticism: "She has the wrong idea on life altogether. I think she should consult the children and let them make the rules more."

chapter sixteen
ETHICAL SENSE

Ethics, like health, is surely a highly individual matter, ranging all the way from the strongly ethical individual to the one who lives a life of crime. Some quite young girls and boys set very high standards for themselves and seem quite dissatisfied with anything less than perfection. Others really do not seem to care.

Some anthropologists tell us that ethics are, to a large extent, determined by the society one lives in—that there are some cultures in which the biggest liar or the most successful thief is the person most admired.

To some extent, this seems to be true. Though in all likelihood in Nature, in Society, and in the case of the human individual, a certain tendency toward achieving some sort of order and predictable pattern prevails, it seems most unlikely that young children are born with the notion that they should tell the truth, refrain from stealing or harming other people's property, or taking things that do not belong to them.

Family example obviously makes a difference. The father who boasts of cheating on his income tax, who boasts of outsmarting other people in business deals, who lies about a golf score, quite obviously sets a very poor example. The highly ethical parent sets a good one. And even the five-to ten-year-old, in fact the child considerably younger, learns very quickly what things the grown-ups approve of or disapprove of.

But even in the culture which is most ethical (from an American point of view) and even in a family which itself sets a good example and a strong ethical standard, many children take quite some time to reach a mature level of ethical behavior.

This chapter need not be long since its basic message is simple. Ethical behavior takes time to mature. Even a ten-year-old—mature as he or she may seem compared with the four-year-old who lies like a trooper, the six-year-old who may bring home from the neighbors anything that is not nailed down—may quite normally be expected to show many lapses in ethical behavior.

This doesn't mean that at ten, eleven, or whatever the age, we should condone serious lapses. It does mean that in the interests of successful parenting and harmonious family living we should not be too demanding of the (still rather immature) ten- to fourteen-year-old in the matter of ethical behavior.

Quite normal ten-year-olds, for instance, admit that they do not take the blame for wrongdoing if they can palm it off on somebody else. And most admit that "sometimes I do and sometimes I don't" tell the truth. However, most are much more strict with themselves about not stealing and not cheating than in the years just earlier. As to behavior in general, a boy may report with admirable candor, "Sometimes I do a few bad things, but I try to be a good boy."

At ten years of age, slightly fewer than half the children questioned by us report that "some of the kids" they know do smoke cigarettes, though only twelve percent hazard the guess that "some of the kids at school" might use drugs. Nearly one third of each sex claim that some of their contemporaries drink, though this may be more bravado than actual fact.

By thirteen, with a well-endowed boy or girl from a favorable home and school environment, most admit that they "usually" can tell right from wrong. And though they say it is sometimes fun to do bad things, they mostly try to do right. Many say their consciences would bother them if they did wrong. Most claim that they do listen to reason, even though "my parents can change my mind but I still might want to do it in my own mind."

Most Thirteens say they wouldn't cheat. Though even now, truthfulness is not complete. "I don't always tell the whole thing"; "I might embroider the truth a little."

Now approximately three quarters of all Thirteens questioned by us claim that they or some of their friends smoke cigarettes, and nearly half say that at least some of their friends use drugs. Also, more than half say that some of their friends drink, though the extent of this supposed drinking is not defined.

If things go well, probably the majority of well-endowed young people who have the advantage of growing up in stable, supportive households have achieved, by the time they are sixteen, what we think of as reasonably adult standards in truth telling and other types of honesty, taking the blame, living up to the demands of their reasonably firm consciences. But we must remember that not all young people are well endowed: all too many grow up in a household or neighborhood where standards are not what one might wish.

More than that, many potentially splendid boys and girls—young people who one day will head stable homes and do their best to bring up their own children to be good and stable individuals—as teenagers will often slip from the path of perfection. These slips, as a rule, are possibly temporary and part of more or less normal growing up.

That any teenager at times behaves in ways that differ rather markedly from the standards that highly respectable adults set for themselves should not be a cause of despair or a reason for their parents and other elders to give up on them. We would all do well to remember our own adolescent rumblings.

PART FOUR
After Fourteen

chapter seventeen
AFTER FOURTEEN— WHAT COMES NEXT?

This book ends officially with the fourteen-year-old, but your boys and girls are going to keep right on growing. Here's a glimpse of what may happen in the years which immediately follow:

THE FIFTEEN-YEAR-OLD

How difficult it must be, after having been a glorious, outgoing, and relatively happy fourteen-year-old to turn fifteen and find that so much of the world—especially the adult world—*thinks, feels,* and *says all the wrong things.* It is difficult to be a boy or girl who desperately needs to be free and independent and to be living in a grown-up world which believes that he or she is not ready for independence.

"I can't stand my mother. She just doesn't *think* the way I do," a typical fifteen-year-old boy will tell you. Another will say, "If only I could be free of my family and just go live in a hotel." When asked who would pay the bill, he will reply, "My father, of course." Father and mother still pay the bills. Father and mother still make the big decisions and lay down petty rules as to where he should go and what time at night he should be in. Humiliating!

One of the greatest desires of the fifteen-year-old's life is to be free of his family. If possible, boys and girls would like to be entirely independent. "They want us to stay home more, but they would have a hard time making us stay home" is the report.

Whether it is mother or father who causes the greater dissatisfaction is sometimes hard to say. A mother puts it well when she comments, "We're still on speaking terms." "Can't stand her" and "Just have to get away from her," unfortunately, all too often represent the fifteen-year-old's own attitude.

In general, things go better with father than with mother. "He understands me better." This slightly better relationship may be caused by the fact that fathers in general stay out of things more; mothers are still trying to improve their teenagers. Father and son may wisely avoid each other much of the time. When they don't, real blowups may occur.

Suggestions and comments by either parent are likely to be met with real scorn. (Embarrassment may be the key to the young person's reaction to parents at fourteen; scorn at fifteen.) Refusals of "reasonable" requests—a motorcycle, a car (even though they do not yet have a license to drive) are not well received.

And many Fifteens object to what they call parental non sequiturs. *Mad,* back in the 1960's, gave humorous examples of what kids say to their parents, what kids think parents will say to them, and what parents actually do say:

What Kids Say: "Great news, Mom! I just got a full scholarship to Harvard."
What Kids Hope Parents Will Say: "Just think: An Ivy-Leaguer in the family. I'm so happy I could cry!"
What They Probably Will Say: "Sure—you can get into an Ivy League School but you can't even keep your room clean!"
Or, *What Kids Say:* "Guess what? That aptitude test I took says I'll make a great doctor."
What Kids Hope Parents Will Say: "I tell you, Ida, if anyone can find a cure for cancer it's our Sheldon."
What They Probably Will Say: "A doctor? You think they'll let you be a doctor when they find out how you tease your sister?"

In general, Fifteens get along better with brothers and sisters than with parents. Things aren't too bad with older siblings. With younger ones, at best they can be quite protective. They may say to parents, "She's a good kid. Let her alone," though they themselves may make substantial efforts at improving this same "good kid."

It is, quite naturally, at the ages when family is most unsatisfactory that friends mean the most. "He wants to be surrounded by his friends, but he can't stand his family" is a typical parental comment. The more outgoing girls who, at home, may be quite uncommunicative or argumentative at best, can be the life of the party when out with their "whole gang" of friends. Parents might well be surprised and might hardly recognize their daughter. The more inwardized girls may restrict themselves to one or two best friends with whom they share confidences and discuss personalities. But these girls too are often quite different at home and abroad.

The same is true of boys. A few restrict themselves to one or two best friends whom they often select on the basis of their personalities: "I like the brainy type." Others seem the center of a large group of friends who, according to parents, "are always calling him up." The idea of mutual help between friends comes in strong: "We help each other out in this and that."

Dating is a big source of pleasure (or pain) at this age. Three quarters of the girls recently questioned by us and close to two thirds of the boys are going steady or have done so, though some may have nobody at the moment. By far the majority say that either they or their friends "make out," and well over half at least have friends (or say they do) who have "gone all the way."

Both sexes, with few exceptions, love going to parties, where at least according to their own reporting, behavior is rather more sophisticated than most parents would wish. The favorite activity of both sexes, they tell us, is drinking, with drug use a close second. Making out, dancing, and talking come next. Long gone are the days when eating and playing games were the big features.

Yes, certainly, friends can be everything. Fifteen spends as much time with them as possible and, for the most part, enjoys them thoroughly. Family, admittedly, is something else again.

So much for relationships with other people—how about the young person himself? At this age there is much concern about one's own personality, but even greater concern about one's mind, thoughts, opinions, ideas. Though this may lead to much arguing (Fifteen calls it discussing) at home and abroad, it is a fine sign of increasing maturity and approach—even though tentative—toward adulthood. One must respect Fifteen's opinions (a strong demand on his part) even when one does not necessarily agree with them.

An interesting aspect of self is the fifteen-year-old's plan for the future. Three quarters of our girls, half our boys (a low point) hope to go to college. More than three quarters plan to marry, and nearly all of these expect to have children. Girls as well as boys plan careers, though most of the girls think they will take time off from work and stay at home while their children are young.

As to ethical sense, we now find a rather substantially increased maturity. Boys and girls no longer think in terms of black and white but can now tolerate certain shades of gray. Many are now influenced in their behavior by consideration of how what they do might affect other people.

Most are trying to arrive at decisions about right and wrong for themselves, though many admit that what their parents have taught them is a strong influence, and consciences are reported to be very strong. That things be fair for other people as well as for themselves is important. And honesty is quite as important as fairness. Most are willing to take the blame (except perhaps in dealings with parents) when they themselves are at fault. And they *love* to argue. Proving a parent wrong can be a tremendous satisfaction.

However, for all that the ethical sense is rather strong in most at this age, the majority of fifteen-year-olds do things which cause their parents great anxiety. All but a very few claim that they or their friends smoke, at least on occasion. Nor is drinking far behind. And close to ninety percent of our subjects claim that they or some of their friends use drugs, either on occasion, "to go along with the crowd," or even more frequently.

Before fifteen, many teenagers with unfavorable personalities or unfavorable backgrounds, or both, do more or less contain any delinquencies within manageable limits. By fifteen, those who are not going to make it within the bounds of society—unmarried girls who will become pregnant, boys who are involved in burglary or street crime, children of either sex who have already lost out to drugs—may already be quite outside parental control. However, Douglas H. Powell in *Teenagers: When To Worry and What To Do* gives the encouraging information that "according to mental health professionals, only about one teenager in ten has *significant* emotional or behavior problems."[18]

Emotionally, except when things really go to pieces, the typical fifteen-year-old has himself rather well in hand. Physically and emotionally violent responses do occur but are much less prevalent than earlier. Most when angry now simply leave the scene or make some violent verbal retort. Some sulk or plan revenge, but others quite maturely try to suppress their anger or may even try to talk things over with the person who made them angry.

Reaction to school tends to be at one extreme or another, partly depending on Fifteen's own individuality, partly on the kind of teacher he or she encounters. Intellectual curiosity seems almost at war with the student's need to criticize and rebel against the person in authority.

Thus Fifteen may show considerable resistance, argue, pit his own ideas against the teacher's to an extent that actually interferes with learning. Or may, on the other hand, be intellectually challenged to the extent that he or she not only learns a great deal and stretches his mind, but may actually identify with and admire his teachers.

One of Fifteen's most characteristic, and actually most touching, kinds of response to any adult's prying, or even mild show of interest in him and his activities, is revealed in his response to our own interview procedures. If it seemed to us at times that Thirteen was the height of noncommunication, it was only because we had not yet become acquainted with Fifteen.

A typical fifteen-year-old interview may go something like this:

Interviewer: "Well, how are things at school?"
Fifteen: "What do you mean?"
Interviewer: "Well, for instance, what kind of grades are you getting?"
Fifteen: "In what subject?"
Interviewer: "Well, say, in math."
Fifteen: "About average."

Clearly, not much was forthcoming. Very shortly we hit on the expedient of keeping the interview going by showing no real interest in the subject or what he or she had to say.

About five minutes (or less) of clear noninterest on the part of the interviewer, and boy or girl starts to warm up. "You type pretty fast," he will concede. "Well, I've been doing it for a long time," the interviewer would reply, coldly.

Another compliment, another comment, and soon it was Fifteen who was trying to warm up the interview. Fifteens really would like to confide, or at least to communicate, if they could only be *certain* that it really does not matter to the adult whether they do so or not.

In view of what we know about this age, then, three suggestions may be in order. The first is that parents take advantage of Fifteen's intense intellectual interests, aptitude for debate, and love of argument. Young people of this age who feel that you have real respect for their intellectual capacities, even though you may not agree with them, can often be led along good pathways of thought and ideation.

The timing had best be theirs. Approach them with the suggestion that the two of you have a good intellectual discussion, and they will probably flee as if pursued. But if you strike while the iron is hot, for instance at a time when they are pointing out to you how wrong you are in something you have said, you can, cautiously at first and then with increasing success, get into a worthwhile discussion.

Your second best bet is to try to appreciate and respect the child's intense need for independence, for being his or her own person. Thus, even though you may feel that your son or daughter needs more supervision and protection than he or she is ready to accept, ask yourself, "Is this advice, this precaution, really necessary?" Try giving even a little more freedom than you consider entirely safe. The boy or girl who is not unduly pressured is often willing to accept more supervision than the one who feels hemmed in. The young person wants so desperately to be treated like an adult, even though so often by word or deed he shows that he is not ready for this kind of treatment! Sympathy and understanding will get you, as a parent, much farther than the impatience which you may at times quite understandably feel.

And lastly, if you wish either to be respected by your fifteen-year-old or to find out what he or she is thinking and doing, don't try too hard or appear too eager. Any mother's plea—"Aren't you going to wear that sweater that I knitted *especially* for you?" or "Aren't you going to eat that piece of pie? It's your *favorite* kind"—will in all likelihood be met with a look of scorn.

The parent who wants to know what son or daughter has been doing all evening "till this late hour" will not pounce with questions the minute Fifteen comes into the house. A discreet show of lack of interest is your best bet for eliciting comment because in the long run and at heart, Fifteen really does like and admire you and would like to share at least some of his adventures with you—if only he were convinced that you are not dying to know.

THE SIXTEEN-YEAR-OLD

Our theoretical schema of human development would lead us to expect that Sixteen would be an age of outgoingness and equilibrium. Things should go well. In this instance, at least, Nature fits with man's intent.

Sixteen is indeed a smooth and comfortable age for many. Girl or boy seems secure in sense of self and, perhaps for this reason, secure and relatively giving in relationships with other people.

One can almost tell this from posture alone. Fifteen was likely to stand and walk with one shoulder forward or perhaps with both shoulders raised. A girl might toss her head in hostile defiance; a boy lower and lumber. Quite different the posture at sixteen: Now a relaxed body suggests an inner relaxation.

The phrase "Sweet Sixteen" is no mere poetic fantasy. Sixteen *is* sweet, especially when compared with the person he or she was just earlier. Fourteens, as we have mentioned, were critical about parents: "You're not going out in that hat?" to mother. "Peanuts—I don't know why you even bother going to work, if that's all you make," to father.

Nor does Fifteen, with his or her incessant argument and discussion and derogatory attitude toward family in general—"I'd rather live in a hotel"—add very much to family life.

Thus Sixteen, who is not only friendly to family but even appreciative, is a breath of fresh air indeed. Up till this age, one of a parent's chief complaints is that son or daughter is all take and no give. Sixteen gives. He or she not only expresses appreciation of parents but even tries, at least at times, to make things go more smoothly in the household. Boy or girl at this age will often put his or her own needs second to general family harmony.

Thus, just as a few years earlier one's tangled eleven-year-old emerged into a whole new level of smooth emotional functioning at twelve, so Fifteen seems to climb out of what often seems like an emotional trough to ride the crest of the wave at Sixteen.

The typical sixteen-year-old is often described by parents and others as cheerful, friendly, positive, outgoing, well-adjusted, matter-of-fact. Some are even interested in attempting to control their emotions in order to make things more comfortable for other people.

Thus temper may now for the most part be pretty well controlled: "I don't get mad the way I used to"; "I'm on a pretty even keel." Not only good nature but also good humor is characteristic of many Sixteens. They now see the funny side of things, and their own spontaneous humor (as expressed in school papers or even in their ordinary conversation) can often be extremely amusing from an adult point of view.

As to sense of self, many now seem to have achieved a new sense of poise and self-sufficiency. Temporarily at least, the earlier frenzied search for self, which so often seems to necessitate putting down other people, appears to be in abeyance. Sixteen seems to like himself or herself and to feel relatively secure. Faced with a problem, girl or boy can now say, "I'll have to work that out myself."

Some, beautifully, can even accept criticism. "Everything is much better now," young people and parents alike may say. Some can actually list, with charming frankness, some of their own faults: "I speak too quickly"; "I argue too much."

Home routines—eating, sleeping, bathing, choice of and care of clothes—even clothes buying—now are pretty much under the young person's own control. Many do a remarkable job of earning and saving money. Many still do a remarkably poor job of keeping their own room in even acceptable condition.

Sixteen's improved (in fact often excellent) relationships with other people seem to result, at least in part, from an increased security with and satisfaction in his own self. Quite obviously the person who is secure personally, and no longer trying to prove his or her worth and independence, can approach others more comfortably than if he were still fighting resented authority.

The beauty of Sixteen's relationship with his mother is that he or she, much of the time, can now see her as a person and not as a jailor. Thus a girl may say, "My mother works so hard and is so unselfish. Everything for us and nothing for herself." Or a boy, who at Fifteen may have told us, "I can't stand my mother. She doesn't think the way I do" now may say, "Oh, Mom and I get on fine. *Always have!*"

Except when dating restrictions seem excessive, most girls get on well with their father and may be starting to admire him again. And unless severe father-son personality clash and conflict has actively begun, many boys show considerable respect for their father's authority: "He's pretty strict. Have to watch your step."

A moderate amount of squabbling with siblings occurs in many families but in others, sixteen-year-olds not only get on well with sibs but can even criticize their own former attitude toward younger ones: "I was too bossy with him."

Some Sixteens will even go out of their way to smooth things out in family living, to put family harmony ahead of their own wants and wishes. And some may even think they are given a "reasonable" amount of freedom and independence.

All in all, life at home tends to be much happier for boy or girl than it was just earlier. And "school is much better than it was,"

Sixteen will tell you. Teachers have improved quite a lot since the year before, we are told. Sixteens at school, as at home, seem to have less need to prove themselves and so are often able to see the good in adults in authority.

To a Gesell interviewer, as to other adults, Sixteen responds in a smooth, friendly, casual manner. Girl or boy seems fully ready to answer any and all questions asked. Many comment politely that the interview is "helpful" or "enjoyable." But with most there is little depth to communication. They respond politely but for the most part do not elaborate.

This is not the withdrawn secretiveness of Thirteen or the cautious and sometimes rather belligerent noncommunicativeness of Fifteen. It is simply that communication with adults may not be as vital to boy or girl now as it used to be. Sixteen is tolerant of adults but often not tremendously excited about them.

As good as many sixteen-year-olds are with their families, most actually prefer the company of their friends. (In fact, it may be partly because family is so much less important to them than it used to be that they can be as calm, friendly, and accepting of family members as they are.)

Friendship means even more, if possible, at this age than earlier and is even more comfortable. Friends are easier with each other, even if no less intense: "I tell her everything and she tells me everything." Girls, at least, in their increasingly intense relationship with the opposite sex find security, comfort, and pleasure in sharing their adventures verbally with their best girlfriend.

Some girls have a whole crowd of friends. Boys even more than girls have many friends, not just one or two. Though some boys, like girls, are interested in the personalities of their friends, boys perhaps more than girls find that shared activities, especially sports, may be their main bond.

As to friendships with the opposite sex, for most things are going rather well. Two thirds of boys questioned, more than three fourths of girls, tell us that they are going steady or have done so in the (presumably recent) past. Nearly all say that they (or their friends) do "make out." And sixty-eight percent of girls, seventy-two percent of boys, say that they or their friends or acquaintances have "gone all the way." A discouraging fifty percent of girls say that some friends have "gotten into trouble" sexually, that is, we assume, have gotten pregnant. (This percentage increases to sixty-six percent at seventeen years).

Reports of what they do at parties throws some light on sixteen-year-old boy-girl relationships. For girls, dancing, drinking, and a rather ambiguous "having fun" are the leading activities. For boys, drinking (fifty-four percent of boys questioned), talking, "having fun," and drug use are the activities enjoyed most. "Making out," which rated so high earlier, is now mentioned by relatively few. Presumably, as dating becomes more settled and satisfactory, couples attend parties together and do their "making out" elsewhere.

Eighty-four percent of our girls say that they plan to combine work and marriage. Sixty-eight percent say they plan to take time off from work when their children are young. As to occupation or profession, thirty-four percent of girls at this age still say they haven't decided. The work most often mentioned is being a nurse. Other choices are highly scattered, though by seventeen, teacher and secretary lead.

Only eighteen percent of boys cannot indicate a choice of future work. Lawyer, architect, and carpenter are leading choices, though with boys there is an even greater variety of choice than with girls.

One aspect of the typical sixteen-year-old that is especially gratifying to parents is the increased responsibility which girl or boy is ready to assume. It may be responsibility for the care of younger sibs, for a share of household tasks, a willingness to take and hold a job outside the home, or even for trying to keep things smooth within the family.

Ethical responsibility grows as well. Most Sixteens believe they can usually tell right from wrong and, for the most part, try to do right. Fairness is important to them, though perhaps more in theory than in practice, since sixty percent of those interviewed were satisfied with what we are doing with regard to integration. Forty percent of girls and forty-eight percent of boys do believe that they might do something to improve "conditions" when they grow up.

The easy ages, as this description of Sixteen suggests, are very clearly less dramatic than the difficult ones. When one's children have reached the usually comfortable age of sixteen, we cannot help wondering what all the fuss was about.

The fuss was about the difficulty and the complexity of growing up. Sixteen is by no means an adult. Yet, briefly, boy or girl has reached a usually highly satisfactory stage of living.

Briefly at least, other people, if not more important than self, are to be considered. Sixteen can look at adult demands with understanding and even compassion—even if he or she does not fully intend to comply with what the adult requests.

Sixteen gives us a beautiful preview of what we hope for our sons and daughters when they become adults and can communicate with us adult to adult rather than, as until now, as child to adult. It tends to be a highly satisfactory time of life for all concerned.

Appendixes

Appendix A:

SOURCES OF INFORMATION

Original Subjects:
Information was gathered by several means. All subjects were given a standard Gesell Developmental Examination, an intelligence test, and three projective tests (the Rorschach Ink Blot Test, the Lowenfeld Mosaic Test, and the Thematic Apperception Test.) Subjects were also given a thorough visual examination and a physical growth evaluation, which included measures of height, weight, and grip strength. Standardized physique photographs were taken for somatotype estimates, and maturity status evaluation was made.

We then conducted a personal interview with each subject covering such areas as self-care and routines, emotions, sense of self, interpersonal relationships, activities and interests, health and tensional outlets, school behavior, and ethical sense. An interview with each parent covered, more or less, these same topics. When possible, the teachers of our subjects were also interviewed.

1977-1978 Subjects:
Our second sample of subjects was interviewed in 1977 and 1978 by means of a questionnaire, which follows. These questionnaires were handed out by teachers in social studies, and related classes, in elementary and high schools throughout the United States and were filled out during class periods.

Occasionally a student would comment, "Who wants to know?" or "What's it to you?" But for the most part responses appeared to be sincere and honest. Students were guaranteed anonymity (they did not put their names on their questionnaires) and thus appear to have responded fully and frankly.

Schools which cooperated with us in this venture ranged, geographically, from the East to the West Coast. Specifically, they included schools in Long Island, New York; Hamden, Guilford, and Taftville, Connecticut; Peterborough, New Hampshire; Mount

Pleasant, Iowa; Gig Harbor and Tacoma, Washington. Number of subjects responding are shown in Table 2.

Table 2

Number of Subjects Responding to 1977–1978 Questionnaires

Age in Years	Girls	Boys	Total
10	75	75	150
11	100	100	200
12	100	100	200
13	50	50	100
14	50	50	100
15	75	60	135
16	50	50	100
17	54	25	79
			1064

We do not have available IQ scores for subject, but can report on socioeconomic status. This varied tremendously and represented all levels from upper-class private school students through middle-class, big-city and middle-class, rural students to lower-class, small-city boys and girls. Parents of children in one Army school ranged from colonel to private. The majority of subjects came from two-parent homes, but some mothers were divorced or widowed; and a few were single parents. Most subjects were white, except for a small number of black students in the New York schools.

Analysis of data obtained from the questionnaires was easily carried out, since all responses could be easily tabulated. Findings were summarized in Tables 3 to 7, which follow. These tables cover the following topics: college, marriage and career plans, marriage plans of 1950 subjects compared with those of 1970 subjects, information about dating and sexual activity, information about smoking, drinking, and drug use, party activity, and use of television. Information from this analysis is also included in the text under appropriate headings.

QUESTIONNAIRE FOR 1977-1978 TEN- TO SIXTEEN-YEAR-OLDS

AGE:

SEX:

SCHOOL GRADE:

Career and/or School Plans:
Do you plan to go to college?

Do you expect to get a job right after high school?

What kind of work would you like to do?

Do you expect to get married?

Do you plan to combine work or career and marriage? (girls only)

Do you plan to take time off from work when your children are young? (girls only)

Do you plan to have children at all? If so, how many?

Ethics:
Do you think we're doing enough to integrate schools and neighborhoods?

Do you think that politicians are dishonest?

Do you feel that you personally might, through politics or otherwise, try to improve conditions in this country?

Television:
On the average, how many hours a week do you spend watching TV?

What programs or kinds of programs do you prefer?

Do you feel that violence on television influences you adversely?

Any conflict between you and your parents about the amount or kind of programs you watch?

Do you feel that television—

Benefits you more than it harms you?

Harms you more than it benefits you?

Drugs or Drinking?
Do any of the boys or girls you know drink? Smoke?

Do any of the boys or girls you know use drugs? If so, what kind?

If they either use drugs or drink, is it just occasionally at parties or to go along with the crowd? Or are they really into it?

Have any of the students in your school or neighborhood gotten into serious trouble with either drugs or drink?

Dating (10 to 12):

Have you started dating yet?

If not, would you like to date?

If you do date, is it a single date, double date, or with a crowd?

Do you think you have adequate information on the subject of sex?

What kinds of things do you do at parties?

Dating (13-16):

Do you do much dating?

Do you believe in going steady?

Do *you* go steady or have you gone steady? If so, how many times and for how long?

What kinds of things do you do at parties?

Supplement to Dating (13-16 Years):

Have you ever had a friend who sometimes or often makes out?

Have you ever had a friend who goes "all the way"?

If your friend goes "all the way," what kind of birth control methods do you think she (he) uses?

Has anyone you know gotten "into trouble"?

APPENDIX B.

TABLES

Table 3

College, Career, and Marriage Plans
(Percentage of Children Responding)

	10 Years		11 Years		12 Years		13 Years		14 Years		15 Years		16 Years		17 Years	
	G	B	G	B	G	B	G	B	G	B	G	B	G	B	G	B
Do you plan to go to college?	84	70	82	70	78	66	84	88	78	84	77	54	74	68	74	88
Do you plan to get married?	87	82	89	72	74	83	86	88	70	72	82	78	84	84	96	86
Do you plan to have children?	84	79	85	72	81	72	86	82	80	78	75	72	86	88	92	86

Marriage Plans of 1950 (G1, B1) Boys and Girls Compared with Those of 1970 (G2, B2) Boys and Girls

Percentages Who Say They Plan to Marry

10 Years				11 Years				12 Years				13 Years				14 Years				15 Years				16 Years			
G1	G2	B1	B2	G1	G2	B1	B2	G1	G2	B1	B2	G1	G2	B1	B2	G1	G2	B1	B2	G1	G2	B1	B2	G1	G2	B1	B2
81	87	50	82	91	89	52	72	85	74	55	83	94	86	75	88	100	70	43	72	100	82	75	78	80	84	19	84

Table 4

Information About Dating
(Percentage of Responses)

	10 Years	11 Years	12 Years	13 Years	14 Years	15 Years	16 Years	17 Years
Would like to start	54 65	57 71	34 52					
Have started	15 26	30 42	35 38					
"Yes" I do "much" dating				30 32	32 56	39 55	48 64	70 32
"Believe in" going steady				56 68	56 74	85 69	78 80	86 56
Am going steady or have done so				40 44	68 54	76 60	76 68	88 56
Any of your friends "make out"?				90 90	82 75	87 72	88 80	90 48*
Any friends "gone all the way"?				25 30	57 55	78 55	68 72	81 44*
Any gotten "into trouble"?				25 40	39 50	53 22	50 32	66 8*

* Boys possibly more discreet than truthful at this age.

Table 5

% of Girls and Boys at Each Age Who Respond "Yes" to the Question:
"Do Any of the Kids You Know Smoke, Drink, Use Drugs?"

	10 Yrs. G B	11 Yrs. G B	12 Yrs. G B	13 Yrs. G B	14 Yrs. G B	15 Yrs. G B	16 Yrs. G B	17 Yrs. G B
Smoke:	52 54	75 46	80 68	84 68	100 88	98 96	86 96	100 100
Drink:	38 34	21 30	52 52	66 64	74 80	94 92	96 92	100 100
Use Drugs:	12 12	21 31	32 39	46 48	90 82	91 88	86 86	82 82
In trouble with drugs or drink*	15 12	9 9	22 18	30 22	52 32	58 53	50 58	46 52

* This is the % who KNOW SOMEBODY who has gotten into trouble, not the % who themselves have gotten into difficulty.

Table 6

What Do You Do At Parties?
Percent of Responses

	10 Years		11 Years		12 Years		13 Years		14 Years		15 Years		16 Years		17 Years	
	G	B	G	B	G	B	G	B	G	B#	G	B	G	B	G	B
Eat	21	15	4	6	24	16	16	16	24	20	8	3	6	6	16	6
Talk	6	0	24	42	28	8	14	20	12	35	22	14	20	28	22	24
Play games	18	30	40	0	28	12	14	6	0	5	13	2	4**	6	2	0
Dance	12	5	32	42	54	8	32	40	24	60	22	14	38	14	40	32
"Have fun"	1	20	0	6	20	8	14	12	16	20	8	11	22	28	30	0
Play records	0	0	0	0	20	8	6	2	10	15	17	16	10	8	18	0
"Make out"	0	20*	20	16	20	16	24	28	16	95	20	23	6	18	6	8
Drink	0	0	0	0	4	12	8	12	16	65	42	31	24	54	56	32
Drugs	0	0	0	0	8	4	16	6	28	50	30	26	16	24	18	24

* Tens may not be certain what "make out" means.
** Games at 16 and 17 consist of playing cards.
# Only 20 subjects respond.
(Outstanding items at each age are underlined.)

Table 7

Television Use

Number of Hours of Watching Which Includes 50% or More of Subjects*

10 yrs.		11 yrs.		12 yrs.		13 yrs.		14 yrs.		15 yrs.		16 yrs.		17 yrs.	
G	B	G	B	G	B	G	B	G	B	G	B	G	B	G	B
20	25	15	25	15	20	15	20	10	15	15	15	15	15	10	15

* This is to be interpreted that 50% or more at ten years do not watch more than 20 hours (girls), 25 hours (boys) and so forth.

Percentage of Subjects Who Say, "TV Violence Does Not Affect Me Adversely"

68	68	82	69	74	70	74	58	50	54	87	67	76	84	72	88

Percentage of Subjects Who Say, "TV Benefits Me More Than It Harms Me"

52	58	52	56	48	59	58	56	50	54	64	62	56	64	54	68

APPENDIX C

NOTES

1. Rutenber, Ralph. *How to Bring Up 2,000 Teenagers.* Chicago: Nelson-Hall, Inc., 1979.
2. York, Phyllis, York, David and Wachtel, Ted. *Toughlove.* Garden City, New York: Doubleday & Company, Inc., 1982.
3. Bayard, Robert T. and Bayard, Jean. *How to Deal with Your Acting-Up Teenager: Practical Self-Help for Desperate Parents.* New York: M. Evans & Co., Inc. 1983.
4. Wells, Joel. *How to Survive with Your Teenager.* Chicago: The Thomas More Press, 1982.
5. Brazelton, T. Berry. *Infants and Mothers: Individual Differences in Development.* New York: Delacorte Press, 1969.
6. Sheldon, William (with S. S. Stevens). *The Varieties of Temperament: A Psychology of Constitutional Differences.* New York: Hafner Publishing Co., 1970.
7. Lightfoot, Sara Lawrence. *The Good High School: Portraits of Character and Culture.* New York: Basic Books, Inc., 1983.
8. National Society for the Study of Education. *Adolescence. Forty-third Yearbook. Part I.* Chicago: University of Chicago Press, 1944.
9. Kovar, Lillian C. *Faces of the Adolescent Girl.* Englewood Cliffs, New Jersey: Prentice-Hall, Inc., 1968.
10. Caplow, Theodore, et al. *Behavior Today,* 1979, 10, 4.
11. Feingold, Ben F. *Why Your Child is Hyperactive.* New York: Random House, Inc., 1974.
12. Smith, Lendon H. *Feed Your Kids Right: Dr. Smith's Program for Your Child's Total Health.* New York: McGraw-Hill Book Co., 1979.
13. Wunderlich, Ray C. and Kalita, Dwight K. *Nourishing Your Child: A Bioecologic Approach.* New Canaan, Connecticut: Keats Publishing, 1984.
14. Crook, William G. *Tracking Down Hidden Food Allergies.* Jackson, Tennessee: Professional Books/Future Health, Inc., 1978.
15. Smith, Lendon H. *Improving Your Child's Behavior Chemistry: A New*

Way To Raise Happier Children into Healthier Adults. Englewood Cliffs, New Jersey: Prentice-Hall, Inc., 1976.

16. Straus, Murray A., Richard J. Gelles, and Suzanne K. Steinmetz. *Behind Closed Doors: Violence in the American Family.* Garden City, New York: Anchor Press/Doubleday, 1980.
17. Wunderlich, Ray C. *Allergy, Brains and Children Coping.* St. Petersburg, Florida: Johnny Reads, Inc., 1973.
18. Powell, Douglas H. *Teenagers: When to Worry and What to Do.* Garden City, New York: Doubleday & Company, Inc., 1986.

INDEX